Richard Needham was MP for Chippenham for eighteen years. During that time he was Britain's longest-serving minister in Northern Ireland, responsible for its economic regeneration. In 1992 he was promoted to Minister of Trade, in charge of the UK's export strategy. In 1997 he left politics to return to industry. He was a director of Dyson for sixteen years and chairman of Avon Rubber PLC for five. He has been involved in many other large, medium and small companies covering many sectors. He has three grown-up children and lives with his wife in Gloucestershire.

Richard Needham has spent a lifetime in business and politics, starting at the bottom and having reached the top finding himself at the bottom again. The one constant in his varied life has been the management theory espoused by Douglas McGregor called Theory X and Theory Y.

RICHARD NEEDHAM

ONE MAN, TWO WORLDS

·THE·
BLACK
·STAFF·
PRESS

Thanks

Without Sissy this book would never have been started, let alone completed and without whom none of what I have achieved would have been possible.

I would also like to thank Helen Wright, my editor, who has corrected my grammar, improved my vocabulary and whose enthusiastic support has carried me along.

First published in 2021 by Blackstaff Press
an imprint of Colourpoint Creative Ltd
Colourpoint House
Jubilee Business Park
21 Jubilee Road
Newtownards BT23 4YH

© Richard Needham, 2021
All rights reserved

Richard Needham has asserted his right under the Copyright, Designs and Patents Act 1988 to be identified as the author of this work.

Front cover portrait by Jonathan Yeo

Printed by GPS Colour Graphics Ltd, Belfast

A CIP catalogue record for this book is available from the British Library

ISBN 978 1 78073 315 9

www.blackstaffpress.com

Contents

Prologue

I CAME FROM a family of barely solvent aristocrats, who distrusted trade and despised politics. For some inexplicable reason, however, I had always been fascinated by both. From the age of fifteen, I was determined that I would first make some money, and then enter politics and change the world. Not for me the uneventful, minor military career, probably in the Grenadier Guards, that had been the fate of generations of Needhams before me.

While I was at Eton, a visiting politician who had come to speak, gave some shrewd advice: 'Know your country from top to bottom, north to south, east to west. Gain as broad an experience as you can in as wide a variety of jobs as you can. Then make up your mind which party you want to join and what aspects of politics you want to make your own.' It was advice that I was to follow and that served me well.

On 1 April 1967, I boarded a flight bound for Jamaica. I was marketing manager at a medium-sized engineering company, Sterling Industries, based in the west of England. Sterling Industries had the agency for a Cleveland-based company called Trabon, which sold oil-lubricating equipment to steel mills. They had invited their distributors from around the world to a conference in Jamaica, for a week's intensive interactive tutorials run by top lecturers from the Harvard Business School who wanted to mix teaching with rum and Coke. The top Sterling management thought all this case-history based learning was a bit beneath them as their careers had already taught them all they needed to know so I, a twenty-five-year-old from marketing – a subject which they believed had little relevance – was deputed to go. The trip was to change my life.

The case histories were indeed fascinating, not least the one on how Hugh Hefner's Playboy company had become the single largest purchaser of Scotch in the USA by only serving the customers in their clubs steak and whisky. But it was the relentless concentration that was placed on the importance of individual motivation and the necessity of engaging employees that had the greatest impact on me. The emphasis on using employees' talents: trusting them, organising workflows that gave them responsibility and engagement and that created a common sense of corporate ambition, making them responsible for the success and profitability of their companies, and stretching them all to the limits of their abilities, gave me a new vision. What I was learning was far from what was happening in strike-torn, class-ridden British industry.

The professor who had more than any other encapsulated the new industrial psychology was called Douglas McGregor and his book was *The Human Side of Enterprise*. His thesis was based on studies of people in work, pioneered by Professor J.A.C. Brown in England in the 1950s and the Australian Elton Mayo's research in the 1920s and 1930s at the Hawthorne Works in Chicago. This work proved conclusively that so-called Scientific Management based on piece work (i.e. paying people for each item produced), far from being a motivator, resulted in shoddy workmanship, as well as high levels of absenteeism, conflict and disputes.

McGregor had brought together the strands of this work into what he called Theory X and Theory Y. Theory X stated that if you give a person the choice between more work or less, on balance they would prefer more leisure time. Give him the choice between more or less responsibility, the average person would prefer to stay where they were. Most people worked for money, and it was the chance of more money that was the major motivator in getting them up in the morning to work harder and more productively. Most working people's loyalties were predominantly governed by their families and their class, not by their employer or the organisation for which they worked. If someone was slipshod or inadequate, fear of the sack was a principal motivator in getting them to change their ways.

Theory Y postulated that of all the factors motivating man to work in modern society, money was the least important. Of course, people would not work for nothing, but in Abraham Maslow's Hierarchy of Needs, money was a reward – a hygiene factor, like clean toilets – not a motivator. At best it was part of a company's reward system. Give someone the choice between more responsibility or less, they would choose more. Give them more work or less work, they would welcome more. It was a natural part of anyone's character to want to be part of a team and to make it ever more successful. An employee's loyalty to their organisation or their employer was as natural as any other loyalty.

The key to a successful company was involving the staff; worker participation, wherever possible; shared ownership; respect for each individual's unique abilities; listening to complaints, both collectively and individually; setting personal goals; and sharing information and minimising unnecessary secrecy (often used as a tool to cover up failure).

What I learned in Jamaica was that Britain's industrial base was dominated by the proponents of Theory X and Scientific Management. If we were not to change our ways to learn from the Japanese, the Germans and the Americans, our manufacturing industry would be decimated and irrelevant in just a few years' time.

Theory X and Theory Y reflect a psychology of management style. People who are attracted by Theory X are usually more interested in results and outcomes than they are in welfare, wellbeing and individual performance. Throughout this book I have referred to individuals whose behaviour and performance exhibit Theory X and Theory Y styles of management, as being Theory X or Theory Y.

Theory Y gave me the foundation on which I could build my political and business career. This is the story of how far I got.

CHAPTER 1

An Uncertain Start

I WAS BORN in Hertford on 29 January 1942, nine months and a day after my parents had married. The colonel of my father's battalion (Third Battalion Grenadier Guards) sent a congratulatory telegram to my mother enquiring whether the amber light had turned green. Whether this was a reference to my mother's earlier flighty reputation, I do not know, but according to her, she could not make up her mind between three men on the same night in 1939.

Queen Mary, who was a friend of Lionel Faudel-Phillips, my grandfather, was staying at Ball's Park, his Palladian mansion in Hertford, while my mother wrestled with her dilemma. When the great Queen was asked what my mother should do, she replied 'Oh, she should choose Patrick Needham. And then, Lionel, we will become quite closely related.'

This advice related to the rumours that my grandfather, Buddy Needham, had been the outcome of an affair between the Queen's brother, Prince Francis of Teck, and my great-grandmother, Nellie Kilmorey. It is true that Francis had left the famous Teck emeralds to Nellie in his will, which caused a terrible rumpus, but there is no proof that he was Buddy's father. However, when my father died forty years later, his only possessions were a pepper grinder that he had had with him since the Battle of Monte Cassino, a pair of German nail clippers, an ivory comb and a pair of gold cufflinks engraved with the initials 'FT'. So, at some stage, Nellie must have helped the prince out of his shirt.

Even without the Queen's advice I am certain my mother would have fancied my father more than the other two. He was very handsome and looked ravishing in his full dress uniform (the Needhams claim to be one of the oldest two families in the regiment) when he was changing the guard at Buckingham Palace.

There was another incentive. My father's uncle, the earl of Kilmorey, had no sons, so my father was in line to inherit his title together with what was left of the Irish estates and Mourne Park, a dilapidated stately home near Kilkeel in County Down. In the meantime, the downside was that he was utterly impecunious, relying on a small allowance from his dragon of a mother who had inherited a small fortune from her father – a Combe of Watney, Combe & Reid, the brewers – after her brother had been killed in the Great War.

The Needhams were an Anglo-Irish Shropshire family, whose generations of raffish and reckless ancestors were interspersed occasionally with a more indolent variety of Needham. Since 1832, the raffish ones had managed to squander twenty acres of Twickenham, fifteen thousand acres of Shropshire, fifty thousand acres of Northern Ireland and two Gainsboroughs. The indolent ones had been incapable of restoring the family fortunes or repaying the debts.

On my mother's side, her father – the Queen's friend Sir Lionel Faudel-Phillips – was the son and grandson of two Jewish lord mayors of London. Sir George Faudel-Phillips had been lord mayor at the time of Queen Victoria's Diamond Jubilee. He was as rich as Croesus. In August 1905 the *Jewish Chronicle* reported that 'Prince Gorchakov (the Russian foreign minister) said to Lord Augustus Loftus, the former ambassador to Russia, "I will give you all the Jews in Russia for half a dozen of yours in London!" It was of such men as Sir George Faudel-Phillips that he was thinking.'

Sir George's eldest son, Sir Benjamin, was reputed to be gay. He was certainly a brilliant code-breaker of the German naval codes in Room 40 during the First World War. His younger brother, my grandfather Lionel, had three beautiful daughters – he had married the granddaughter of a Scottish marquess and had hastily abandoned his Jewish faith. In fact, the Jewish connection was not discussed in our family when I was young! It was only when I was called 'Budgie' and 'Beaky' at my prep school that the truth came out.

My mother was the youngest and least-wanted daughter. She was brought up downstairs by the servants, surrounded by enormous wealth. She had little love from her mother, who was more interested in the Chows that she had had brought from China than she was in her daughter.

When my grandfather and grandmother died in 1940 and 1941, the Balls Park estate was split up, and after death duties and disbursements, my mother was left with the income from some small trusts and a house full of 'things' to share with her two sisters.

What the Faudel-Phillips girls did have were wonderful looks, wonderful taste and a wonderful sense of humour. My mother was a very knowledgeable gardener, an inventive cook, an innovative flower-arranger and an imaginative photographer. She had a highly developed sense of style and dress. She could be great fun and she had an infectious laugh. But she also had a sharp tongue and was too often unkind and hurtful both as a mother and, when the time came, as a mother-in-law.

She also occasionally liked the boys and the booze more than was sensible and, as my father put it, 'she had ants in her pants'. Every few years she got bored and moved from one admittedly beautiful and wonderful place to another: Cornwall to Dorset, Dorset to Devon, Devon to Castiglione della Pescaia in Tuscany, Castiglione to Florence.

My father, Patrick (and his father, Buddy) were of the gently indolent variety of Needhams – both professional soldiers in the Grenadier Guards, who retired as majors in their early thirties and did nothing very much thereafter until they died of heart failure, one at the age of 69 and the other at 62. They were unfit for a world outside soldiering and had no idea how to make money, let alone earn it. The topic was never discussed. The nearest I got to a financial tutorial was the instruction I received with my first pocket money: I was always to pay the milkman, the butcher and the greengrocer. Everyone else could wait.

My earliest recollection is sitting on my potty sticking a Union Jack on a pole into the bars of an electric fire to see if it would catch alight. It did. My second memory was hearing a doodlebug fly overhead, and my third is of Maurice Willes, an old family farming friend, lying in the bath with a large sponge over his willy telling me I was to go back with him to become a shepherd's boy. I screamed.

I think I remember Nellie Burton – who was a hereditary baroness in her own right, descendant of the founder of Bass Brewery and a lady-in-waiting to Queen Mary – coming to tea when I was five and telling my mother that I had the head of a future prime minister! I certainly recall her explaining to me that a 'settee' was called a 'sofa' and the only time one said 'pardon' was when one farted. She had also set the precedent for all the eldest daughters of peers who wished to claim their fathers' titles ahead of their brothers.

When my father returned from the War he took me into his classroom at Sandhurst, where he was an instructor, and gave me a small carved tank that he had sculpted from wood with his penknife. It was the first time I had ever seen him.

Soon afterwards he resigned his commission and we moved to a stunning little Georgian house called Menehay in the far west of Cornwall where my two brothers, Christopher and Jonathan, were born in 1948 and 1951. It had a most beautiful garden of azaleas, camellias and rhododendrons. Hundreds of miles from anywhere, it looked out over Falmouth Bay and was idyllic, but lonely for a boy of my background looking to make friends. As my brothers were so much younger than me, I was sent away at the age of six to a school in Eastbourne.

The school was owned and run by Major John and Betty Maxfield, great friends of my parents. He had a tin leg having lost his real one serving in the Marines at Walcheren. He was great fun when sober, which wasn't that often, and had a vile temper, backed up by a ruler that kept his charges in order. I don't remember what, if anything, I learnt, only that it took a day and a half from Cornwall to get there and that we did a lot of excursions around Sussex.

I do remember my landlady being a sour old witch who used to send us to the loo every morning with three sheets of Bronco. One was to come out dirty, one nearly clean and the third spotless. Bronco came in a yellow pack with a window in the front. The Bronco box was adorned with printed gold medals which claimed that the company had won 'Best in show' at the Paris Exhibition of 1848 and was similarly successful in Berlin and London. Why anyone should have an exhibition for shiny, hard, non-transparent loo paper, let alone be awarded gold medals for their efficiency, I never discovered – nor did I work out as I sat there what their methods of inspection and quality control were.

After two years at Eastbourne I was moved further away to a proper preparatory school in Broadstairs called Selwyn House. Broadstairs was a hive of prep schools: St Peter's Court, where my father had been, Wellesley House, which was a feeder for Eton, and Stone House. Broadstairs, even in the fifties, was a drab, cold, soulless resort, which had been popular with Londoners from the East End for a day by the sea in the nineteenth century.

On my first day we were told to report to Victoria Station to catch the 3.20 train to Broadstairs. I was handed over to the deputy headmaster, Walter Meade-King, and met Peter Davies, who was to become my best friend. His mother, like mine, was sobbing, while another new boy called

Morgan was being sick into a paper bag. There were eleven of us new boys in the autumn term of 1950.

The wind howled through the dormitories and we eight-year olds were tucked up in mattresses on metal-springed beds. The mattresses formed canoes for the homesick, who spent most of the night blubbing away. I was one of them. In the distance we could hear the bleak sound of the North Foreland Lighthouse rising and falling in the storm, reminding us 'of those in peril on the sea'.

The school was run by John Green and his wife. He was tall and gaunt but sympathetic and an invigorating teacher. His wife was enormous and taught us to swim in the spring once the temperature of the pool reached sixteen degrees. She put us in a canvas sling at the end of a pole, dropped us in and dragged us back up the side of the pool. If you looked up you could see her grubby underwear and if you looked down, you drowned. We all learnt to swim quite quickly.

The deputy headmaster, Walter Meade-King, was a ghastly man. He was tall and burly and smoked incessantly. He had a nicotine-stained moustache and fingers. He corrected your work while puffing smoke in your face. He had an infuriating habit of doing this while writing on the blackboard at the same time. Every morning after breakfast, he sat at a desk and did *The Times* crossword while he organised the boys in squads to go to a row of sit-downs in the cloakroom. We were allowed three minutes to complete our business before the next team arrived. His passion was cricket and his temper depended on how England were playing, particularly against Australia. I remember him in a towering rage when Denis Compton was brought on to bowl in one of the tests with Australia at about six hundred for three. For minor misdemeanours he used to force the boys to drop their short trousers before he spanked them on their bare bottoms. He was a bachelor, but nobody seemed to think there was anything particularly strange going on.

I was rather an asthmatic boy and was often ill in the winter terms, spending most of my time in the sanatorium. On one occasion I caught pneumonia and couldn't breathe. My parents sent some clotted cream up in a tub from Cornwall and I was allowed to put it on my cornflakes. After I had recovered somewhat, I was sent home and we all went off to the Scilly Isles for me to recuperate. It was my first flight in an aeroplane. I was terrified and vowed never to go up in one again.

At school we all had little gardens that we were allowed to cultivate with seeds of our choosing – I used to grow nasturtiums. The food was revolting: powdered egg, tough over-cooked venison every week with boiled potatoes and over-cooked smelly cabbage swimming in water.

Once a term my parents would drive up from Falmouth for the weekend to take me out. They stayed at the Albion Hotel, overlooking the sea. We used to sit in the conservatory watching the ships in the Channel while my father read *The Times*. For excitement we would visit Dreamland, a local funfair, and then head off to the Omar Khayyam Cafe in Broadstairs for fried egg and bacon followed by a knickerbocker glory. For exercise we would walk along the cliffs. I always brought Peter Davies for company.

The highlight of the week was the letter from home. My mother wrote every week and my father perhaps twice a term. Her letters were full of news about the dogs and cats, the weather and my brothers. His letters were about what was going on in the garden. My replies were a summary of my results, a description of the weather and a request for sweets. The letters settled into a pattern over the years, rather like saying your nightly prayers. 'God bless Mummy and Daddy, Granny and Grandad, Christopher and Jonathan'. They were unimaginative and banal but at least they were links. I had good friends at Selwyn House who I never kept up with. My other enjoyment came from collecting stamps and cigarette cards. I was happy because I knew nothing else. I was diligent and terrified of failure.

At the end of my time, and just after I had taken Common Entrance, I was called to the headmaster's office to be told the 'facts of life'. There was a lot of explanation about vaginas and penises but nothing about what really mattered. Pretty little boys going on to their public schools were likely to be targets for older boys. I was going to Eton where small boys wore tight striped trousers, a white shirt and stiff collar with a black tie, and a short cut-away black coat – a 'bum freezer' – that finished at the waist. All very fetching. But of the dangers facing us, we remained blissfully unaware.

CHAPTER 2

Eton: 'A sombre grey patch upon the chart of my journey'

(Winston Churchill on his time at Harrow)

I PASSED MY Common Entrance quite comfortably and my first term started in January 1955 when I was just thirteen. My grandmother had sent my father to Stowe, which had opened after the First World War and was meant to be a more civilised version of Eton. As she was paying, when it came to me she insisted that, as a future earl, my education reverted to tradition. My grandfather, great-grandfather and great-great-grandfather had all been to Eton as had probably generations of Needhams before them.

But we were not a particularly academic family. We had not done much to trouble the scorers. I have one of my grandfather's reports that was written in 1902 when he was sixteen:

Dear Lord Kilmorey,

Buddy is a nice, kind and hard-working boy. He applies himself as best he can but he is held back by his recurring illnesses and finds it a struggle to keep up. I think he will find it too hard to get into the Household Cavalry, but the Grenadiers might have him.

They did.

My parents distrusted intellectuals as being too clever for their own good. I don't remember my father ever reading a book, with the exception of Nicholas Monsarrat's *The Cruel Sea,* which had been given to him by a naval friend.

The point of sending children to Eton is that, by and large, the masters there are better than the masters at other public schools. Secondly, the extracurricular subjects and hobbies on offer cover a huge gamut of cultural, political, sporting, literary and artistic activities. No school in the world offers more. Thirdly, many of the boys come from extremely powerful establishment families. If your little mite befriends one of them, it may lead at best to a job in the City and at worst to numerous invitations to go shooting and fishing.

Eton manages to instil in its pupils a patriotic fervour to go out and conquer the world, whatever their chosen career. I do not know why that is – it is perplexing. Maybe son following father; maybe the breeding stock! Maybe privilege. Or maybe, and probably, the school is so steeped in history, tradition, success, self-belief and self-confidence that it imbues these characteristics in its students.

In the 1950s there was a dark side to the school. Eton prided itself on giving responsibility to the boys to run the houses where they boarded. Each house consisted of about sixty pupils, looked after by a housemaster and a dame, a matronly figure who was there to ensure the house ran efficiently.

If you were tall, tough, sporty and spotty when you arrived, you could get by. But if you were tubby, short (too small to wear tailcoats), pretty and your balls had not dropped, you could be in trouble.

Every new boy started off as a 'fag' to one of the members of the Library, the room in which the prefects sat. The task was to clean the fag master's shoes, run errands, take messages to his friends and prepare his toast for tea. If he thought you had failed in any of your duties, the remedy could be to have you beaten by the head of house.

A 'beating-up' was a ritual. After prayers in the dining room, which came at the end of each day, the head of house – who was eighteen years old and often well over six foot – would follow the housemaster to his study to get agreement for the thrashing. Because Eton ran on the principles of the boys being in charge, the housemaster invariably concurred, regardless of how petty the alleged misdemeanour was. If members of the Library thought that so-and-so would benefit from a good whacking, the offence might even be made up.

After prayers the boys all returned to their rooms. The members of the Library took off their tailcoats, put on tweed 'change' jackets and took down their canes. They then proceeded to run around the house beating their canes against the walls and rattling them up and down the staircases. Everyone, particularly the little ones, prayed it was not their turn.

The junior member of the Library would then throw open the door of the culprit's room (every boy had his own room, however tiny) and shout,

'Get outside the Library!' Up you went. The Library door was slammed. As you stood outside, you could hear the furniture being moved around to form the circle for the kangaroo court.

You were summoned inside, dry-mouthed, shaking with fear. You were told of your crime. In my case, a member of the Library had seen me playing around in the gym with some of my friends instead of concentrating on my exercises. What had I to say? Nothing, unless I wanted an extra three lashes.

I bent over a chair. I had my tails flipped up over my backside by the head of house with his cane. Then I was beaten – in this instance the so-called offence warranted six strikes. The maximum was around twelve. The key test was to remain silent. Then out I went, back to my room, to examine the red ridges on my bottom. This ritual was repeated on different backsides once or twice a month. There were different sorts of canes: long thin whippy ones and the 'Pop' canes which had knobbles all the way down the shaft. (Members of Pop are the School's elite six formers who wear white stick-up collars, brightly coloured waistcoats, sponge-bag trousers and carnations in their buttonholes. They also have the special canes and were allowed to fine boys for minor demeanours.)

There was an additional form of punishment called 'a swiping', carried out by the headmaster for poor performance or cheating. The head of school (Eton's term for the head boy) would burst into a classroom unannounced and order the victim to the headmaster's room immediately. The headmaster then commanded that the miscreant dropped his trousers. He knelt on a block and was 'swiped' on his bare bottom with a birch. A bill was sent to his parents at the end of the half (Eton's name for term) for eleven shillings to pay for the birch. On account of the blood, birches could only be used once. The head boy was in attendance as a witness.

The very threat of a beating-up was enough to send many into a funk. I've often asked myself what purpose these beatings-up were meant to achieve. The only semi-satisfactory answer I dug up was in a Russian communist encyclopaedia, which stated, 'Eton is a school where big boys beat little boys and when the little boys grow up, they go out to Africa and beat the natives!'

There were other subtle forms of bullying – by threat and innuendo, for example – that would go unnoticed if a housemaster was not on top of his job. My housemaster was Peter Lawrence, a former Royal Naval Reserve officer who was un-affectionately known as 'Wetty'. He had a powerful wife and six children and spent more time keeping on top of them than on running his house.

Houses in Eton compete for results and trophies. Many had sideboards groaning with silver and noticeboards covered in news of academic triumphs. Our sideboards were bare and our noticeboards empty. Lawrence was fearful for his job and so any new boy who didn't cut the mustard academically early on in his time was asked to leave in case his failure would rub off on Wetty. My brother, Christopher, was one of them.

Nothing lasts forever and after four years the bullies had left and I joined the Eton Corps. My father and Wetty were delighted. Neither of them had any idea what to do with me: my father had done nothing other than soldiering; Wetty had been a sailor in the RNR and then a schoolmaster.

The Eton Corps was run by Colonel William Gladstone and his regimental sergeant major was called Ayling. He had been my father's sergeant major in North Africa and he was determined to take me under his wing. He had hopes I might follow in the family footsteps but I was not a model pupil. I was not particularly fit so I was slow, I didn't like taking orders, I couldn't hit the target with my rifle and, worst of all, I had two left feet on the parade ground.

Once a half we used to go on exercises on Salisbury Plain for forty-eight hours. My map reading was not the best and we often ended up on the wrong hill. I was hiding, not very convincingly, when Dickie Birch-Reynardson, the Corps adjutant, rode by and bellowed at me to become invisible. As I was attempting this manoeuvre, my rifle went off, scaring Birch-Reynardson's horse and dumping him on the ground.

That was the end of my military career. As I was dressed down by Sergeant Major Ayling before he removed my cap badge, he whispered an inch from my nose, 'The best part of you, Needham, ran down the inside of your mother's leg.' Then he paused. 'I apologise,' he said. 'Her Ladyship's leg.'

I liked acting and I was a good mimic. I got taken up by Raef Payne, a truly inspirational teacher, who gave me confidence and self-belief, unlike the pusillanimous Wetty. I became the fool in *King Lear*, the school play. Lear was played by a huge boy called Bill Grosvenor who spent most of his adult life trying to work out how he could get rid of the relatives that stood in the way of him becoming the Duke of Westminster.

At the first performance, after my last line ('I'll go to bed at noon'), I dashed round to the back of the audience. Raef was a chain-smoker and he had a line of Lucky Strike cigarettes standing on their filters on the balustrade. 'How's Bill doing?' I asked, as mist clouded out of a machine in the wings, thunder cracked and lightning shot across the stage. Bill seemed to be in majestic form. 'Not very well,' said Raef, 'we haven't had any Shakespeare for the last ten minutes!'

In those days *The Times* theatre critic reviewed the Eton school play. He wrote: 'The Fool was an energetic little fellow whose accent swung violently between Yorkshire and Lancashire.' I had never been to either.

I was also taken up by Norman Routledge, another inspirational beak (the Eton word for teacher). He was a mathematician who had taught at Farnborough with Alan Turing after the War. We put on a house review that consisted of half-a-dozen or so sketches: some set to music and dance and some pale reflections of Dick Emery. I was the lead player. I loved it. In one of my song-and-dance routines I was dressed in ill-fitting tights, wearing a French revolutionary cockade and singing, 'I am the public prosecutor, for my sins I had no tutor!' In the next sketch I was a farm labourer. 'I had rabbit on the Monday, boiled rabbit Tuesday, fried rabbit Wednesday and by Thursday I got a shockin' stomach ache. "Wot I needs is castor oil," I told the missus. "No, you don't, you needs a ferret!" '

Wetty showed no interest although he tried to take some of the credit from Norman when we got a rave review in the *Eton Chronicle*.

The only subject I shone at was history. I sucked up the stories of great battles, great generals, great statesmen. My heroes included Henry de Navarre ('Paris is well worth a mass!'), Cardinal Richelieu, Gustave Adolphus, Wallenstein, Marlborough, Wellington, Garibaldi and Rommel. I wanted to believe that crucial moments in history were decided by men – not by movements or by economic and social trends. In Giles St Aubyn's history class I sat next to James Loudon and Edward Mortimer. (Edward later became a fellow of All Souls and director of communications for Kofi Annan at the UN.) Both were scholars, and under real pressure from them and St Aubyn, I managed to come top in the junior Rosebery History Prize with my essay on Napoleon's Italian campaigns. That was the apex of my academic achievement. After that it was downhill.

My Latin and Greek master Robin McNaughten was nicknamed 'Cauliflower'. He had a head like a cauliflower and ears like their blooms. He was very short-sighted, wore thick bifocals, and spoke very quickly and very quietly. Most of the time the boys just ignored him. He wasn't helped by having a classroom that ran north–south, with windows in the south-west corner. As the winter light beamed in, he was always fully illuminated and the rest of the class was in Stygian gloom. On one occasion, unseen by Robin, a fight erupted. 'Sit down!' bawled Robin into the dark. Nothing moved. 'Sit down or I'll give you a hundred lines!' Still nothing. 'A hundred lines in my room by lock-up (this was when boys had to be in their houses)!' The boy's coat hanging on the back wall failed to respond.

I passed my Greek O level without understanding the alphabet, let alone Homer, which was rather sad as ancient Greek plays are rather invigorating, as I have since discovered. Robin went on to be a very fine headmaster of Sherborne School where his disabilities became irrelevant.

My German and French teacher was called A.J. Marsden. He had had a very good War but had been rather shaken by his experiences. His interests were rowing and whisky, not German, French or his pupils. So, fairly regularly he failed to turn up to teach us and I failed my German A level with ease. His report into my attempts at French stated, 'Quiet as a mouse. I was hardly conscious of him though he sat two feet from me. He never gave any sort of trouble and learned his work reasonably well.'

When I was seventeen, I decided that politics was the career for me. I wanted to get to the top of whatever I did and I certainly didn't want to go into the army or the law (although my uncle said there was a lot of money to be made in patent litigation!). I had been brought up to believe in public service. The Foreign Office was out – I wasn't clever enough – but politics sounded glamorous, and with my acting abilities I thought I might be rather good at declaiming my own words rather than somebody else's. It was time to be thinking about the next steps after Eton. Pa and Wetty put their heads together.

The outcome was far from satisfactory. It consisted mainly of 'don't knows' from my father or 'you can't possibly do thats' from Wetty. Sometime later Wetty came and sat on the end of my bed on one of his evening rounds of the house. Had I any idea of what I wanted to do before politics? I told him my family had no money, that we lived in Cornwall, and that my parents' contacts were limited to some retired army and navy friends. They had lived, apart from the War, a very narrow and parochial existence, occasionally enlivened by family visits and local highlights, such as entering the Falmouth Flower Show. I once spent several hours organising an arrangement in the children's section, only to forget to put any water in the bowl. Unsurprisingly a prize eluded me as everything had died by the time the judges did their rounds.

Although I was set on politics, I wanted and needed to go into business to become independent. 'What sort?' demanded Wetty.

'Advertising,' I ventured.

'You can't do that – one day you'll be an earl!' he replied.

'That won't help if I have no prospects and no money,' I countered.

'Oh well,' he said. 'I'll try and get you into Oxford or Cambridge.' He got off the bed, shunting the can down the road.

Eton didn't do 'careers advice'. Generally there was no need for it as the boys could walk effortlessly from Oxbridge into the City or the Foreign Office, run their estates, take over from their fathers or wait to inherit generations of capital in tax-efficient trust funds. For a significant minority Eton was a blight on their prospects. Those who didn't move in rarefied self-perpetuating circles or whose families had fallen on hard times through death and death duties found it hard to gain a place in the real world. For them, going to Eton was the crowning achievement of their careers and finding success outside eluded them.

In all I applied to three Oxford and three Cambridge colleges: Christchurch, Exeter and Pembroke at Oxford, and Trinity, Corpus Christi and Magdalene at Cambridge. They all declined to give me an interview bar one. Christchurch told me to write an essay on one of three topics, none of which I knew anything about. I sent it; they told Wetty (whose college it had been) that I was well below the standard required. Years later, as I was walking into Christchurch, I looked up and saw the Kilmorey crest on the ceiling of the entrance. My great-grandfather had been a benefactor and a friend of Charles Dodgson (Lewis Carroll). Had Wetty or my father known about the connection, it might have improved my chances in those nepotistic times.

There had been no attempt by Wetty or my other tutors to prepare me for Oxbridge entrance, any more than there had been any form of careers advice. Other universities were not even considered. Magdalene College, Cambridge, said I was a 'nice' boy but too limited in my outlook and insufficiently academically gifted. Magdalene was right on both accounts. I was extremely young for my age and I had little or no intellectual stimulation at home. Cornwall in the 1950s was not renowned for its theatres. My topical reading consisted of the *Daily Express* and the *Illustrated London News*, which my grandmother gave me every year as a Christmas present. I had started life with Alison Uttley's *Grey Rabbit* and *Hare Joins the Home Guard*. These were followed by Enid Blyton, *Just William* stories, Biggles and romantic novels such as *Angelique* by Anne Golon, topped off with war stories about Colditz and the Great Escape. I was left on my own and told to 'get on with it'. Whatever 'it' might be, it did not include reading the classics. Arguments with my parents petered out after I told my father that it was the Russians who had won the war and my mother sent me to my bedroom for the rest of the day. As I grew older I realised I had less and less in common with either of them.

I had little in common with my contemporaries in my house at Eton either. One was a boxer who lived on Dartmoor, another became a seller of hotels in Scotland having commanded a nuclear submarine and the rest have faded from memory.

I left Eton in the summer of 1960 with two A levels and a tie called 'the Scramblers' which was worn by those who had done little or nothing of consequence. I had no idea what I was going to do next but I was sure of something: I would never go back, I would never send my children there and I would never keep up with those I had boarded with. These were vows that I kept for the next fifteen years.

CHAPTER 3

The Godfathers

THERE WERE PEOPLE in my childhood who were profoundly influential. The first was Nigel Nicolson, son of Harold Nicolson and Vita Sackville-West. He arrived out of the blue as the Conservative parliamentary candidate for Falmouth and Camborne in the summer of 1950. He had fought Leicester North in the February election and lost by 7,600 votes to Greville Janner's father, while the Labour MP Harold Hayman had hung on to a majority of two thousand in Falmouth. Why Nigel was coming so far to another Labour-held seat, I have no idea. He was very tall, very nervous, very shy. He blushed very easily and was extremely scruffy. He always arrived at Menehay out of the blue, and always with a great case of dirty washing.

He was also very kind and understanding to me. I worshipped him and used to follow him around to wherever he was campaigning. He had been in the Guards Armoured Division in the War, ending up on the Austrian-Yugoslav Frontier. So, when looking for a place to stay, I suppose he looked up the ex-Grenadiers in the area and came across my father.

He took me to his public meetings when I was just eight or nine. One of them was a terrifying confrontation with the 'red' dockers in the Falmouth shipyard. I think the only reason they didn't throw things at him was because I was on the platform next to him, holding his hand!

At a garden party at Killiow, the home of legendary, gin-swilling Annie Penrose, he began his speech, 'Ladies and gentlemen and Richard.' I was hooked. Nigel became an idol to me. He was a hopeless politician who I think went into politics to please his parents and because he had a tremendous sense of duty. After losing Falmouth by almost the same number of votes as the previous candidate, he was elected to Bournemouth East and Christchurch. But he fell out with the government over Suez in

1956 and was kicked out by his right-wing activists. He was a true Tory 'wet' – and years later I was to follow in his footsteps.

My father's closest friend, also an ex-Grenadier, was David Beaumont-Nesbitt. He was the son of a general. His sister married a general and his nephew became a general. He was a bachelor colonel. My mother insisted she was the only love of his life. After the end of the Korean War, he left the army and ended up, a fish out of water, at ITV. He was killed in 1963 when he crashed his blue MGA on Putney Bridge. I called him 'Uncle D' and he was my godfather. He introduced me to red wine at Christmas when I was eight. The wine was called Auberge and I was allowed two full glasses diluted by half. He had spent time in India and used to dress up in a kaftan and wear a turban when cooking curries, which were always very spicy and were always followed by what he called 'a hot squat'. There were joss sticks stuck in oranges all over his kitchen.

He always supported me against my mother's ever-changing moods and allegiances. I would stay with him in his little house in Hampstead and he would talk about anything and everything. I once asked him about sex. He said he had had very little experience of it. He had been, he said, to a brothel in Seoul with his brigadier but the rice paper walls had done nothing to increase the intimacy of the occasion – he could hear the brigadier going about his exertions and from time to time blurting out, 'Don't touch that, it's got nothing to do with you!' As a child, he was my closest confidant but like my father, he lived in a bygone world.

When I was fifteen, I was given a sixteen-foot sailing boat called *Margaret*. She was a Plymouth One design. She had been built thirty years earlier for sailing in Plymouth Sound so she had a very tall mast, a very large sail area and she was a handful for a small boy. I used to race her in handicap competitions, but my parents were the only crew I could muster and my mother was better at being a passenger than a deckhand. Occasionally we caught mackerel, which I had to clean. The boat required constant maintenance, particularly scrubbing down, sandpapering, anti-fouling and painting. This took place during the Christmas holidays. I was glad when after two years *Margaret* broke her mooring and sank, even though she had taught me how to sail.

My youngest brother, Jonathan, was born prematurely in 1951 when I was nine and Christopher was three. It was a difficult birth and afterwards my mother employed a nanny who was to stay with us for the next twenty-five years. Her name was Inez Williams; we called her Nan. She came from

Bodmin. She was a true Cornish liberal Methodist and she found it difficult with me being a Tory MP. She never had a chance to marry because she also looked after her parents as well as bringing up the three of us. As I was the eldest by several years, she looked after my brothers more than me. She was a wonderful cook, cleaner, carer, confidante and supporter. She was a clever, well-read woman who in different times would have become matron of a large hospital. She made enormous, delicious Cornish pasties in the Aga with our initials baked on the top.

When Jonathan was small, Nan used to take us in the summer holidays on long walks down to the slide in the Botanic Gardens in Falmouth, or along the cliffs at Rosemullion and down to the beach to find tiny, pink cowrie shells, with Jonathan in a pushchair, Christopher aged five and one or other of our dogs, usually Chows. Christopher had an extraordinary knack of finding a recently encrusted cowpat, which he would fall into, covering himself from head to toe, and then scream. Occasionally I would push him in the right direction to see what would happen. My brothers were so much younger than me that we only really got to know and love each other once we had grown up.

Our house was semi-detached to the farmhouse next door. The farm was run by the Dunstans and they had a son, Roger, who was roughly my age. My father nicknamed him 'Roger-the-lodger-the-sod' and, as he was smaller than me, he used to take instructions with some semblance of discipline. The gardener, Willy Rashleigh, had a daughter called Rosemary. The three of us used to play in the sandpit, go shooting pigeons with a 4.10 on cornstalks in the fields and fool around. Aged thirteen, I was caught kissing Rosemary in the walled garden when I was supposed to be feeding my pet tortoise, which ended that happy relationship.

When I was sixteen, a cousin of my mother's died, leaving her some money. Having decided that Cornwall was too remote for us all, my mother moved us into a large Victorian rectory, Broadwindsor House, near Beaminster in Dorset. As market gardening in Cornwall had failed to pay the bills, my father turned to battery chicken eggs and breeding pigs for Unilever in the stables. Neither proved any more remunerative than anemones or hydrangeas. But for me, after ten years in Cornwall, Broadwindsor was nearer to the action than Penryn and I was able to ask my friends to stay. When I turned eighteen I was given a second-hand green Morris Minor with a fold-down roof. It was meant to be Britain's answer to the Volkswagen Beetle and probably would have been if the workers at Morris hadn't spent so much of the time on strike. It was excellent for getting out and around the local pubs at weekends, when we played darts, cribbage and skittles. We drank cider, which tasted like vinegar but was improved by adding blackcurrant cordial.

On 11 January 1961, just three years after we had moved to Dorset, my great-uncle, 'Minor' Kilmorey, the fourth Earl, died at Mourne Park, Kilkeel, County Down. I was staying in Castle Drogo, a mock Norman castle in Devon. The butler arrived during dinner in the great hall with a message on a silver platter telling me that my father was now the earl and that I, as his eldest son, was the fifth viscount Newry and Mourne. I had realised that sooner or later this was going to happen, but it seemed completely irrelevant to me, other than the fact that it might give me a slight advantage with the girls and help me make reservations in restaurants I couldn't afford. I had never been to Northern Ireland. I had only met my great-uncle once, at my grandfather's memorial service in the Guards' Chapel. I had no idea where Newry was and it was always unlikely that any money or 'nice things' would come in my direction, not least because of my parents' extravagance and lack of income.

My parents had no desire to live in the wilds of the Mourne Mountains and my father had had little connection with his uncle or cousins, so he was dispatched to Belfast with the family solicitor, Stephen Robinson of Radcliffe's, to collect what money and boodle he could. My cousins had had many years to work out how to deal with this eventuality and had laid careful plans to ensure that my father came away with not a farthing more than he was entitled to.

The mother of my great-aunt Nora came from a rich Northern Ireland linen family and she had got together a hundred thousand pounds, which they offered to my father in return for buying out his inheritance. This consisted of Mourne Park, several hundred acres, most of the town of Kilkeel, considerable slices of Newry and a large number of family paintings and a significant amount of silver.

Over ever more generous helpings of gin it was explained to my father that the house was falling down, the debts were enormous, the UVF had stolen the silver and most of the pictures were copies. It was a tribulation of St Jude to collect the rents from the tenants, control the thieving habits of the locals and avoid the IRA. As a sweetener they added a pillowcase of heirlooms – including a diamond tiara, some brooches and earrings and what little silver they claimed was left. They also threw in some ugly seventeenth-century portraits of fierce-looking bewigged Kilmorey ancestors with armoured breastplates. As soon as they arrived at home, my mother stuck her finger through each of them.

My father came back happy. A hundred thousand pounds was a fortune in 1961. He took the pillowcase into Garrard's on Regent Street and sold the jewellery and silver for half what he would have got had he gone around the corner to Sotheby's or Christies to have them sold by auction.

This sudden arrival of riches allowed my mother to take on a butler and his wife. He was called Horner, and he used to wake us up every morning with a cup of tea and a cheery exclamation about the weather and where the wind was coming from. We had two gardeners, two dailies and Nan. The cost of this establishment rose to twenty thousand pounds a year. My father's income was £3,700 and with tax on unearned income of 97 per cent, it was not long before the assets ran out and they were forced to sell up.

CHAPTER 4

Finding My Feet

IN THE SUMMER of 1960, with no university place on offer, I was struggling with the question of what to do next. I signed up with a crammer in Holland Park called Davis, Lang & Dick to retake my German A level with the futile plan of persuading an Oxbridge college to take another look at me. It was a miserable time. I was living in digs in Earl's Court with an almost speechless Pom-hating Aussie; trekking up to the crammer and then going back to my bedsit in the late afternoon with no money, no friends and no notion of what lay ahead. It was the first time in my life that I was really lonely and depressed.

At the end of the cramming course I managed to find a Christmas job at Harrods, serving in the cooked meat department. This involved coming in at 7 a.m., going down to the cold storage rooms in the basement, and retrieving the haggises and the hams before displaying them in refrigerated display cabinets. One morning, as I was carrying an armful of haggises up from the cellars, I met the rat catcher. He had a couple of rats hanging on hooks from one side of his belt and a venomous-looking Colt .45 revolver strapped to the other. He must have been a very good shot. The haggises were sometimes a bit worn on one side after drying out in the light cabinet during the previous day, and on the other damp side they attracted a fine layer of mould. However, a wipe-over with a sponge had them looking good as new and back on display they went. After the store closed at 7 p.m. we had to spend the next two hours packing up boxes for customers who had ordered by post. One Warwickshire woman had ordered a large box of Smith's crisps, which seemed extravagant when she could have ordered an identical box from the local greengrocer.

It was a long day and any attempt to lean on the counter behind brought an immediate blast from Percy Peacock, the manager. He and his assistant,

Wally, had been in the War together and Wally had been wounded. At lunchtime they repaired to the Bag 'O Nails pub for a couple of hours, leaving us in control.

At the end of the Christmas season, they asked if I would come back the following year but three weeks had been enough for me. Wally died soon after I left and Percy's trips to the pub led to cirrhosis of the liver and his demise.

What was I to do with my life? I had to try to get some sort of qualification. I wanted to change the world for the better, particularly the pink bits on the atlas. I was captivated by politics. I had told my brother when I was fifteen that I would be prime minister one day! But I was scared of making a fool of myself in debates. I considered myself of average intelligence and I was average at sport – but I could make people laugh and I could act. I was passionate but my self-confidence was not based on any rock of achievement or substance, and it was superficial. I could not expect to inherit much so I would have to do it myself. I had no career mentor other than my mother's brother-in-law, the incredibly successful John Sheffield, who told me I should be prepared to do it all on my own, as he had done!

I was inquisitive and realised that to achieve my ambitions I would have to go into business. I wanted to make things. I wanted to set up factories and reverse Britain's industrial decline, of which I was vaguely aware. I wanted to understand my country. At eighteen I was beginning to grasp the necessity of gaining a broader experience of life and society beyond my narrow and privileged upbringing. I had a plan at the back of my head. I would be married by twenty-five – she would have to be beautiful and different. Millionaire by thirty. Member of Parliament by thirty-five. Prime Minister by fifty. This was a dream that lacked a theme, a foundation, an overarching political message or a philosophy. It was egotistical, personal and self-centred. But, nonetheless, some of it was to come true.

After two months cramming, I passed my German A level but still had no place at Oxford or Cambridge. It was John Montagu, one of my friends from school, who came to my rescue. He was a year younger but he lived a couple of miles from us in Dorset. His father was a famous right-wing controversial politician who had made his reputation as Lord Hinchingbrooke, member of parliament for South Dorset. They lived in a beautiful manor house outside Beaminster, and his father Hinch, as he was always called, held 'court' every weekend with his reactionary friends as they plotted Harold Macmillan's downfall. Hinch had recently been on a tour of South Africa as a guest of Verwoerd's government and the South Africa Foundation. John had left Eton at the same time as me and had a year to spend before going up to Cambridge. While he had been in South Africa, Hinch had met one of the most successful Afrikaans businessmen, Anton Rupert. He suggested to Hinch that John went to work for his company, the Rembrandt Tobacco Corporation, for a few months during his gap year and John asked me if I would go along.

In February 1961, John and I boarded a South African Airlines Boeing 707 and set off for Johannesburg. If I didn't like flying between Penzance and the Scilly Isles, I took serious fright on my first trip in a Boeing 707. Even though the plane was half empty and the stewardess let me stretch over three seats, I remained terrified as we flew from Amsterdam to Rome and on to Brazzaville in what was then French Equatorial Africa, one of the few countries left on the continent where SAA could land and refuel. The airport was not much more than a line of shacks with a petrol tanker on the tarmac. The parking stand was patrolled by the hard-faced men of the French Foreign Legion, dressed in camouflage fatigues and their famous flat, green berets, and touting sub-machine guns. By the time we approached Johannesburg the pilot announced that in order to increase the rate of descent from thirty thousand feet he was going to lower the landing gear and we should not be alarmed. The plane seemed to jolt to a stop in mid-air and then we plummeted earthwards. Alarm was an understatement. For the next twenty years, flying was to remain my greatest phobia.

We were met by an Afrikaner couple, the Moolmans, from the South Africa Foundation and a small troop of reporters. I decided it was appropriate to say a few words, which were fortunately attributed to John in the following morning's papers. Neither John nor I had realised that Rembrandt were keen to use us as a PR tool against their rivals, British American Tobacco. Business and industry were almost entirely in the control of the English colonialists and Rembrandt was one of the very few successful Afrikaner-dominated corporations. To have a Lord and the son of a Lord working for Rembrandt was a nice little snub to the snobs of BAT. At the same time, South Africa was about to leave the Commonwealth and the shadowy South Africa Foundation was keen to attract gullible young school-leavers to their cause. We woke up to headlines of 'Two nobles have a job at Paarl', 'Boland Lord' – with a picture of me wearing a badly-tied silk bow tie – and 'Viscount starts first job in Paarl'.

On our first weekend, the Moolmans drove us to Pretoria to see the Voortrekker Monument. On the way, we gaped at the pyramids of goldmining waste on the way. That Sunday we had lunch with a very swanky English lady, lay in her pool and then caught a plane to Cape Town. Even after two days we grasped how divided South Africa was. Not between blacks and whites, because we hadn't met any yet, but between the English colonialists and the Dutch settlers.

To the Afrikaners, the English and the blacks were interlopers. It was the Afrikaners who had arrived first when the only inhabitants of the country were the Khoikhois. They had settled it. It belonged to them. The only natives the Afrikaners recognised as being more local were the indigenous people of the Cape who had long interbred with the white immigrants to create a separate, slightly less-inferior coloured community that sat somewhere between the whites and the blacks, along with the Indians and the Chinese. The Dutch did not use the word 'native' in the sense of belonging, but to refer to someone who they believed had lower intelligence, culture and ability; who had come to find work; and who would never be able to rise to the standards required to run or manage a sophisticated European society. The English settlers still thought of England as 'home'. They were South African but only second to being British. They looked at the 'natives', as the British did wherever they went, with patronising condescension and a belief that perhaps one day, after many generations of education and civilising British rule, they would be able to participate in the governance of the country.

Rembrandt had worked out a three-month programme to enable us to cover as many aspects of the business in the shortest possible time. It involved us doing different jobs in different places for two-week slots and then joining up at the weekends to have fun. In the Cape I was put up in the local hostelry, the Paarl Hotel, run by Papa Sachs and his daughter, Bella. Every morning at 7 a.m., I walked down to the cigarette factory, jostled by a noisy crowd of Africans. On one occasion, crossing the Berg River Bridge, I found myself face to face with an enormous local woman carrying a baby. She pushed me aside with a look of contempt and hatred. With her in mind, I stupidly asked one of the men working in the suffocating tobacco leaf department whether he was happy. 'Of course,' he said. 'What else do I know?'

Every evening I propped up the bar with the white locals. I drank Oude

Meester brandy diluted with Canada Dry and played Liar's Dice. After a fortnight I got quite sharp at fibbing and it helped to pay for my rising intake of alcohol.

My menial task was to go around with some of the local management trainees to check quality in the various departments. It was an international Commonwealth team, headed up by Afrikaners who kept to themselves. They spoke to each other only in Afrikaans. Many of them wouldn't have been too unhappy to have seen us lose the War.

Because of John's and my notoriety in the local news, we were not short of invitations come Friday night. We also had two highly sophisticated Afrikaner minders, Willy Malherbe and Wynand van Graan, who took us fishing or on trips to wineries and fruit farms. They were men who would never have gained access to international business careers had it not been for the arrival of Anton Rupert and his commercial genius. Apartheid did not only affect the blacks.

One weekend we were invited to stay with the high commissioner, Sir John Maud. I was ushered into his study after lunch. He was a very grand establishment figure, every inch a Foreign Office mandarin. He was about to give a speech at the inauguration of a new mayor for Cape Town, Mrs Joyce Newton Thompson. He told me whenever he made a speech in English in Cape Town, he always included a quotation which made him popular with the locals. He had found an address that Field Marshal Jan Smuts gave on 25 February 1923 having climbed Table Mountain to unveil a memorial to members of the Mountain Club who had fallen in the Great War.

> Not only on the mountain summits of life, not only in the heights of success and achievements but down in the deep valleys of drudgery of anxiety and defeat we must cultivate the great spirit of joyous freedom and upliftment of the soul.

John Maud had this translated into Afrikaans, and he taught me an early lesson: flatter your audience whenever you can. He then lay down on the sofa and went to sleep for exactly fifteen minutes. I was ushered out and told to reappear for dinner, during which he explained how Macmillan's 'Wind of Change' speech had sounded the end of the British Empire in Africa.

The weekends were rounds of party-going, trips to the races, sightseeing and drinking. The smart mothers, all of English background, were keen to have their daughters meet the two young English Lords. They were unaware that one of them had no money and no obvious prospects. Unfortunately, the daughters were not the slightest bit interested. They had a wide range of bronzed, muscular, beautiful rugby- or cricket-playing boys to choose from. A shy, lanky seventeen-year-old and a talkative, long-nosed, pale-faced, red-necked nineteen-year-old did not cut the mustard.

It wasn't through lack of trying on my part. The nearest I came to success was with Nicky Caras who was Miss Durban, Miss Universe the Third and one of the Miss Rothmans who handed out free cigarettes at cocktail parties. I was rewarded with a kiss on the cheek after taking her out to a Chinese restaurant in Johannesburg. John said he was put off by her orange hair! He was no more successful.

There were two major political events while we were in the Cape. One was the first anniversary of the Sharpeville Massacre; the other was South Africa being forced out of the Commonwealth. In both cases it was the British South Africans who were most concerned and unnerved. Although they found apartheid 'distasteful', for most of them it ensured a way of life and a standard of living that they could never aspire to in Britain. They were fearful of the future and they were right to be. For the Afrikaners, international opprobrium reinforced their bunker mentality, their nationalism, their determination to fight for supremacy. For they had nowhere to retreat to.

It was extraordinary to spend our lives so completely cut off from the black and coloured majority. Once, in Johannesburg, we discovered a multiracial nightclub which gave us an unforgettable evening of music and dance. In general, the only conversation we had with black people was with the servants in the rich houses we stayed in. They were always smiling, polite and kind. They wore immaculate white uniforms and the head 'boy' wore a red sash and a black kepi. At the dances, you could see them watching from the sidelines.

Almost all our Afrikaner and most of our British friends bombarded us with the horror stories of what they thought would happen when black people had greater control. At worst it would lead to tribal war between Xhosa and Zulu; smaller tribes would be annihilated; whites would be massacred; the country would fail. It would become a Marxist chaos like the Congo. It was not for us teenage, privileged outsiders to tell them how to run their country, they told us. After all, we couldn't even beat them at rugby or cricket.

Of course, there were some we met who denounced it all as racist rubbish, which it was. But for two young boys straight out of school, the passionate opinions of most of those we came across was bound to leave an impression, particularly as many of those who supported apartheid were, in every other way, kind, descent, hospitable and reasonable people. They often likened themselves to the Israelis.

Although for the mother country, Britain, cutting the umbilical cord was traumatic, it was what would happen when America took an interest that really threatened them. Sitting in the bar one evening in Paarl, one of the locals confided to me that he would be happy to shake Louis Armstrong by the hand. I told him I doubted the gesture would be reciprocated.

When our time in the Cape was up, we flew together to Johannesburg and I went on to Durban. There, for three weeks, I was a Rothmans rep, driving around in a big decorated limo, selling cigarettes to CTNs (Confectionery Tobacco Newsagents). My role included filling up the cigarette dispensers in the canteen of a mental health facility. It was hot and humid but at least the role was more stimulating than sitting all day in a lab or quality-control office.

We were passed around like curiosities from family to family, pampered and spoiled. One day I was an 'extra' in a South African B-movie called *The Hellions*, starring a five-foot-two Richard Todd and a sinister Lionel Jeffries. We went to Kruger National Park for two days, but never saw a lion. We were never lonely; we never missed home. I got the occasional letter telling me about the cats and dogs. John's mum, for some reason, told him about his outstanding bill at Billings & Edmonds and the size of his overdraft at Coutts.

After I had changed places with John and spent three weeks in Johannesburg, we were moved to Salisbury (now Harare) in Southern Rhodesia, part of the Federation of Rhodesia and Nyasaland, for the last part of our trip. The atmosphere in Salisbury was very different from Cape Town. The whites in Rhodesia were facing the full force of Macmillan's 'winds of change'. Southern Rhodesia was part of a federation that included Northern Rhodesia and Nyasaland, though nobody was quite certain why the backwater of Nyasaland was included. Each country had its own system of government but all three came under the control of the Colonial Office and Commonwealth Relations Office.

In the years between 1946 and 1960 there had been a tripling of white immigrants. But the 223,000 settlers in Southern Rhodesia were hugely outnumbered by the three million blacks, and the numbers in Northern Rhodesia and Nyasaland were much lower.

Many of those who came out from Britain were ex-servicemen, refugees from Communist Europe and those fleeing from French and Belgian decolonisation. For a time, the Federation's economy boomed as investment keen to escape the Labour government's nationalisation and taxation policies flooded in. The government was overwhelmingly white and was driven by attempts at paternalistic reform, which included a mild form of condescending racism. However, the mood was one of anxiety and doubt. The prime minister, Sir Roy Welensky was a fearsome Northern Rhodesian ex-heavyweight boxing railway man. Born to a Lithuanian Jewish father and an Afrikaner mother, he described himself as 'half Jewish, half Afrikaner and a hundred percent British'.

John and I got invited round to tea and the prime minister was captivating, charming and very persuasive. He told us if Britain abandoned Africa too early, chaos and bloodshed would follow. The African tribes, the Shona and the Ndbele, would go back to murdering each other as they had done a hundred years earlier. There would be ethnic cleansing and mass murder. The whites would leave. The Africans would be incapable of developing and maintaining the economy, and the three parts of the Federation which were blessed with every sort of resource from copper to tobacco would be blighted for generations. Unfortunately, that's exactly what happened.

Roy Welensky begged for time to educate, train and involve the black population. But it was not to be. The British, prodded by the Americans, had had enough of Empire. There were charismatic black leaders waiting in the wings, often backed by left-wing Communist agitators keen to foster revolution. Violence was around every corner. For many black people, it was preferable to be ruled chaotically by people of their own colour than governed by rich masters of a paler complexion.

Rothmans put me to work fitting out a new factory they were constructing in Salisbury. I was in charge of a gang of Africans who were cleaning the copper domes of the tobacco mixing machines before they were sprayed. It was hard work. My team all came from different tribes. We all got on and had fun, but I could feel their underlying resentment of my position – and they were, of course, right.

We became friends with Peter Smith who was the mild, liberally-minded, stuttering chairman of the 'Young Feds'. Under the influence, I got into serious trouble for bawling him out with my plan for uniting European industry, which would be fed by raw materials from the Commonwealth. Then, according to John, I started arguing the opposite of what I had been advocating until finally admitting that at nineteen I had no idea what I was talking about.

We toured the tobacco auction rooms and stayed with a delightful tobacco farmer called Johnny Dankworts. He was in the process of moving his workers out of their mud huts and into corrugated iron roofed concrete shelters, which was a step up but hardly a flight.

On the way back, over Easter, we took a few days off to fly up to the Murchison Falls at the head of the Nile in Uganda. Africa is so huge. We could see hundreds of miles over to the Mountains of the Moon in the Congo, shrouded by electric storms and lit with huge lightning bursts – but so far away as to be noiseless.

We were almost charged by a bull elephant by driving between him and his herd. Whenever we stopped beautiful smiling children appeared suddenly out of the roadside bushes. We slept in tents, devoured by mosquitos and kept awake by the roar of the lions. We were aware that the 'Queen's Writ' no longer ran in Uganda. We managed to send a silly cable to our parents: 'Happy Eastie from your wildebeestie'!

CHAPTER 5

Coming Out

WHEN I GOT home at the end of April 1961, I signed up again for the College of Law. All my other friends were at university and I didn't have a job. So, much as I disliked the idea of the law, it seemed sensible to get a qualification. Soon after I started the course, Wynand van Graan, one of the Afrikaners who had looked after us on our trip, rang me. He had been moved to London and he offered to take me on as an informal management trainee whenever I had time off from my studies. This suited me well as I found learning the law tedious – and the money was welcome too.

I also needed somewhere to live. One of my friends from school, Simon Davie, told me that his parents had bought two houses in Kensington's Onslow Gardens and that they were letting the rooms as bedsits to the children (both sexes) of the 'well-to-do'. John Davie, his father, asked me if I would like to rent one at three pounds and twenty-five pence a week, including breakfast.

As most upper-class children went to single-sex private schools up to the age of eighteen, they had little chance of putting into practice the scanty information on the opposite sex that they had been given by their parents. The 'season' was designed to remedy this. It began with the grand Queen Charlotte's Ball, at which virginal debutantes dressed in white had, until 1958, been presented to the Queen. The rest of the season consisted of dances and balls in London during the week, and at great country houses at weekends. To be invited, an applicant had to be on the 'list', which was prepared by a doughty journalist, pen-named 'Jennifer', who worked for *The Queen* magazine. Jennifer had originally been at *Tatler* but she was poached by its rival. *The Queen* was managed by an extremely handsome, blonde, square-jawed extravagant young 'catch' called Jocelyn

Stevens (later Sir Jocelyn). He drove around London aged twenty-five in a Continental Bentley, and succeeded in hooking my first cousin, Janey Sheffield. Her father, my uncle, was concerned that Jocelyn did not have a career so he bought the magazine as a wedding present for him. Jocelyn, who came from a publishing background, set off on a stellar career that encompassed three fortunes and three partners. He gained the reputation of a posh bully and was nicknamed 'Piranha Teeth' by *Private Eye*.

Jennifer's list was comprised of all the available, well born, well endowed offspring of the aristocracy, the upper middle-class and the thrusting parvenus whose parents wanted them to marry well. Unsurprisingly, I found myself on it, along with other residents of Onslow Gardens. There was always a competition to see who got the most invitations. They adorned the mantelpiece like prizes in a raffle. The more you had, the more desirable you were deemed to be. They were embossed on thick white card; thermography was considered naf. *Tatler* and *The Queen* carried extensive accounts and photographs of the 'deb parties' – pages of pictures of young-bloods in their dinner jackets, grinning gormlessly at the camera while posing with a glass in one hand and a deb in the other.

For the weekday dances we dressed up in black tie and caught a taxi to some grand apartment for a dinner party of twelve to fourteen. These were designed to give the parents an opportunity to check out our manners and behaviour before we decamped at around half-past ten to Claridges, The Ritz or The Dorchester.

Each party had two parts. For the first hour or so, we were in the brightly lit main ballroom with a live band. Confrey Phillips, who scored more often than the most handsome of the debs' delights, was the most popular bandleader, although the parents frowned on his Goan roots. The second part of the evening was a disco. At about 2 a.m. the blades, who included the likes of Sir Toby Clark (the original 'chinless wonder'), would make it off with their girls to a darkened disco where the DJ's playlist was dominated by the Beatles, the Rolling Stones, Lulu and Cilla Black. There it was easier to get really close and dance cheek to cheek, followed by crotch to crotch. This might at some stage have to led to something more, or maybe not. Those of us who lacked confidence, good looks, style or determination – such as Johnny Wills, Christopher Donald and me – would remain outside with one or two of the wallflowers and wait for breakfast, which usually arrived between 3.30 and 4 a.m. It consisted of scrambled eggs and smoked salmon or bacon buns and coffee. Most of the participants would be in bed by 5 and at work by 9. This went on three nights a week. Occasionally I would end up in the disco and enjoy a kiss and a cuddle on the way home. It was an exhausting existence.

As an Irish viscount, I was only considered a 'desirable' match for the second daughters of the aristocracy as I had no land or money and no obvious prospects of inheriting any. From my side, I was never very keen on the London girls and had already decided that the Needhams needed new and different blood if the line was to be regenerated. My half-Jewish mother had helped bring in some desperately needed shrewdness, intelligence, wit and ambition, but it was not enough and I was determined to fish in a different sea.

Much as I enjoyed my nights out, I was ambitious to get my career going. I wanted to run my own business and become an MP. But how? One of the guests living in Onslow Gardens was Adrian FitzGerald, later to become the knight of Kerry. Through his mother's family, he was employed at Molins, manufacturing cigarette-making machines that were used in the Rothmans factory in Basildon, where I was occasionally working in the quality control department. He was a bigger catch on the circuit than me, although he never married. We would often go to parties together. In the autumn of 1961, he introduced me to Paul Bristol who had, with three others, founded The Monday Club.

The club's patrons were Lord Salisbury and Sir Alan Lennox-Boyd and the members met on Monday nights at Paul's house in Knightsbridge. The Monday Club was a right-wing pressure group that stood against the rush for decolonisation, particularly in the Federation of Rhodesia and Nyasaland. It opposed handing over immediate power to African despots and it was concerned about the leftward drift of Macmillan's government, which was, by the early sixties, losing drive and purpose.

As I had just come back from Africa and was working part-time for a South African company, I had considerable sympathy for these views, particularly over the speed of withdrawal, which I believed would lead to disastrous consequences for many of our former colonies. I did not, however, want to become part of a youthful anti-Macmillan tirade against the government's Africa policy. I wanted to talk and write about the social, economic and industrial problems facing Britain. Paul, who is an adventurer and has had a colourful and varied life full of both successes and crashes, was delighted to welcome someone who would give the Monday Club a broader base and a wider audience. He introduced me to Julian Amery, who was Macmillan's son-in-law and whose brother had been hanged for treason. 'Right-wing abroad and one-nation Tory at home, dear boy!' he advised me.

Anyone serious about politics needs to have passion, belief and a burning desire to improve the country's lot. But it is impossible to care about everything and a young politician should concentrate on those areas that he or she knows most about and most wants to see change for the better.

I realised that failing to get to Oxbridge to read PPE meant that I would have to educate myself. I had two antagonists, both Rhodes scholars, to spar with. One of them was Steve de Klerk – brother to Val, a friend from South Africa – and the other, Christopher Mitchell-Heggs, who was studying to be a lawyer like me. Night after night we debated the metaphysical world. I started my education with Bertrand Russell and his book *The Problems of Philosophy*. I read Hobbes's *Leviathan*, Thomas Paine's *The Rights of Man*, Edmund Burke's *Reflections on the French Revolution* and Hegel and his contention that 'the march of God on earth, that is what the State is'. I dipped into Schopenhauer's theories on pessimisms, then on to Kant, followed by Malthus's Iron Laws of Economics. The problem with all this reading was that, without a tutor to guide me, half of it was way over my head!

However, what stuck was that in the debate over whether the individual was there as the servant of the state to serve the community, 'from each man according to his ability, to each man according to his needs', I was on the side of the individual. It was the State that was the servant of the people. Man had come together of his own free will to form associations and communities to improve his economic and physical security. It was the individual around which the universe revolved. The problem, however, was complicated; nothing was black and white. Could workers have gained and maintained their rights without the rise of trade unionism? Surely the worker owed his loyalties to an organisation that had helped him from his knees? Men and women were free to vote for whomever they wanted. They could determine who governed them in their private lives but at work, they had no say in the running of or decision making within the organisations that employed them.

There were three books that had a seminal influence on my thinking. Karl Popper's *The Open Society and its Enemies* gave me the intellectual certainty to defend and promote liberal democracy. Ruth Benedict's *The Patterns of Culture* gave me a broad understanding of how circumstance, environment, history and social convention can lead to widely different variations of behaviour, and the establishment of values that appear bizarre and sometimes irrational. Lastly Milovan Dilas's *The New Class* provided me with an analysis of the Communist system, and gave me a comprehensive destruction of dialectical materialism and how a Marxist state would always end in dictatorship. All this was enough to turn me into a 'wet' Tory at an early age! There was room for the State to take initiatives to help the poor and intervene for the improvement and defence of society and of its values, but only up to a point.

What my new-found intellectual self-confidence did not provide me with was a solution to the issues of motivation, reward, incentives and participation in the world of work. I cared about industry, and about manufacturing and innovation. Most of all, I thought I cared about the people who worked in industry. I believed Britain survived or died through the power of its industrial heartlands. By the early sixties, it was clear that Britain was in real trouble.

The next three years were a whirl of activity. For the first eighteen months, I was studying at Gibson and Weldon (the College of Law) for my Bar exam. My fellow pupils included Simon Tuckey – the rare medical condition of having two hearts didn't stop him from becoming one of the few judges of the Appeal Court who had not been to Oxbridge – and Bhai Patel, a Fijian Communist, who went on to become the senior UN official in Gaza and then the Philippines. He once, most provocatively, proposed at the Oxford Union, that 'this house supports apartheid'. He now writes cookery books in Delhi and has recently completed a soft-porn novel which has some carefully crafted gay encounters. Then there was the most beautiful and clever Heather Meredith-Owens, over whom everybody lusted but in vain. After qualifying she married, went to America, got divorced, returned, became an artist, applied to become a Conservative Parliamentary candidate and at a tragically young age, died of lung cancer.

Our tutor was a terrible man called Padfield, who wore black-striped trousers, a black jacket and a black tie. He did not have a very high regard for his black pupils, whom he often insulted. After eighteen months of Mr Padfield teaching me Roman Law, together with having to attend Lincoln's Inn dinners (which were inedible), I passed Part 1 of the Bar exam.

But the Law was not for me and I took up Wynand van Graan's offer to become a full-time management trainee at Carreras Rothmans on a salary of 750 pounds a year. The business consisted of two Jewish-owned English companies that had been taken over by Anton Rupert in the 1950s. Both had begun at the latter end of the nineteenth century making pipe tobacco, hand-rolled Turkish cigarettes and cigars. They both traded out of smart, exclusive shops in London's West End. Both had royal appointments and early in the last century they had started manufacturing machine-made cigarettes, which widened their appeal. They were small, top-of-the-market, well-run establishments with brands capable of rapid growth with the right marketing and finance. Carreras was also an enlightened employer. Its Arcadia works was the first factory built out of pre-stressed concrete. It was the first to have air conditioning, to introduce proper dust extraction and to provide a full welfare service to its employees. It practiced Theory Y whilst slowly killing its customers.

Rothmans was more bespoke and received its royal warrant from Edward VII in 1905. Both were ideal stepping stones for Anton Rupert to force his way into the international tobacco market through his own Rembrandt company, the motto of which was 'Rembrandt. Every cigarette a masterpiece!'

The English management of both companies were very much hired hands. The head of Rothmans was Major Ron Plumley who was a moustached former soldier of fairly average ability. Our competitors were all run by former generals or admirals and it was always felt a bit demeaning by the staff that we only warranted a major. The key decisions were taken by Rupert and his closest Afrikaner colleagues.

My boss, Wynand van Graan, came over to London to act as a coordinator between the UK and South Africa. He soon dumped his South African wife for his pretty English secretary, which limited his career progression. But he mapped out a training course for me which covered every aspect of the business. There were three of us on the programme: Patrick Brown, who ended up as permanent secretary at the Department of Transport, Robin Garran, whose father was ambassador to the Netherlands, and me. It was open ended, so when Robin had finished a year, Rothmans decided he knew enough that they could pack him off to run Cyprus, which was in the middle of a civil war.

I was more fortunate. I worked in the trademark department under John Joyce, a clever Dublin lawyer, who claimed he'd got the scar on his back from a Tommy soldier's rifle when he was trying to plant a bomb in the North. It was more likely to have been caused by an accident with his javelin. He was the Irish Olympic javelin thrower, but the ladies and the 'juice' led him often to being late on parade and well out of the medals. He had several wives of differing shapes, sizes and colours, and he ended his career working for the government of Hong Kong. He taught me that if you declaim with authority what you believe the law to be, even if it isn't, you'll usually get away with it. Years later he became my eldest son's godfather, to the horror of some of my more 'loyalist' relations.

I spent a couple of months working in Carreras' massive new factory in Basildon. I was attached to the quality control department and strutted around in a white coat, holding a clipboard and occasionally scooping handfuls of cigarettes from the machines and taking them for analysis to the laboratory. In the canteen I became friendly with one of the shop stewards, who persuaded me to join the Tobacco Workers' Union. This caused some raised eyebrows amongst the senior managers and even a quiet word from Cedric Bulpitt, the managing director. But I felt strongly about the demarcations that existed at almost every level within the company. 'The working class can kiss my ass, they've made me foreman at long last.'

I then spent some time working in an advertising agency and then in the marketing department, laying out the merchandising budget on a huge spread sheet that had to balance both vertically and horizontally. I worked in the PR department, promoting Rothmans' sponsorship of a wide range of sporting events. The best and most stimulating fun was the months I spent on the road under the semi-watchful eye of my sales manager, Bill Sutton. I became a 'Rothmans Rocket' aged twenty.

We had a fleet of Ford Zodiacs emblazoned with the Rothmans' logo and colours. We bombed from town to town in these beautifully decorated wagons, staying in local hotels and trying to pick up girls with an offer of free cigarettes and a ride in 'the Rocket'. Our role was to call on the CTNs and to persuade them to give us top-up orders; to try to fix up Rothmans Kingsize pack dispensers; to take on new brands; to accept Rothmans shop facias; to fix Rothmans wall signs above the shop door; and, wherever possible, to cover the counter with show cards of semi-naked models smoking a pipe or puffing on a Kingsize. For some reason I was the champion Peter Stuyvesant salesman.

Peter Stuyvesant came in a US-type soft pack which was designed to fit in a breast shirt pocket. How and why they sold, no one seemed to know. The tobacco was a common-or-garden Rhodesian leaf. The name was of some Dutchman who had founded New Amsterdam until we threw him out and called the place New York. No one could pronounce his name, no one knew who he was and, as most Brits wore pullovers, the pack stuck out like some breast orthotic while the cigarettes were crushed between the pully and the chest. However, anything American was all the rage.

My sales area was the West Country and South Wales. It was a hard sell as Bristol was the headquarters of Imperial Tobacco, an employer of thousands, and South African interlopers were not welcome. The Welsh valleys had hardly heard of Rothmans. I hatched the idea of pushing Consulate menthol cigarettes, which had the strapline 'cool as a mountain stream'. Ideal for the valleys, I thought.

As soon as I arrived at a dingy little newsagent in Newport I could hear the proprietor hacking away in the back room. At the tinkle of the bell on the door, out he came. 'I want you to try a new type of cigarette – it's menthol and as cool as a mountain stream,' I said. 'It's the new experience.' He looked at me warily. I took one out, lit it and gave it to him. He took an enormous draft. Slowly his face turned purple and he started to slip down behind the counter until he disappeared and all that could be heard was a rasping, gasping groan as he tried to gather breath. Finally, his fingers grasped hold of the counter. He rose, puce with fury, and invited me to leave, never to return. After that I gave up on Consulate.

I learned a lot from my time repping. It took me to places of real poverty and hardship, from where hope had departed, and where the prospects for many were an early death, helped by beer and cigarettes.

After eighteen months, at the end of 1963, my training was over. I was called into van Graan's office and he offered me the role of assistant packaging design manager. This small section was a vital part of the Rembrandt empire. Rupert's success had been built around repackaging and marketing the Rothmans and Carreras brands. His creative designer, Piet Morkel, who lived in Capri, was the genius who introduced the white, uncluttered design. Rothmans looked smart, sophisticated, modern and desirable. The advertising was of a hand holding a packet. The lower arm was wearing a blue jacket with three gold rings to represent the captain of an international jet. In today's parlance the brand would be described as cool and aspirational. Morkel once said that he aspired to his designs being so clean and simple that they would not look out of place in a chemist's shop.

My new boss, Dick Rogerson, who later became my partner, was competent, creative and fun. We were both a bit prone to panic in an emergency. His task was to take Morkel's and his cockney accomplice David Taylor's crayon mock-ups and turn them into the finished article. This involved the most intricate lettering skills, as the directors wanted to see every item as if it were the finished article. Hours were spent layering gold leaf on to gold leaf to achieve the embossed effect so that Major Ron and Dr Anton could compare their prototypes with their competitors' existing offerings, such as Benson & Hedges' Kingsize or State Express 555s.

Everything was done in the greatest secrecy. Dick and I divided our roles between brands. He rightly took the big hitters while I was responsible for Schimmelpenninck cigars in Holland, Murray's chewing tobacco and Erinmore's pipe tobacco in Belfast, together with some of the ageing brands such as Craven A Full Strength and Guards. Long-forgotten symbols of an age when smoking was acceptable, ubiquitous and supposedly non-life-threatening. We also had direct relationships with the large packaging printers, Fields of Bradford and Gestel & Zoon in Eindhoven. They proofed up our prototypes before they went into mass production. Unfortunately, Fields of Bradford have long since gone.

CHAPTER 6

Power of a Pamphlet

M EANWHILE I HAD my political future to consider. By 1963, Macmillan's government was on the skids. To use Dean Acheson's famous one liner, 'Britain had lost an empire and not yet found a role.' Germany and France were on the point of overtaking us economically. The country seemed incapable of sustaining growth without running into deficits and high inflation. Our manufacturing industry was racked with demarcation disputes, inter-union rivalry, wildcat strikes and low productivity. The government's weak response to the rise of militant trade unionism and its patrician out-of-touch, laid-back attitude, exemplified by Harold Macmillan's hang-dog demeanour, had lost it public trust and support. Harold Wilson – who arrived in 1962 as Labour party leader after Hugh Gaitskell's premature death – talked of modernising Britain through the white heat of the technological revolution and struck a chord, particularly amongst the young. It was time for a change.

At a grand ball held by Sir Harold Wernher for his debutante granddaughter Sacha (later Duchess of Abercorn) at Luton Hoo, where all the strawberries were exactly the same size and served in identical solid silver bowls, I asked Lord Salisbury, who was wearing white tie and tails together with the blue ribbon of the Garter, what he thought about an incoming Labour government. 'No point having a democracy if the other chap does not get a chance sometimes,' he insouciantly replied.

In July 1963, after two years of research, dinners, discussion and debate, we (the Monday Club) managed to persuade the Conservative Political Centre, who up to then had concentrated mainly on the Bow Group, to publish a thirty-two-page pamphlet called 'Strike Out or Strike Bound?' When we launched, it we got coverage in the *Financial Times*, *The Times*, the *Telegraph*, the *Scotsman*, the *Yorkshire Post* and the *Daily Herald*.

We were unbelievably pretentious. Our average age was twenty-three. We had persuaded the chancellor, Reggie Maudling, to have dinner with us. On another occasion George Woodcock, general secretary of the TUC, came along. We were never short of advice from the great and good. Our most prominent headline was in the *Communist Daily Worker*: 'Peer advises unions – pay rises worry him a bit!' We advocated 'a new look' for the TUC, giving it much greater power to reach a national wage agreement with the British Employers' Confederation. Unions should rid themselves of the class stigma, amalgamate more, charge more for their services, pay their staff more. Employers employed too many technocrats, unable to lead men. Many managers lacked tact on the factory floor. We suggested setting up work councils like the Germans. There should be much greater worker participation in the running of businesses. The government should set up new industries in unemployment blackspots. There was no end to our advice.

It seems extraordinary that we should have gained such access at such high levels and that we received such broad, in-depth reporting of our work. There was I – wet behind the ears, twenty-one years old, with little experience, a management-trainee in Rothmans – telling the TUC and the employers how to run British industry. The press covered it as if we were the CBI or the Engineering Employers' Federation. The pamphlet fired the engine that became the driving motivation of my political and business life: I was a businessman in politics. It was a document New Labour would have been proud of.

During the summer of 1963, Paul Bristol suddenly decided in his enterprising way to go off to Aden and the Yemen to find out what was happening. This gave those of us who thought Paul had lost the plot the opportunity to replace him, which we did with a committee member called John Howe. John was a quiet, sensible, consensus-style moderate who we thought would be less antagonistic and confrontational than Paul. After several weeks Paul came back, phoned up all his old friends and reinstated himself, leaving us looking weak and ineffectual.

John Howe resigned and disappeared. No one ever heard of him again. He could not be traced. There was no reply from his address or his contact number. He had told me that he ran an import–export agency with Eastern Europe, and that at one time he had been a spy and that he had listened in to Khrushchev's tirades from a tunnel that had been built from Austria to tap the Moscow phone lines to Prague. We then realised that

'John' was in all probability an MI6 agent who had been planted to keep an eye on our dangerous, youthful, extravagances. He must have been deeply embarrassed to have suddenly found himself as chairman.

In the autumn of 1963, the Tory party was in uproar. Macmillan's attempt to refresh his cabinet in the 'night of the long knives' had failed. His prostate started playing up, causing him enormous pain. The medical advice was that it might be cancer, so he decided to quit. During the previous six months and at the same time as writing 'Strike Out or Strike Bound?', I was involved in writing another more explosive leaflet entitled 'Conservatism Lost, Conservatism Regained'. Its co-authors were Robin Garran, Simon Tuckey and Jeremy Francis. Our pamphlet fitted the bill of Macmillan's opponents perfectly. We represented the rebellious youth who wanted change in the leadership and despised the moral decay of the British establishment, exemplified by the Bessell and Profumo scandals. Our appeal to Party members was to persuade the leadership to hand over power to the next generation, embrace technology, reform the civil service, protect individual freedoms and broaden our base. 'Conservatism is falling short in its attempts to escape being labelled the party of privilege.' Too much of the old-school tie, of nepotism and clubbiness still remain under a facade of Victorian institutionalism, we claimed.

Stirring stuff from a twenty-one-year-old Etonian Irish viscount, writing with the son of the British ambassador to the Netherlands. Our final line was:' "The arrogance of age must submit to be taught by youth" – Edmund Burke.' We launched our pamphlet twelve days before Macmillan resigned and on the opening day of the party conference. The impact was electric. The *Daily Mirror* published a brilliant cartoon by Franklin of Macmillan being clobbered by Salisbury and Lennox-Boyd, both of whom immediately took to the letter columns to deny any treachery or knowledge of our pamphlet.

The *Daily Telegraph* honoured us with an editorial that concluded, 'The demand for his resignation (Macmillan's) is either an unpleasantly indirect attack upon him by his former colleagues or as seen much more likely, it is the twitterings of a handful of youths and therefore meaningless.' We made front page of the *Observer*: 'Macmillan Must Go, Hailsham For Premier', which was slightly at odds with our call for new young thrusters at the top of the party. But Hailsham was the party faithful's idol after ringing a handbell on a Blackpool beach.

None of this was to be. Macmillan resigned and a small coterie of men in grey suits decided the fourteenth earl of Home should be his successor. The Tories went on to a narrow defeat in the 1964 election.

Meanwhile, The Monday Club was falling apart. The Federation of Rhodesia and Nyasaland had collapsed. Ian Smith had taken over from Winston Field and was determined to make a unilateral declaration of independence. Those of us who believed Ian Smith would be a catastrophe for Rhodesia decided to leave rather than support him, and my flash of fame and publicity was soon forgotten.

A funny thing happened on the way to the Forum
[Frankie Howerd's new Roman comedy musical]

CHAPTER 7

Sissy

THERE WAS ANOTHER aspect to my life which became every bit as important as work or politics. In June 1963, Steve de Klerk invited me to the Merton Commemoration Ball. He asked if I would take his sister, Val. He was bringing a German girl called Sigrid. Sigrid turned out to be the most strikingly attractive blonde I had ever set eyes on. She had a captivating smile, an infectious laugh and legs that went up to her armpits. She did not show the slightest interest in me. So, I wrote down my telephone number and slipped it into her bag. This was neither chivalrous to Steve's sister nor gentlemanly behaviour towards Steve, who was her boyfriend. When I woke up the next morning, I was full of remorse, but comforted myself that nothing was likely to come of it.

Several weeks later, Steve went back to Cape Town for the summer holidays and to have a minor operation to unblock a sinus in his nose. He died under anaesthetic aged twenty-one. My godfather Uncle D had just died six months earlier. Steve's death was another terrible blow. It was the first time I had had to confront disbelief followed by heart-wrenching grief. Steve had unbounded self-confidence, drive, intelligence and ambition. He was attractive to everyone who came across him. Had he lived, he would have become a very powerful force for good in the future of South Africa.

A month or so later I got a telephone call from Sigrid, who turned out to be Sissy. She was staying in London with her father, John Gairdner, on her way to finishing her English A level at St Clare's in Oxford. Would I like to come round for a drink at the Durrants Hotel off Baker Street? I put on my best Billings & Edmonds dark grey, single-breasted suit, with covered buttons and purple satin lining. I learned later that John thought I was an overdressed cocky young cigarette salesman who left him with a half-finished packet of Rothmans.

It turned out that John was Sissy's stepfather. John was the half-Thai son of a Scottish hydrographer who had mapped South East Asia for the Royal Navy in the early 1900s. John had escaped from Singapore and then through Java when the Japanese overran the British garrison. He found his way back to Europe ended up part of the occupation force in Hamburg in May 1945.

He had requisitioned as the sergeants' mess the house in which Sissy was being brought up by her mother, grandmother and great-grandmother. He took pity on the four generations of women and allowed them to live in the cellar. Sissy's father, Ernst Thiessen, had been a lieutenant in the Luftwaffe Flak Abteilung (artillery) of Army Group North. He saw his daughter for the last time, in early 1945, before returning to his unit in the east Prussian pocket around Königsberg. At the end of the war he was captured by the Russians and shot, having jumped from a train that was taking him to Siberia. His brother Hans had been killed two months earlier in the same area. Ernst was twenty-four. He was a tall, brave, handsome young man who had been decorated with a golden cross and two iron crosses.

After the War, John stayed on in Hamburg, working for a German engineering business. In 1953 he married Sissy's mother, Ilse, and decided to go to Indonesia to represent a German steel company involved in the construction of the Krakatau steel works. Sissy and her mother went along. Sissy was educated at the American International School in Jakarta until she contracted cholera and was sent back to Hamburg to her grandmother to recover. She was then sent to a boarding school in Neuchatel, Switzerland, for a year to catch up with lost education time and then back to Hamburg, where she attended the Rudolf Steiner School. As a result, she ended up speaking German, English, French and Indonesian. At nineteen she had come over to Oxford to polish up her accent-less English and do an English Literature A level.

Finding a permanent man was not part of her mother's game plan for her. Unfortunately, I appeared on the scene and spent the rest of 1963 driving up and down to Oxford in my smart new MGB that my parents had bought me for my twenty-first birthday. The MGB was a gutsy lady-killer but like so much of British engineering in the 1960s, it was shoddily produced and spent most of its life in the garage under repair. The main gasket kept bursting, the electrics kept blowing, the hood didn't fit properly and there was swarf in the fuel lines.

By the summer of 1964, it was clear to all that things were getting serious between us, so Sissy's mother, Ilse, and my mother, Helen, decided to get together for a chat about how to bring the affair to a conclusion. The meeting took place over lunch at my parents' house in Devon. My father asked Ilse what she would like to drink. 'A sweet sherry,' she replied. We didn't 'do' sweet sherry, so my father was dispatched to the local pub to find some. Ilse was desperately bothered that my parents would think that their son was marrying beneath himself. Not knowing my mother was half-Jewish, she had prepared a short speech outlining Sissy's impeccable German pedigree. She had come, said Ilse, from exemplary north German stock. 'In fact, she is thirteen generations pure German,' she announced proudly.

'Oh,' said my mother, 'how do you know that?'

'Hitler said so!'

This statement had the merit of being true, since everyone had had to prove their racial purity in the 1930s, but it was not necessarily what my parents had been expecting.

For me, Sissy was perfect: fun, international, clever, gentle, sometimes moody, incredibly hard-working and happy to be involved (or so she said) in my efforts to enter politics. She brought what the Needham bloodline had badly lacked during the previous four generations as the family fortune had disappeared into an Irish bog. We needed an extra infusion. Sissy had thirteen generations of it.

In a desperate attempt to reverse the ill-judged match between two children too young to marry, Sissy was summoned to Indonesia to allow her breathing space as far away from me as possible. The day she left, I flew to Berlin in a rickety Dakota with fifteen others to attend the Junior Königswinter Conference.

The Königswinter Conference was founded by Dame Lilo Milchsack after the War as a way of bringing together the leaders of Germany and the United Kingdom to create understanding and friendships. It was designed to ensure that never again would war break out between the two countries. By the early sixties a 'young' version of the conference had been organised to bring together young politicians of both countries to map out the future. I had been proposed by Sir John Biggs-Davison. He was a right-wing Catholic with Anglo-Irish connections. He was also one of the most vociferous and influential supporters of the Monday Club in the House of Commons.

The Königswinter conference took place over a two-day weekend and we were allowed plenty of time to explore Berlin, both east and west. The German participants were smart in their blue blazers and grey flannels, polite, international and spoke perfect English. The British side were rather scruffy, argumentative (particularly with each other), spoke no German and made little effort to make lasting friendships with their opposite numbers. We had separate dormitories and my bed was next to a twenty-one-year-old Marxist intellectual who wanted to start a revolution of the proletariat. We argued all night and made little sense at the plenary sessions the following morning. However, I did make one life-long friend, Nick Montagu (later Sir Nicholas Montagu, head of HMRC). We joined up on the Saturday afternoon and were determined to catch the S-Bahn into East Berlin. I dressed up in my smartest suit and my bow tie, and I stuffed my pockets with packets of Rothman's and Cadbury chocolate bars, intent on promoting capitalism to the East Germans.

Once we made it into the Russian sector, we searched for somewhere to eat. We found a restaurant that was almost as empty of customers as the streets were of cars. We asked for a menu. It was long and detailed but when we came to order, the only item that was 'at home' was *Eisbein mit Sauerkraut. Eisbein* is the hock of a pig, this one still covered in its hairs, and boiled for several hours. We then took a train to the Soviet War Memorial, a hideous piece of Stalinist architecture which was besieged by tour groups of badly dressed Russian veterans. Finally, we ended up in a bar in the Tiergarten district. We were greeted with frosty silence and disdainful glares from the regulars. I decided to hand round cigarettes and chocolate. Surprisingly this broke the ice and we spent the next two hours talking about anything and everything in broken English and fractured German. Nick made a friend who he corresponded with for several years. His friend's greatest ambition was to own a Lada.

We had to travel back through Checkpoint Charlie. There was a passport control about seventy-five metres before the actual gate. We had to have our passports checked. As Britain did not recognise the GDR, there was no way of getting assistance except through the Russian military government if anything went wrong. Something did go wrong! As I arrived at the gate, the VoPo demanded to see my passport and asked for the receipt that had been inserted at the customs' post of entry. There was no receipt. I went back to the post. The policeman behind the counter told me that I must have dropped it between the hut and the crossing, so I should get down on my hands and knees and look for it. Furthermore, if I could not find it, they would not let me through and as the UK did not recognise his country, I would be trapped.

I realised that wearing my best suit and bow tie, and stuffing my pockets with cigarettes and chocolates had not been such a clever idea after all. Nick was already on the other side. Panic. At that moment the policeman smiled and pulled the receipt out of his pocket. 'Don't come back here dressed like a parrot or you may never get back to your cage' was his final remark. That night I suggested to my Marxist bed mate that he might like to come across and see how life was in a communist utopia. He declined and spent the next day at a museum.

I learned two things: East Germany was as dreadful and the life there as awful as the Western press reported. And secondly, that in the West, the young Germans were well down the road of building a powerful, sophisticated, liberal, ambitious and ordered society with which we would find it hard to compete. They had embraced Theory Y while we were still fighting the class battles of the twenties and thirties.

When I got back, I continued working for Carreras Rothmans. Sissy stayed in Indonesia for three months. She was packed off to parties at the German embassy in the vain hope that she would find a nice young German – a fairly scarce resource in Jakarta in 1964. At the time we were at war with Indonesia in Northern Borneo so the British embassy was off limits. I managed to hang on to her by writing her passionate love letters. On her return we announced our engagement to two sets of doubting parents. I took her off to Garrard's, the Queen's jewellers, to buy an engagement ring that I discovered years later had a flawed sapphire.

I was then reluctantly invited to Hamburg for Christmas to meet her German family. Hamburg was and is a wonderfully friendly place and remains extraordinarily pro-British even though, when I first went, it was only twenty years since the RAF-induced firestorm that had wiped out the city centre, killing tens of thousands. On a personal level, however, the visit was as disastrous as my mother-in-law-to-be's earlier lunch in Devon.

I arrived with a battered suitcase that did not contain pyjamas or a dressing gown. This was deemed highly suspicious and I was immediately taken off to Karstadt to be properly kitted out. All the German relatives were summoned to meet Sissy's 'English Lord' at a *Kaffeetafel* in John and Ilse's smart townhouse beside the Alster. Between 4 p.m. and 6 p.m. we all sat around on bright pink Sanderson chintz sofas sipping coffee and eating cake from the best china with our little fingers stuck in the air. The conversation was made more difficult by my failure to have taken advantage of two years' learning German at school. I was an expert at getting words nearly right but not quite, which often caused considerable hilarity or embarrassment or both.

I was saved by Sissy's grandmother, Omi Boysen, who was built like an air-raid shelter, bred St Bernards and drove a Volkswagen Beetle. She ran a 'pension' for war widows and, most importantly, she loved schnapps. At every opportunity she would whisk me off for a nip or two with 'Komm her, mein Junge'. She adored Sissy, so Sissy's choice was her choice. I adored her.

On Boxing Day, having been initiated into the German habit of celebrating Christmas on Christmas Eve with the main course consisting of steamed carp (which, even with the most exquisite of mustard sauces, tasted like mud), I was invited out for a day's shooting. Before proceedings began, I inquired whether the rules in Germany were any different to ours. 'No, no – exactly the same!' I was assured, although as it was nearing the end of the season, we would only shoot cock pheasants, not hens. I assumed that everything else was fair game. Unfortunately, it was thick fog and it was hard to pick out what was coming over. The German for cock is *Hahn* and the German for hen is *Huhn*. So, in the confusion of people shouting '*Huhn! Hahn! Hahn! Huhn!*' and disorientated by the mist, I shot a hen pheasant.

In the next drive I shot a partridge. I was pulled aside by John who told me that shooting wild partridge in Germany was a criminal offence. To complete my humiliation, I fired at a rabbit coming out of a hedge – that was closely followed by one of the beater's dogs. Luckily, I managed to miss them both. The following day's invitation to a boar shoot was quietly withdrawn and I returned to London with my tail firmly between my legs, but at least equipped with a very nice pair of silk pyjamas and a dressing gown.

If the engagement announcement was problematic, it was nothing compared to the run-up to the wedding. The first row to erupt was over what Sissy was to do now her course in Oxford had finished and she had moved to London. Ilse was determined that Sissy should learn shorthand and other secretarial skills so that when the marriage collapsed, she could look after herself. My mother, on the other hand, believed that learning to cook, sew and become proficient in flower-arranging was crucial. Ilse maintained that setting the dining room table was more important than the food that went on it.

In the end, it was decided that there would be two weddings: one in Hamburg followed, after the honeymoon, by a reception in London, in Kensington's Pavilion Road, for the British family and friends. My father, as usual, was out of funds and wondered whether there was any chance of a dowry to help pay for the English end.

Then out of the blue I received a phone call from the Private Office of the Foreign Secretary, who at that time was Michael Stewart. Madame Dewi Sukarno, the beautiful Japanese wife of the Indonesian president, who had close connections with Japanese business, had asked if she might attend the London reception. She and Sissy had had the same language teacher in Jakarta, and Dewi and Ilse had become friends. The real reason for the request, however, was that the Indonesians were looking for ways to close down their insurgency in Borneo, which was going nowhere, and Madame Sukarno's visit was a signal that Indonesia wished to negotiate. The foreign secretary, I was told, would be most grateful if we could do everything to accommodate Dewi and her entourage.

This did not play well with the military members of my extended family who were already muttering about the German connection and were suddenly confronted with the arrival of a Japanese-Indonesian who was the wife of the president of a country we were at war with. We could not explain the diplomatic niceties, so a number of angry wedding invitation refusals landed on the doormat.

The wedding in Hamburg on 5 June 1965 was a grand affair. I invited my seven best friends to partner Sissy's six bridesmaids. There was inevitably a considerable language problem – the girls' English was in a different league to the boys' German. My mother-in-law was not impressed that the boys' stag night ended in a lengthy trip down the Reeperbahn. I was packed off to learn how to dance the Viennese Waltz which was the traditional opening dance for newly-weds.

Despite the temperature being in the thirties, which melted all the starched shirt fronts of the ushers, the day itself was a triumph for Anglo-

German relations. The misconceptions that both sets of parents had about each other were temporarily glossed over. The *Hamburger Abendblatt* picked up the story of 'their girl' marrying a British lord and provided a white carriage pulled by two white horses with accompanying footmen.

The wedding concluded with a magnificent dinner and a ball in the Hotel Atlantik, the Claridge's of Hamburg. We slipped away at midnight and left for our honeymoon in Minorca at 6 a.m. the next morning. Lufthansa gave us a champagne breakfast and a large bouquet of roses.

The evening after the wedding, the bridesmaids had persuaded the ushers to take them to a casino in Travemuende, some fifty miles away. By the time they got back, with the taxi meters spinning like roulette wheels, they were broke and had no money to get from Heathrow to London. David Abel Smith, who was the only one with a proper job and salary, came to the rescue, not for the first time – he took those he could fit in his hired limo, and lent the others the money so that they could get home.

David was a serial debs' delight and had arrived late in Hamburg due to his previous social engagements. He fitted into the scene as if he were at a cocktail party at the Ritz although he did not speak a word of German. Luckily for the others he had brought with him a large number of spare studs, buttons and cufflinks as they had failed to ask for the accessories when hiring their outfits from Moss Bros.

After the honeymoon, we had a buffet reception in Pavilion Road. It was dominated by Dewi Sukarno and her entourage, some of whom appeared to be bodyguards and hid behind the massive flower arrangements. Nicknamed Madam Mitsubishi, Dewi was charming, elegant, international and extremely extravagant. She travelled around London, shopping at the most expensive stores in Knightsbridge and Bond Street, with my mother-in-law acting as her lady-in-waiting, and also attended by a clerk with a notebook who took down all the details of her purchases. It was an eye-opener to discover that Bung Sukarno, the Marxist dictator of an impoverished country, should allow his wife to indulge in such conspicuous excesses. I still had a lot to learn about corruption.

CHAPTER 8

Taking the Plunge

S INCE LEAVING THE Monday Club in the summer of 1964, I had been kicking my heels when it came to my political aspirations. I was not a great supporter of Alec Douglas-Home and he had narrowly lost the October 1964 election.

Out of the blue in early 1965, I received a call from Michael Spicer (later MP, chairman of the 1922 and member of the House of Lords). Michael had set up a left-wing Conservative pressure group called – in a rather juvenile fashion – PEST (Pressure for Economic and Social Toryism). The group's mentor was the Charterhouse-educated William Rees-Mogg, deputy editor of *The Sunday Times*. The idea was to force Douglas-Home to stand down, banish the grouse moor image inherited from both him and Harold Macmillan, and promote Ted Heath as an answer to the meritocratic, technocratic Harold Wilson. PEST was to be the bold young motor of the new classless, all-embracing Conservatism. Strange how history keeps repeating itself, regardless of party.

Spicer got in touch with me because he had followed the hatchet job we had perpetrated on Harold Macmillan with the Monday Club, under the patronage of Lords Salisbury and Lennox-Boyd. Would I help to do the same on Douglas-Home? At the princely age of twenty-two, I had no difficulty moving from one end of the Tory spectrum to the other. My pamphlet for the Monday Club had been left of centre, while the importance of Africa and the Empire had never been of overriding significance to me. So, over a couple of months the same team wrote another pamphlet entitled 'Will the Tories Win the Next Election?' We argued that could only happen if Home was ditched in favour of Heath. Much of our discussion took place in a run-down Chinese restaurant called The Old Friends on the Commercial Road, opposite the Seamen's

Union Headquarters in the East End. Sissy used to join our dinners and, having been brought up in Indonesia, she was the only one proficient with chopsticks. Too often we sat, enviously watching delicacies disappearing before our eyes as Sissy's chopsticks darted in and out while we haplessly tried to keep up.

The Sunday before the pamphlet's launch, Rees-Mogg devoted an editorial to supporting our case and hailed us as the party's new young challengers. We agreed to hold a press conference for the launch at the Waldorf Astoria, which was within easy distance of Fleet Street. When I arrived, to my horror I found Michael Spicer dressed up in a smart tweed suit with waistcoat, brown brogues and sporting an old Wellingtonian tie. Sure enough, after our introduction, the lobby correspondent of *The Scotsman* enquired of Michael what club tie he was wearing. 'Wellington,' he replied. The correspondent then went around the rest of us, asking which schools we had attended. Eton and Marlborough predominated. Our cover was blown and the press coverage reflected it.

A few weeks after the wedding Michael rang me again and said my services were no longer required. I had done the job requested of me. But after being involved in the knifing of two prime ministers he was afraid that he could not trust me to be a reliable colleague. Had my political career ended before it began?

A few years later PEST changed its name to the Tory Reform Group, which remains the most influential 'one nation' pressure organisation on the left of the Party. I am still a member.

After Sissy and I were married, David Abel Smith left the rented flat we'd shared in Wimpole Street and Sissy moved in. I walked to the Carreras Rothmans' office in Baker Street every morning. I wanted a break from politics. I wanted to widen my business experience, put Theory Y into practice and to work for a smaller industrial company, preferably in engineering. I wanted to get to know the country better and move out of London. Sissy and I also wanted to start a family. My grandmother had died in early 1965 and had left me £25,000 so we had enough money to buy a house. But where to go to and what to do?

Meanwhile an opportunity had opened up in Rothmans. Dick Rogerson, my boss at the time, had realised the two of us were not easily replaceable. We were the vital link between the conceptual designers of the packaging, the senior directors and the printers. We believed that we could set up on our own, with the highly skilled lettering artists who were already subcontracted to Rothmans by us.

We approached two of them, who agreed to join us, and started our first company, which we called RGM. I put in £1,000 of my grandmother's money to get us going, for which I received 10 per cent of the shares while the others had 30 per cent each. My shares had four voting rights for each share so I and one other had effective control. We rented offices at 240 High Holborn and, after some grumbling from our former boss, Wynand van Graan, we took the Carreras Rothmans business with us.

Dick and I agreed it would be best that, even if we left together, it would be less damaging to our relations with Rothmans if I did something else for a couple of years while we looked for a printing point of sale company to partner with. This company could be fed work from RGM under Dick, and I would run the printing side.

While we were still discussing our plans, luck intervened. My mother met a businessman on the train from Waterloo to Ottery St Mary who offered to make me his personal assistant. I jumped at the chance. We bought a beautiful little dower house with an acre and a half of garden on the outskirts of Yeovil with the princely sum of £5,500, with the help of my grandmother's inheritance.

The businessman my mother met was Ray Harding – a dapper Brummy who was executive chairman of Sterling Industries, the engineering subsidiary of Union Castle, the South African shipping group that was controlled by the Cayzer family. The Cayzers wanted to diversify so they had bought three small engineering companies that had relocated to Crewkerne in Somerset. Ray had brought with him a small management team. Win Denman, the CEO, lived in St George's Hill, Weybridge, and drove down two or three times a week in a white Aston Martin. 'Tubby' Giles, the engineering director, was a moustachioed, Brylcreem-using, Black Countryman who had made Sherman tank sides in the War for the Eaton Yale company. He told me that the reason our tanks were so small was because our railway gauge was so narrow and the height of our bridges so low that it was impossible to transport larger machines to the ports – one of the reasons why German tanks were so much more effective than ours. He and I used to have a sirloin steak and chips twice a week in a pub called Wynyard's Gap and plot how we could turn the beautiful Somerset Valley into dark satanic mills. The sales director was Dusty Miller, another

Midlander, who drove a large Wolseley, sat behind a large desk with a large telephone and never went out. 'I've done enough repping in my time,' he would exclaim through a cloud of pipe smoke (they nearly all smoked pipes), 'and I can control my sales staff from head office!' Not surprisingly, new customers were few and far between.

The three companies were in quite separate manufacturing sectors. SMC Sterling made pressed, sintered metal components for the automotive industry. Exactor Sterling fabricated hydraulic cylinders and self-sealing couplings for forklift trucks, tractors and other lifting equipment. Sterling Instruments produced electrical timers for the general appliance industry. The one thing they had in common was that they were component suppliers to the huge British original equipment manufacturers: Ford, British Leyland, Vauxhall, Massey Ferguson, Lancing Bagnall, Hotpoint and Hoover.

They relied on receiving blanket orders which were then called down over six-monthly periods depending on demand. The R&D departments were non-existent. The sales force brought in design drawings from the customer, which were then priced up to form part of a tender for a new model.

The key to success was the 'time and motion study man', invented by Frederick Winslow Taylor, the high priest of Theory X. Every worker was treated as an automaton or a piece of machinery to be measured, controlled, programmed and paid.

Ray Harding didn't really need a PA but he liked the idea of being able to show the main board of Caledonian, the investment arm of Union Castle, that he had a lord on the board. I did not really have enough to do and had to carve out a niche for myself. After I had been there for six months, Ray had a heart attack and was off sick for several weeks. Then one morning I came in and he had gone. Something to do with his expenses was the rumour in the canteen.

The sales office processing function for the three companies had been amalgamated into one organisation under the command of a martinet former naval lieutenant commander. As the companies were entirely different from one another, there were no savings to be made. The general managers lost control of what happened to their orders as soon as they arrived, and there was constant bickering between the naval commander and the factory managers. I suggested devolving the functions back into the original separate companies and moving the processing staff into the factories where there was plenty of space. Win Denman and Tubby Giles gave me the go ahead and the lieutenant commander was made redundant. 'You've taken my job in order to save your own,' he raged. He was partly right.

I realised very quickly that the salesmen needed properly designed catalogues and data sheets of our own products. So I used RGM, the company I had founded with Dick Rogerson, to redesign the company logo and produce proper, colourful, well-presented engineering fact sheets. I promoted myself to marketing manager and asked Dusty Miller's permission to go out selling. He was more than pleased to have someone explore what was happening in the market place.

One of my first calls was to the shipyards on the Clyde. I was horrified by the tenements as we drove through the Gorbals. Toothless old men and women sitting in their windows with nothing to do and nowhere to go. My next astonishing discovery was the reason why all the foremen in the shipyards wore bowler hats. It was to stop them being maimed by the bolts the disgruntled workers dropped on their heads from the top sides of the ships they were constructing.

There was a multiplicity of trades, from the welders to the outfitters. There were degrees of skills represented by different unions paying different rates. There was the power of the shop stewards, led by such men as James Maxton, whose agenda was to destroy the capitalist system rather than satisfy the customer.

By the mid-1960s, the Japanese were embarking on a huge investment in tanker production. The Germans at Blohm & Voss, the Italians at Fincantieri and the French at Chantiers de l'Atlantique were all investing in the construction of modern, world-class passenger liners. Each yard worked together as a team across every discipline to provide excellence, quality and value for money. The British shipbuilding industry, rooted in Theory X, never saw what was coming and their yards and their industry, with the exception of subsidised naval construction, collapsed.

Geof Mole, Sterling Instruments' general manager, asked if I could help him. He had recently invested in a new plastic moulding machine that punched out the covers that protected his timers. These components were cheaper, lighter and as robust as the metal versions they replaced but his sales were plummeting. Why? The competitor was a French company, Crouzet Motors. Their timers were heavier and capped with elegantly designed anodised aluminium covers that gave them the appearance of

My father, Patrick Needham, 5ᵗʰ Earl of Kilmorey.

In the band (centre of front row). Frensham, 1945.

Me, aged two.

Me (left), with my mother, Helen, and my younger brothers, Jonathan and Christopher.

With Nigel Nicolson (Conservative politician and family friend), Falmouth, during the 1951 General Election campaign.

Learning tennis aged eleven, 1953.

Ernst Thiessen, Sissy's father.
He was shot fleeing the Russians in May 1945.

Taken to celebrate our engagement in 1964.

Me and Sissy on our wedding day, Hamburg, 5 June 1965.

Election family photograph, Pontefract, February 1974.

Electioneering with Ted Heath, October 1974.

Me with my daughter, Christina, at the opening of the
new Site Signs factory on Lynx Trading Estate, Yeovil, 1979.

solidity and permanence. They looked like the back of a Swiss watch. Our product in comparison looked cheap and utilitarian, but as Geof Mole said, it worked just as well, was lighter and the ultimate customer would never see it. Unfortunately, the buyers in the domestic appliance factories did. I got Richard Hazelton at RGM to redesign the cover to be heavier, with a smart new logo and a shiny anodised fitted top to make the motor into a sealed unit. It looked magnificent. We added 50 per cent to the price and within months we were once again neck and neck with Crouzet. The lesson I learnt was that appearance, design and proper presentation are as important as price. Years later with James Dyson, we were to revolutionise the vacuum cleaner industry, in part on the same basis.

Sterling Industries have long since disappeared, as has SMC and Exactor Sterling, although Caledonian Investments still have the company which now makes heat exchangers. Crouzet continues to make timers and motors.

After nearly two years it was time to move on. Our first son, Robert, had been born in 1966. Sissy was keen for more and I had to reboot my political ambitions.

RGM under Dick Rogerson's direction was expanding and thriving. Jamie Robertson, who was our main client at Rothmans, had left and joined Mars. He took us with him and we still managed to hang on to the Rothmans' account. Our sales doubled. We were also generating an increasing volume of print work which we were sub-contracting at low margin. Now was the time for us to put into play the second leg of our strategy and build our own print company.

There were problems. Most of our print orders were wanted yesterday as they were short-run promotional aids for the sales force. I lived in Yeovil. Secondly, we had not nearly enough money to buy into a proper printing business, let alone a lithography company.

I took my life in my hands: I handed in my notice to Sterling Industries and set up a small company to create corporate logos, which Richard Hazelton was a genius at designing. I then hoped to get orders for all the clients' stationery needs as they launched their new modern images. I set up a partnership with Bill Snell, a local printer, and he agreed to give me special prices if we sent down the artwork from RGM in London.

It was a hard slog. I concentrated on estate agents, motor dealers and builders. I was quite successful at selling the idea of them taking on a modern logo but when it came to the printing I was up against their existing suppliers and the margins were tight. It would never make a stand-alone business.

After six months of no pay I was getting desperate. I would have to sell up and go back to London. Fate intervened. Jolyon Ward owned Site Signs, a small silkscreen and sign-writing workshop above a bar, sometime strip club, next to the Odeon cinema in the middle of Yeovil. He specialised in large, six foot by four foot, sign-written 'for sale' boards for the estate agents that were selling land around Somerset and Dorset. He employed two sign writers and his brother David did the sign erections and removals. Jolyon also had a basic silkscreen studio with hand-cut stencils and hand-stretched screens that he used to print posters advertising local community events. He had three 'apprentice' fifteen-year-old printers who he paid £3 a week until they were indentured. He then fired them and took on three more. He and his vivacious wife were going through strained times both personally and financially, and they decided to emigrate to Australia. The company turned over £10,000 a year and he wanted £5,000 for it. I pledged the house to the bank, borrowed the money from NatWest and took it over.

I very quickly realised it was worth nothing. It occupied two floors above the bar. The shop floor was reached by a rickety, outside, wooden staircase. It had a tiny office. It was filthy. Everything was covered in dust, sticky ink and paint. It smelt of sweat and paint thinners. It had rudimentary shared 'bathroom' facilities. Within a few weeks of my arriving, the local fire officer came to inspect and as he was leaving, burst into hysterical laughter. I demanded to know what he found so amusing. 'Fear!' he replied, as he clambered down the stairs.

In every other way, it was perfect. It turned out that the 'workforce' – with the exception of Marion, the receptionist-bookkeeper and Rose Stidson, our cleaner, – were well known to the police and the probation services. The rest of the workforce had recently started migrating from scrumpy laced with blackcurrant – that after several pints turned them into fighting machines – to cannabis, which made them happy, flaccid and idle. This was the chance of a lifetime to see whether Theory Y worked in practice.

Jolyon had also left behind one really clever idea. Fifty years ago, estate agents' flag boards were made out of stove-enamelled cast-iron. They were extremely heavy and therefore limited in size. They could only be bought through the *Estate Gazette* magazine. In the countryside, estate agents would erect these boards on collapsible, anodised metal poles. Jolyon's idea was to develop melamine laminated boards which would be much lighter and larger and therefore more eye-catching. He had just started discussions with Taunton Vale Industries, a company which had been brilliantly successful in designing and laminating kitchenware and was now looking for other products to put through their laminating presses.

I very quickly discovered that there's a big gap between the idea and its execution. I first had to become a silkscreen printer. I learnt how to cut and iron on a stencil, how to stretch a screen, how to use a squeegee, how to expose a positive and how to make a photo-stencil. The challenge was that silkscreen inks were so much denser than litho or letterpress inks that it was almost impossible to laminate them. Once the printed posters were placed in the press, the heated formaldehyde sheets would not penetrate the ink and the boards bubbled. We spent months struggling to find an ink supplier and finally Coates of Glasgow came up with a solution. I also realised that the 'apprentices' needed a master.

I found an old-fashioned retired silkscreen printer, Tom Hawthorne, who had spent his life in the US, wore size 15 boots, and was incredibly slow but incredibly methodical. He agreed to start us up. Now I had to go out and find some orders. My pitch was not only that our boards were brighter, lighter and larger but – because of the RGM connection – we could redesign them using modern type faces and logos.

My first customer was a Welshman, Mr Jones of Lewis's in Bridgwater. He was prepared to be the guinea pig. His board was redesigned from a size of 24-by-18 inch to 36-by-24 inch. The artwork was prepared, the special ink ordered. The heat under the roof of the workshop in summer meant we could only print at six in the morning or the ink dried into the screen. I took twice as many posters as necessary over to Taunton Vale for laminating on to double sheets of hardboard. The signs came out perfectly. They were trimmed on the bandsaw, edged with white protective plastic strips and drilled to fit on to their metal posts.

I delivered them personally to Mr Jones. He was delighted. 'Only one small issue,' he said. 'Bridgwater doesn't have an "e" in it!'

CHAPTER 9

Theory Y in Practice

O N THE FIRST day after my takeover of Site Signs, I told everyone to call me by my Christian name. Some of them knew I was an Irish lord but I told them that from now on, as I was one of them, I would be Richard Needham, not Lord Newry. I stopped using the time clock for clocking in and out and said we would work thirty-nine hours a week but we would be flexible about when we worked, and we would take lunch and tea breaks as and when there was time. I did away with overtime. Every month I made the profit and loss figures available, and shared the profits between us all every quarter. Everyone knew everyone else's pay. We had monthly meetings to discuss how we were doing and where we were going. Every six months I held one-to-one personal development interviews – the only time personal criticisms were allowed to be raised – that concentrated on individual strengths and weaknesses. The company introduced a training programme, with recognised national certificates at the end of the courses. Twice a year we had a party for everyone in the office and their families. I handed out shares to all, depending on their job responsibilities. It was agreed that I would set the rates of pay and collectively they would decide mine. They had to take responsibility for their actions. Anyone who messed up was expected to talk directly to the customer to explain what had gone wrong.

Did it work? It was not easy. With the exception of Tom Hawthorne, the lads were all aged between fifteen and twenty-five, had left school at fifteen, and came from dysfunctional families. They had little self-discipline and a natural desire to take advantage of the boss. Consequently, there were several unedifying events that caused me to question my new-found solution for the nation's industrial problems.

We had decided to replace tea breaks with a tea machine, as allowing everyone to decide when they took their breaks was not working. I left the choice of machine and what it dispensed to them. The only stipulation, which they agreed to, was that they would pay for whatever they consumed. Any surplus could go towards a day out. Tea-machine salesmen came and went. Finally, a choice was made. The gleaming model arrived and 'pantechnicons' of supplies were humped up the stairs. The security and operation of the machine was put in the hands of Bernie the Bolt, one of the printers. He went around with a large chain of keys tied to his waist and was responsible for ordering supplies.

After a couple of months, as I noticed the bills mounting, I suggested to Bernie that it was time to empty the machine to allow us to see how much money we had collected. He looked glum. 'I think you'll be in for a bit of a shock, Richard.' He jangled the keys and unlocked the cabinet. Inside was one pound, five shillings and sixpence. When I examined the cabinet, I saw there was a plastic seal between the door and the machine. The boys had left a three-foot metal ruler on top of the tea maker – they stuck it through the plastic seal and flicked up the inside cup holder to release the tea. I inserted a metal strip in place of the plastic one.

Another six weeks went by and I summoned Bernie the Bolt. Another long face. 'I don't think you're going to be very happy, Richard.' I wasn't. This time there was four pounds, seven shillings and sixpence in the bucket. The bills by then had mounted to over a hundred pounds. One of the boys had cut out a thin piece of Perspex and put a hook at the bottom – they inserted this through the plastic seal at the top of the door and flicked the lever from above. I got them all together. I told them it was their idea – that they had chosen the machine – and that I had had enough. I wanted them to own up and tell me how many free cups they had each stolen. Bedlam broke out. The sign writers had said that all their plastic cups had been used for mixing paint for their boards. The printers said all their cups had been used for mixing up and thinning their inks. I told them I knew how many cups had been consumed and how much tea, coffee, soup and powdered milk had been ordered. I would divide the bill between the lot of them and take the money out of their wages. 'Do you want to go on with this arrangement?' I asked. 'No thanks,' came the reply. 'The temptation is too big. We will abandon tea breaks all together if you will allow us an hour's less work a week.' So that was what we did and it worked.

By the end of the swinging sixties the miniskirts had got shorter and shorter, and the excitement raised the testosterone levels of the lads at the same time that they started experimenting with drugs. As sales soared, I hired Andrew Hodgson, a dour but solid New Zealand-born professional cricketer to bring order and discipline to the factory. Soon after his arrival I was out selling in Yorkshire. When I returned to my hotel there was an urgent message to phone him. After I got through to him, he told me the entire workforce, including the secretary, were in the cells. Apparently, the window boxes that lined the windowsills were not full of geraniums but cannabis plants. To make matters worse, the secretary's husband was also inside for being a drug dealer. He had been persuaded to provide the boys with LSD when he came back from his trips to London. When I returned from Yorkshire, the head of the Yeovil drug squad was waiting for me. A huge, ugly Glaswegian, with a face that looked as if he had only recently recovered from smallpox. He was not very interested in my explanations as to how I was running an industrial experiment based on Theory Y as opposed to Theory X.

He wanted to know how it was that I was unaware of what was going on in the window boxes. Having searched everyone's houses from top to bottom, why shouldn't he do the same with mine? I admitted that I knew that they had been taking LSD as a manager of the cinema next door had rung me about the behaviour of the young printers while they were watching *Easy Rider*. (As an aside, please don't anyone tell me that films full of violence, sex and drugs do not influence the behaviour of the vulnerable young.) 'Well,' he said, 'as we have most of Yeovil's young drug offenders working for you, we can at least keep an eye on them.' The next day, I managed to arrange bail. Very sheepishly and very remorsefully, they returned to work. As they all had jobs, the magistrates were content to fine them and give them a final warning.

The next Saturday night one of the apprentice printers, suffering no doubt from some kind of withdrawal symptom, was caught kicking and smashing a milk bottle. He was taken down to the station and charged with theft. Off to court we went to try to avoid him being tarnished with a criminal record. Fortunately for him, the magistrate found it was impossible for him to have stolen the milk bottle, because he had smashed it.

The most serious and egregious run in with the law involved our wonderful cleaner Rose Stidson. In the late 1960s and early 1970s, supermarkets were mushrooming across town centres. When they opened, they were invariably plagued by an initial rash of shoplifting. As it was their intention to get people to buy more than they could afford, they should not have been entirely surprised by the level of 'shrinkage' that occurred. To minimise this criminality, they employed teams of roving store detectives, sometimes former policemen of doubtful reputation, who travelled from town to town, blitzing the shoplifters. Their tactics were to announce to the local police station that they would be around for a couple of weeks and that they would ring as soon as they had apprehended a culprit. The police would then come down, arrest the suspect, charge them and bring them before the magistrate. This suited the supermarkets perfectly. Their only cost was the store detective and the call to the station. The follow-up publicity as the culprits – who were almost invariably mothers both young and old – pleaded guilty and had their reputations trashed in the newspapers acted as a strong deterrent.

Unfortunately, the methods used by the store detectives turned out on occasion, to be stings of the most disreputable kind. There was a common pattern that repeated itself. 'I saw the suspect go to the back of the store, where she looked furtively around before placing the goods from the wire basket into her own shopping bag.'

In the case of Tesco's newly opened branch in Yeovil, the store security was covered by a former police officer, who had been kicked out of the Met, and his girlfriend. A considerable proportion of their earnings was paid through commission on the number of successful prosecutions that the police obtained. This was a clear incentive to accuse the innocent along with the guilty, and the police – who, by and large, have never had a high regard for the honesty of the general public – were content to go along with it.

When Rose visited the store, she got to the till and had been chatting to a friend on her left while the till operator had been distracted by something or someone on her right. As a result, Rose had not been charged for a bag of apples. The hawk-eyed girlfriend stood a few feet away from the tills to pick up any such event and, as Rose left the store, she arrested her for shoplifting. Rose, scared and shocked to be accused of stealing, offered to pay. This, of course, made her position worse as it gave the impression that she was trying to get out of it. Down came the police and took her off to the station where she was charged and then they took her home, so that the police could check there were no other stolen goods in the house and then tell her husband that her life was about to be ruined.

At first, Rose didn't want to tell anyone what had happened, but finally it came out and the factory rallied round. I contacted my family solicitor in London and he suggested it was important for Rose to opt for trial by jury as the magistrates were less forgiving and more likely to take the side of the prosecution. He suggested we use Richard Du Cann – the brother of Sir Edward Du Cann, former MP for Taunton and chairman of the 1922 Committee – as our barrister. Rose had to wait months before her case came to trial. Finally, on the appointed day, the police offered no evidence and the case was dismissed.

The next day I received the following letter:

> "Shiloh"
> 36 South View,
> Bradford Abbas,
> Sherborne,
> Dorset.
>
> 28th May 1971.
>
> Dear Mr and Mrs Meecham,
>
> It was a pleasure to meet you today, and in particular to meet those who in these past weeks have given my Mother, Mrs Rose Stidson, much comfort and encouragement.
>
> The suffering which my Mother has undergone as a result of these proceedings, can only be known by those close to her, and by those who have similarly experienced the trauma and distress of being wrongly accused. Your compassion at a time when my Mother must have felt her world crumbling helped to give strength, and your magnanimity in the matter of court costs must surely have given assurance.
>
> The events of today have made an indelible impression in my mind of many things, and I would wish to record my deep and lasting appreciation of your involvement and Humanity. It has been a day of vindication for my Mother, but for you both, it has been a day of honour.
>
> Yours sincerely,
> Geoffrey Neate-Stidson

I accept that a significant majority of those arrested were probably guilty, but the failure of the supermarkets to take account of the honesty of their customers together with their use of unscrupulous store detectives – who were 'rewarded' for successful persecutions – was scandalous. The police's unquestioning acceptance of the word of an investigator against that of a previously blameless shopper, and the use of public funds by them to do the work of the supermarket without proper investigation into the background of each case was equally shocking.

I demanded to see the board of Tesco as Rose's case and others in Yeovil had caused something of a media storm. They agreed and for an hour, I explained as best I could what had happened to the three top directors Jack Cohen, his daughter Shirley Porter and Hyman Kreitman, chairman and his other daughter's husband. They listened in silence. They were a tough family from a tough background and I'm not sure that they saw any reason to change their ways, but Theory Y had worked for Rose, if not at Tesco.

The business was a success. Theory Y was a success. Our signboards started to sell the length and breadth of Britain. Our sales went from £10,000 to £50,000 in three years and the factory was running out of space. However we were better at booking orders than we were at making profits and a Jewish lawyer friend, Lyddon Simon, suggested I needed a sharper accountant. So, we took on Casson, Beckman & Rutley. It was rumoured that Rutley was the name of Casson's greyhound and that the name was used to give the firm a more English-sounding slant. Our man was Peter Ohrenstein. A huge, voluble man of strong views, he soon put us right. The key to running a small business is simple – up-to-date monthly financial reporting. It requires a balance sheet and a financial profit and loss statement. These need to marry up, so an increase in profit needs to translate to an increase in assets, preferably in cash rather than stocks and debtors. Underpinning this is the gross margin. The percentage taken up by labour and materials in the sales price needs to be as low as possible. I have learned this simple formula is the key to everything. The higher the gross margin, the more is available for marketing, innovation and expansion.

On the flag boards the gross margin was around 35 per cent. On the big sign written boards it was less than 20 per cent. We could not increase our prices on the bigger boards because we faced competition from other self-employed sign writers with lower overheads. On the smaller boards, we needed to raise our prices and increase the minimum order size. I realised that in order to get my foot in the door with customers, I was taking business and losing money on every sale we made. I also realised that sign writing would never be profitable and we would have to find alternative products with a higher gross margin. But what?

At the end of 1970 we had outgrown our increasingly dangerous and cramped quarters above the bar. We decided to build a new factory in the Pen Mill Trading Estate on the outskirts of Yeovil, once again with the help of the NatWest. Printing was in the front half of the new premises and sign writing was in the back. One of our customers was Paddy Ashdown, who was at that time a buyer at Clarks Shoes. Whenever we had not lived up to his expectations, he would waltz on to the factory floor and give a Royal Marines' bollocking to whoever he thought responsible. I finally took him aside and told him that while I appreciated that we were country yokels who sometimes made mistakes, it was I who was responsible for any failures and I was the person he should berate.

I had been concerned for several years that Taunton Vale, the company we used for laminating, could undermine our business by either refusing to laminate our boards or by starting to encourage our competitors. I approached their operations director, a strange man called Malcolm Wigg. He had been a flight lieutenant in the RAF Regiment during his National Service and was jealous of Dick Jessop and Douglas Forbes, the founders of Taunton Vale. He wanted to move out and set up on his own. We were happy to oblige him. If we could build our own laminating presses, we could move into the kitchen, tableware and dining room place mats market.

We could not have chosen a worse time. Malcolm Wigg decamped – to the fury of his former friends – and set up in a garage in Taunton. It was January 1974, in the middle of the miners' strike. Britain was on a three-day week. And when the power was on it was so reduced that our electrical elements were never hot enough to bond the laminates to the prints. Most of our production had to be scrapped.

It also became clear, very early on, that our avant-garde, brightly coloured, silk-screened kitchenware (which was designed by Brian Aldridge, one of RGM's packaging designers) was not to the taste of the average housewife.

Malcolm's wife was put under intolerable pressure by his former employers. She could see the business was struggling. She had lost her friends, her social standing and stood to lose her savings, on which Malcolm was living. One morning in early 1974, she was found dead in Malcolm's elderly Bentley, having gassed herself. It was an appalling shock.

As we were still reeling from this terrible turn of events, it became clear that the laminating part of the business could not stay in Taunton. The short term lease on the garage had run out. We had to find space in our factory near Yeovil for Malcolm. The sign-writers were continuing to lose money so I had no alternative but to make them redundant. One of the first awful realisations that the world is not always a highway to heaven came when I had to make people who had become loyal, hard-working friends redundant. John White (who later became a tennis coach), Robert Maddick and Dick Lawrence had become part of the factory family. It was little consolation that they could set up on their own and take the business with them. Theory Y was not meant to be about redundancy.

Malcolm came to work in Yeovil every day from his home outside Taunton and we hired additional youngsters, some from difficult backgrounds. There was Eddie 'the Bomber' Painter, who blew a massive hole in the bank of the local river, having mixed fertiliser and sugar to make a mini IRA-type explosive device. He was also an accomplished locksmith, who could find his way into any building and from there into any filing cabinet and finally into the cash box. Then there was Colin, aka 'Compost', whose hygiene left something to be desired and who had gained a reputation at a certain council estate in Yeovil for removing ladies' underwear from clotheslines. Robert Janes, who had been fully involved in the cannabis window-box fiasco, once complained that it was impossible to get a decent day's work out of Compost. I told him that I had found it extremely difficult to get a good day's work out of him a few years earlier! Although it would have been preferable if Compost had been German or Japanese, we had to work with the material we had. A couple of years later, Compost turned out to be hardworking and reliable, as did the Bomber. Theory Y was working again.

After a few months of working in Yeovil, and with the melamine production bay in full swing, Malcolm – who had an infuriating habit of always demanding to use the ladies' loo in the office, rather than the less salubrious facilities in the factory – came to tell me of his future plans. He had been left £30,000 by his wife and intended to spend this over the course of the following year. Firstly, he would marry his very attractive, much younger former Taunton Vale secretary with a slap-up wedding and reception at The Dorchester. Then he would take her off on an expensive honeymoon. When all the money was gone a year later, he would drive up to his wife's grave in Norfolk in his ancient Bentley and gas himself. Despite my repeated protestations, this is exactly what he did.

Three years earlier, in the middle of 1971, Bill Snell, my partner in the logo printing business, had told me that a small greetings card company in Crewkerne that had gone into administration was up for sale. Was I interested? I got hold of the receivers who told me that Ray Tuff Cards was bankrupt, with debts of a hundred thousand, and that they were looking for bids. The company published 'Slim Jim' humorous cards that sold from revolving metal stands in outlets such as WH Smith's up and down the country. Tuff's most popular and successful offering bore the message 'This card can only be opened by a virgin'. It was stuck together. The competitor was Hanson & White, whose founders went on to become Lords Hanson and White. Ray Tuff had fallen by the wayside. Ray was a funny, innovative, hardworking man but he couldn't add up. He had moved his business from Surrey to Somerset to save costs but he never had enough cash to fund the endless demand for new card designs.

We did not have £100,000 so I asked Peter Ohrenstein what we might do. He discovered that Ray Tuff Cards Ltd had a subsidiary called Tuff Ltd, which owned both the premises and the printing side of the business. He suggested that we should buy a majority stake in Tuff Ltd for £51 and then make an offer to the liquidator for the outstanding unsold stock in Ray Tuff Cards. We did this, and we also gave an undertaking that we would take on all the redundant sales staff and transfer them across to the printing company. So, for £51 and an increased overdraft facility guaranteed against the building, we became owners of a litho-printing business. This dovetailed with the silkscreen laminating business. We could now offer a wide range of products, sold through a combined salesforce, as well as taking on substantial litho-work from our packaging business in London.

We were proud of our modern kitcheware products, and hoped they might appeal more to avant-garde European consumers than to the so far unimpressed UK market. My best man, Robin Garran, ran a successful consultancy for companies setting up in the European market. He had come across a Glaswegian diplomat in Stuttgart called Hughie Muldoon.

He was the Foreign Office vice-consul but had decided to leave and set up an import company specialising in British giftware. It was ideal. The company was called Brimpo and I was tasked with finding a range of high-quality specialty British novelties for him to sell. As well as our melamine chopping boards, table mats, trays, key racks, and drying-up cloths and oven gloves (made by Ulster Weavers), we had smart trays depicting fox-hunting scenes and Grecian urns. We also took on a licence to sell hand-painted prints of small birds and flowers for a business run by one of the Clarks Shoes' family members.

We found a business in the Mendip Hills which specialised in corn dollies. We were keen to offer him something uniquely English. I went off to Stuttgart with my samples and Hugh Muldoon took me around the department stores and gift shops. One challenge was that we had no funds for marketing or promotion. Once we had paid the import duties, the transport costs and the local sales taxes, our beautiful range was far from cheap. We did, however, engineer a trial order for two gondolas of corn dollies from the department store Kaufhof in the centre of Stuttgart. We had to prepare marketing materials and packaging in German. I hired a TV cameraman from Bristol to film rustic English ladies, dressed in smocks and caps, knitting corn dollies in an aristocratic landlord's barn. The brand name was 'Lord Richard' and we borrowed the Milton Abbey estate as 'Lord Richard's' family mansion, showing contented workers packing corn dollies in the village's thatched cottages.

Very quickly we ran into problems. The expansive lawns were covered in football and rugby posts as Lord Richard's mansion was in real life a well-known public school. This meant painting out the offending posts frame by frame in the film. Secondly, the owner of the corn dolly company had decided, unbeknownst to us, to use up his stock of last year's corn heads and stalks.

I hired a self-drive five-tonner from Vincent's Garage in Yeovil and, laden with Korn Puppen, Tabletten (trays) and boxes of hand-painted bird prints, I set off for Stuttgart. Two days later, when I arrived, I had to spend several hours explaining to customs officials that the corn dollies were not an unapproved agricultural product full of English pests likely to contaminate the German wheat industry.

The next morning, Hughie had arranged to meet with the Kaufhof's chief buyer and a camera crew from Sud Deutscher Rundfunk, who would conduct an interview with 'Lord Richard' in his halting German as we drove down into the city.

First, I had to fill up with diesel. I drove into the petrol station, only to wedge the top of the lorry under the canopy above the pumps. The canopy was hung with strip lights that rained glass all across the forecourt as I tried to extract my wagon. Undeterred, I collected the camera crew and we started the descent into Stuttgart with the cameraman sitting on a copy of *The Times*, which I had placed prominently on the dashboard, and the considerable Herr Meyer, the buyer, in the passenger seat. As we plunged, the remaining glass from the canopy lights crashed from the roof of the van on to the pavements, causing elderly ladies with their smart shopping baskets on their way into town to take emergency evasive action. The camera was rolling. 'Ah', said Herr Meyer. 'In the last War, the RAF bombed one half of Stuttgart. Is it your intention to now bomb the other half? That is a yoke! A good English yoke, no?'

Finally, we arrived, unpacked the lorry and carted the corn dollies on to the shop floor – only to discover that most of last year's corn kernels, which formed the skirts, had bounced out of their ears on the trip across and were now rattling like maracas. We had to repack and reseal all of them. As we completed our work, on the gondola next to ours appeared a Romanian gypsy with basket loads of enormous and beautiful corn dollies, all shiny new, in bright colours and at half our price. Unsurprisingly, our sales were minimal. Our desperate attempts to persuade German housewives to hang our *Korn Puppen* over their beds to reinvigorate their sex lives fell on deaf ears.

The sales of the kitchenware and the painted prints, if not as disastrous as the corn dollies, were mediocre at best. A year later and fifteen thousand pounds wiser, we called a halt to our assault on the German market. I had learnt lessons about exporting which stayed with me for the rest of my career, not least when I became Minister of Trade, responsible for the UK's export strategy, and, later still, when I spent sixteen years working with James Dyson.

First: if a product sells for £5 in its home market, it will need initially to sell for £10 in an export market. Second: depending on the market sector, without a gross margin of at least 50 per cent, it is impossible to conduct proper research, have a sufficient marketing budget and give the agent enough margin to distribute and promote the product. Third: because it sells well at home, doesn't mean it will travel. Fourth: learn to crawl before you walk. Start in Ireland, rather than Germany. Fifth:

make sure you have sufficient time and money to manage market entry until you are established. Sixth: quality and reliability will make you or break you. Finally: spend time learning basic phrases, read the history and understand the culture of the countries you are targeting. Don't talk in slow, loud English about your family, your dog, your football team or your golf handicap. Consult others who are already there. Use our embassies. Get in touch with the local UK trade promoters, fix up financing through letters of credit or bank covenants, check out payment conditions – Italy is 120 to 150 days if you're lucky.

There is something magical in running your own small manufacturing business. The intimacy with the employees; the lack of class distinction; the anticipation of opening the mail on Saturday morning to see how many cheques have come in; the need to be involved with every aspect down to the last detail, particularly when someone becomes sick or leaves.

There is also the dreaded disaster sitting on your shoulder. On one occasion Coates, the only producer of laminating inks in the country, rang up to say they were reducing their range and would in future only produce black. We were finished. I had to beg and bribe to keep them supplying. The price doubled as did the quantities I had to order.

The whole family was involved. Whenever we had a big order from RGM for supermarket displays, our two boys used to come into the factory to rack the cardboard units after they had been printed. On one occasion, Andy climbed up a rack and fell on his head on to the concrete floor. He got up, shook himself and carried on. Andrew Hodgson, our laconic manager from New Zealand, nicknamed him the 'silver bullet'.

For me, the most rewarding, exciting and fulfilling role was repping, or getting in the orders. I travelled everywhere. There was no town or city centre that I did not know. I had three sample cases in my car. Signs for estate agents, humorous cards for stationers and tableware for gift shops. They were very different pitches requiring very different techniques. I became a commercial chameleon. It was the greatest apprenticeship for my future career as a politician on the doorstep and at the hustings.

By 1974 we were turning over £3,000,000 across the group and employed over 30 people. Had Theory Y worked?

In a small organisation it is always easier to establish close personal relationships and for everyone to feel part of a joint endeavour. John Garnett, Virginia Bottomley's father, had brought new life to the Industrial Society because as a naval officer in the war, he had seen how much more complicated it was to manage men on a battleship than a destroyer. But our little company had gone much further than just building trust and transparency – we had increased our productivity, enhanced our skillsets, minimised staff turnover, become friends, and taken on youngsters from dysfunctional, deprived backgrounds and turned them into well-rounded, motivated individuals.

What were the downsides? We didn't concentrate enough on our profit margins. Sometimes we were too easy-going, too prepared to overlook a mistake and give someone another chance when threatening them with the sack might have been more appropriate. However, as everyone worked as a team, the other members soon took exception to one of their colleagues not pulling their weight or trying to pull a fast one, and their disapproval was often more effective than stern words from me.

I had considered turning the West Country companies into a cooperative based on the Scott Bader Commonwealth model. But I was not convinced that ownership should be transferred from individuals to a corporate identity. Although Scott Bader has survived and is an extremely successful company, it has never taken off as a model for others. Instead we amalgamated the different companies into one and offered shares to everyone. But as some of the companies always struggled to generate sufficient cash, the value of the shares failed to increase and their importance declined in comparison to the pay-outs from our company-wide, individually-tailored bonus scheme. There was an intense rivalry between the smart boys from RGM, our company in London – who believed they were always bailing out their Somerset country bumpkin cousins – and our West Country employees.

Once a year we had a company party to draw the sting. It kicked off at 11 o'clock in the morning with a poorly refereed football match. The main purpose for the Yeovil side was to show up the 'city slickers' by fair or foul means; the Slickers aimed to get the opposing captain (me) red carded. They were invariably successful.

After the match we all piled into minibuses with partners, wives and children to head off to Lyme Regis for an afternoon's mackerel fishing. Regardless of my pleadings, the partners and girlfriends were invariably dressed in skimpy miniskirts and high-heeled shoes. After an hour's fishing, most of the men had consumed enough beer to fill a brewery and the girls were frozen. We then returned to Little Aldon, our home, and set up a barbecue for the mackerel (if we'd caught any!) steaks, chops and all the trimmings.

After about 11 o'clock, those who had not disappeared into the bushes would either fall asleep or start fighting. One year Terry Laver, our factory foreman, was so incensed with Richard Hazelton, the captain of the Slickers, that he started waving a broken bottle around, and Mick Lawrence, our star card salesman, took exception to something I had said and was found wandering around, threatening revenge, with a bread knife in his hand.

It all sounds a lot worse now than it seemed at the time but those who think that the Brits are a law-abiding, peace-loving, fair-minded and tolerant people have not followed our imperial history, let alone considered the RGM annual summer party.

CHAPTER 10

Back to Politics

I N THE SPRING of 1967, there were the Somerset County Council elections. 'Nick' Nicholson, who was John Peyton's agent in Yeovil, had asked me if I would stand in Yeovil South, where I lived. He had read about my stuttering performances in the Monday Club and PEST. I was keen to get local government experience on my CV and also to see how Theory Y might be introduced into the public service.

No other candidates were put up for the ward, so I was selected. During the campaign I contracted a nasty chest infection, made worse by smoking thirty Rothmans King Size a day. My doctor, Derek Kibblewhite, told me that, as an asthmatic, if I didn't give up tobacco, I would soon be unable to blow out a candle eighteen inches from the end of my nose. Admittedly I have a very large nose, but the distance is not that demanding. I never smoked another cigarette.

Sissy had to go out leafleting and canvassing on my behalf, which she had not foreseen as part of our matrimonial contract, not least because Robbie was only just two years old. I was elected as the youngest county councillor in Somerset.

In the early 70s, following the Maud report, local government was undergoing radical reorganisation. New local government areas were created, split into two tiers. Large county councils were responsible for education, highways, social services and strategic planning and district councils dealt with refuse, housing and local planning.

The reforms were necessary, although they were laced with as much gerrymandering as the government could get away with. Much of northern Somerset was hived off into a new county, Avon, which was designed to act as a Conservative counterweight to Labour-controlled Bristol City. However, nothing was done to improve or introduce modern management techniques, increase efficiency and productivity, or concentrate resources on providing a professional multi-disciplined public-sector workforce.

The council was dominated by independents as a cover for their Tory pedigrees. George Wyndham, the chairman, was from an old upper-class Somerset family. Educated at Eton (as was his vice chairman John Wills of the tobacco family), he was kind, conciliatory and gentle. He generally deferred to his clerk, who was a bewigged tetchy solicitor.

Sitting immediately in front of me in the horseshoe council chamber was Matthew Waley-Cohen. He was as broad as he was tall. For most of the time he sat like a slumbering volcano but occasionally he erupted with fury, banging the desk in front of him.

One such occasion was when John Vincent, the owner of Austins motor distributors in Yeovil and chairman of the finance committee, announced that Dutch elm disease had arrived in Bristol docks and was fanning out across the county. The council had no resources to handle it. The government would not assist and in time it would kill all the elms in England. Waley-Cohen jumped to his feet and exploded at the council's complacent ineptitude. The chamber's seating comprised wooden planks, twelve feet long, nailed into and connected to the side arms of the neighbouring seat. Next to Waley-Cohen sat the chief fire officer, dressed like a Christmas tree. Next to him was David Young, an eccentric architect who was always sipping from a Schweppes ginger ale bottle. As Waley-Cohen sat down there was a crash. He, the chief fire officer and David Young disappeared as the seat broke away from its support. When they reappeared they received a rapturous reception. The only casualty was David Young's reputation: when his ginger ale bottle spilled over his neighbours, its contents turned out to be dry sherry, which largely explained why he was speechless for most of the meetings.

I was determined to improve the management of the council by introducing Theory Y. George Wyndham and John Wills supported me. The county surveyor flatly refused to be involved as he was a passionate advocate of scientific management – the bible of Theory X.

In spite of his opposition I pushed on. I discovered that the only firm promoting Theory Y in the UK was the consultancy company Coopers & Lybrand. They described their offering as Management by Objectives. This sounded more reassuring and more practical than Theory Y. They were given a trial contract and the chief education officer reluctantly agreed to be the guinea pig. He was a gruff, bossy, humourless little martinet. He told the consultants that he set the objectives for his senior team and as far as he was concerned, they carried out his instructions to the letter.

When his staff were interviewed it transpired what they actually did bore very little resemblance to what the chief education officer was telling them to do. As he had no system of involving his managers or taking into account their varied personalities, prejudices and preferences, it was not surprising that his department lacked coherence, leadership and imaginative policy initiatives. The education committee endorsed the · recommendations of the consultants and Somerset became one of the first councils in Britain to adopt the principles of Douglas McGregor.

The chief education officer was a chastened man. Management by objectives became embedded in the Education Department's management. The county surveyor remained in his bunker.

By 1970 I had been re-elected as a county councillor, the business was doing reasonably and I wanted to try to break into the national political scene by being accepted on to the prospective parliamentary candidates list.

John Peyton, Yeovil's MP, agreed to sponsor me, along with George Wyndham. Nick Nicholson, the agent, told me to write to Bill Elliott MP, chairman of the candidates committee. Eighteen months later I was called for interview at 1.30 p.m. on 10 May 1972 at Conservative Central Office in Smith Square. It was a catastrophe. I had arranged to have an early lunch with David Rawlins and Robin Garran, two of my oldest friends, at Antonio's in Dover Street. As European consultants to Carreras Rothmans, they enjoyed very long lunches involving plates of antipasti followed by spaghetti alle vongole, drenched in garlic, washed down with litres of Antinori white wine. I could have weathered the storm but at 1 o'clock, just as I was about to leave, Bill Elliott's secretary Doreen Hudson rang through to say Mr Elliott would be delayed, and could I come at 2. The same thing happened half an hour later and then half an hour after that, until I was finally told to report at 3.30. I arrived at Central Office, reeking of garlic and, as Dr Paisley would have said, 'with the drink taken'.

Doreen appeared with a copy of *The Times* and said that Mr Elliott had been further delayed and would I like to borrow his paper. At 4 p.m. she reappeared and asked if she could have the paper back as the vice-chairman had returned and wanted to read it. At 4.30 I was ushered in and asked to sit in a very low armchair opposite the MP while he peered down at me like an owl from behind a large Queen Anne desk.

I was wearing a Disraeli black frock coat with brass buttons, a Mr Fish psychedelic bright pink shirt and matching tie, bell-bottomed sponge-bag trousers and black patent leather shoes with gold buckles. As I lowered myself into the armchair one of the brass buttons popped off and flew across the desk landing on his blotter. He picked it up gingerly, examined it and, as he returned it, remarked that he was not aware which regiment it represented.

He asked me why I wished to be an MP. I then handed him a summary of how the Conservatives should accept the Theory Y approach to management if the country was to reverse its long industrial decline. Bill Elliott was a delightful man on the left wing of the party, representing a northern seat, but I could see as his brow furrowed that he was not convinced. As he handed back my précis he pointed out of the window and said, 'Mr Needham, are you sure you have come to the right building? Transport House is just on the other side of the square.' Several weeks later a roneoed, unsigned letter arrived saying that the standing committee on candidates had refused my application.

I immediately went to see John Peyton, Howard Davies, the West Country central office agent, and John Hannam, the newly elected MP for Exeter who had been a county councillor with me in Yeovil. They wrote to Bill Elliot, explaining that I was not as awful as I looked and that I had worked hard for the party in Yeovil. In September 1972 I received another letter welcoming me on to the list. I was on the way. Or was I?

1972 was a bad year for the Heath government. Twenty-three million days were lost to strikes. The country was on the verge of a general shutdown. Unemployment was close to one million, growth was stagnant and inflation at 8 per cent. The old right-wing union leaders were being replaced with left-wingers, like Jack Jones – who was later found to have had contacts with the KGB – and Hugh Scanlon – a former communist, who wrote everything in shorthand as he could not read, and once famously remarked, 'It's lucky we are not going to have another war as if we do, we will lose it.'

With my background in business large and small, my experience as county councillor and entrepreneur, together with my earlier pamphleteering for the Monday Club and PEST, I believed I was everything the Tory party most required.

I started applying to the candidates' department for my name to go forward for safe seats as they became available. I received no response. I then downgraded to Tory marginals – nothing – then Labour marginals – still nothing. Next safe Labour seats, from which I sometimes received the standard response thanking me for my interest. I was left with hopeless Labour seats, mainly in South Wales and South Yorkshire. There was not much competition as most Tories did not fancy taking on striking miners who were determined to overthrow the Heath government. I did find one other friend in a similar position: Brian Williamson, (Sir Brian Williamson) who had been Maurice Macmillan's personal assistant and who later became a hugely successful banker. He was finding it as hard as me to be selected. We travelled around Yorkshire together. There was usually a local councillor or property developer as the only competition. The Association much preferred a local, however tongue-tied, to a smart, slick talking, self-confident, southern public school boy. The developer thought selection might help with planning permissions.

On one occasion Brian didn't help himself. He was always dressed immaculately in a pinstripe suit and highly polished Church's brogues. He had driven up early to Goole, in the East Riding of Yorkshire, so as not to be late for the interview and had parked his new BMW on a large empty parking lot overlooking the dock. Above the back seat, for all to see, he had left his Territorial Army officer's cap, his swagger stick and some Conservative leaflets. He went to sleep. When he awoke the dockers had offloaded a further five hundred BMWs that completely surrounded him. It took him two days to retrieve his car and Goole never had the chance of considering him.

Meanwhile I had landed Pontefract with a Labour majority of twenty-five-thousand. My rival for the position was an aggressive, touchy builder, Ian Bloomer, who had married the boss's daughter. The interview took place in the Pontefract Conservative Club under the watchful eye of the agent, the formidable Suzanne Hick, who used the bar as her office, controlled her members with a rod of iron and didn't like Bloomer. She had been in charge of elections since 1955 and continued until she died aged 93. The Bloomer supporters thought they had the killer question. Would I live in the constituency if I won? 'Yes,' I said, 'of course I would!' I could think of no part of the country I would prefer more. Anyway, I had an ancestor, William Nedham, who had been MP for Pontefract between 1780-1784 before coal was discovered. I was in.

I was hugely advantaged by having Sissy, who has a wonderful ability to make friends and talk to everyone about anything. The elderly in Pontefract particularly adored her and marvelled at her ability to bring up a young family and spend time in the Yorkshire coalfields.

Just as I was selected, we decided to go to the 1972 party conference. It was a thoroughly dispiriting occasion. We found a dreadful Blackpool boarding house on the seafront, about a mile from the conference centre to which we walked every day in driving rain and wind. Our room was next to an ancient lift that rattled up and down throughout the night. The communal toilet also required relentless flushing. At the conference we hardly knew anyone and certainly not anyone who mattered. We listened from the back of the hall to the speeches of the great and the good and then wandered aimlessly around the rooms and exhibition stands hoping to meet someone we might know. But those we did always seemed to be in a rush to meet someone else and while we talked to them kept looking over our shoulders to see if they could find someone else more important. I put forward my name to speak in the industrial relations debate but did not get called. After two days we went home. Clearly I was at the very lowest rung of the ladder, which selection for Pontefract had done little to alter. I needed to find a way of making myself known to the makers and shakers, and become involved at the centre.

I decided to approach James Douglas, who was head of the Conservative Research Department. He was a gentle, middle-of-the-road academic who drove around London on a Lambretta, wearing a crash helmet, striped trousers and a black jacket. He found time for me and was genuinely interested in my ideas. Against the background of manufacturing accounting for 44 per cent of the economy, we agreed a brief that I would write a paper on how the government and the Conservative party should adapt to lessen the harsh and unacceptable face of capitalism. It was certainly a highly effective way of getting rid of me.

A year later, I completed my project. It concluded:

The Theory X concept of social responsibility is that of minimum involvement. The company through corporation tax and the rates pays for the services it requires from the community. By providing employment in creating wealth industry is the basis of the state's continued existence. That is its only responsibility. Theory X management would feel that any imposition of further outside tasks would weaken management's primary function which is to make profits. Theory X aims at fulfilling fundamental social needs by using money as the exclusive yardstick.

Theory Y is the more inclusive theory of motivation because it includes higher needs and considers them to be more important. An enlightened factory will not only make products and concentrate on excellence but also help people to become better citizens, better husbands or better wives. This is an asset to the population at large in the same way as a school or hospital. This, of itself, is fulfilling a social function as it reduces community stress and therefore social costs. It is to be hoped that as Theory Y enterprises take root, they will force others to change if they need to keep their labour. We must of course assume that people want to improve both as workers and consumers and they want to make or buy finer quality products. If cheapness is the only criterion Theory X will triumph.

Industry must be persuaded that Theory Y is not a way of pampering workers which will lead to falling output or that social responsibility is another burden placed on overworked management by interfering government. Theory Y is not only the answer to greater job enrichment, it is the way that businesses in the future will grow and profit. Social responsibility is not another stone around the neck of industry, it is a vital area of corporate responsibility. Disregard for safety, pollution, misuse of people or raw materials will cause consumer hostility. If this country continues to follow social advance reluctantly rather than welcoming it, if it continues to discuss its industrial relations in terms of inevitable conflict, the future for all of us looks bleak indeed.

I sent in my report. Nothing happened. After several weeks I rang up. Mr Douglas was not available. Mr Douglas never seemed to be available. Finally, he agreed to see me. He was effusive. The report was wonderful and contained everything he believed the Tory party stood for. He was a strong supporter of Theory Y and hoped it would be universally applied across British industry. However, he had a problem. He didn't know what to do with it. It was impossible to change the attitudes of management and trade unions through legislation. He found a suitable pigeonhole for it in Central Office where it has remained to this day.

Meanwhile, the government was falling apart. The miners, supported by the Transport and General Workers' Union under Jack Jones and the AEU (the Amalgamated Engineering Union) under Hugh Scanlon, were determined to bring down the government. In the autumn of 1973, the miners rejected a 13 per cent pay rise. They followed up with an overtime ban and the lights started to go out. The country was reduced to a three-day week, a State of Emergency was declared and 81 per cent of the miners voted for strike action. In February 1974, Heath called a snap election with the rallying cry of 'Who governs?' For me, it was time to pack up and go to Pontefract, where the colliers were waiting for the Tory candidate to call!

CHAPTER 11

The Miners' Strike and the February 1974 Election

PONTEFRACT, CASTLEFORD AND Featherstone in West Yorkshire have been mining villages since the early nineteenth century. Between February and April 1785, during Pontefract's rural past, a William Nedham had been its Member of Parliament. He was a distant relative of the Kilmoreys. He had fallen out with his nephew and had left his huge estates around Newry to General Needham who became the first earl of Kilmorey. No one in Pontefract recalled his stay.

Pontefract is famous for its black liquorice cakes, which Yorkshire people love and most others find disgusting. The other towns are famous for their rugby league teams and their colliery bands. With the exception of the present distinguished incumbent Yvette Cooper, most of the past MPs have done little to be remembered by.

I was keen to get down the Prince of Wales mine, which was Pontefract's main employer. I contacted the colliery manager, Arthur Ramsbottom, but as tensions increased, he became impossible to reach. Finally, he answered Suzanne Hick's call when the miners had already gone on a go-slow. He told her that, while he could guarantee to get me down there, he couldn't guarantee 'to get the little bugger back up again'!

By chance I knocked on his door during the election. He was a huge man with a bristling moustache, broad brown corduroy trousers, braces and a brass-buckle belt. He winked at me and shut the door.

The average age of the local supporters was anywhere between seventy and eighty. There was no way that either physically or mentally they could go head-to-head on the doorsteps with the striking miners. Using her office on the bar in the 'Con Club', Suzanne operated like a mother hen, shepherding her flock to write up the envelopes for the free election address.

We had some other assets. The members of the sixth form of the local grammar school were, almost to a pupil, young Conservatives. They wanted to have a good time. My other advantage was a team of mates, including some of the boys from the factory, who wanted to pay a visit. They bed-and-breakfasted at the homes of elderly members.

We wanted to present ourselves as young and with it in contrast to old and stuffy Labour. I wore a pale blue denim jacket with a huge blue rosette, and matching jeans with a sign on one buttock depicting a grinning prime minister entitled 'Ted Teeth' and a patch on the other buttock with the message 'kiss my patch'.

We divided each day into knocking on doors, finding a pub for lunch, visiting outside a school as the mothers collected their children, more door-knocking in the evening and finishing off back in a pub. On a few occasions we would visit a shopping centre to hand out leaflets. Sometimes we received a fair amount of abuse with people turning their backs on us. We did not make too much noise and put the girls at the front.

The national campaign passed us by, as did any visiting minister. We handed out literature that talked about anything and everything other than the miners and their fight with the government. For the most part miners and their families were hospitable and took pity on our inevitably hopeless cause. A surprising number of others thought that the miners were taking advantage of their position.

The candidate's team was a combination of beauty and the beast. Sissy invited one of her best friends to provide company and comfort. Debbie Idiens is stunningly brave and beautiful. Born in Zimbabwe, she has all the settlers' grit and determination. She is mother to Kristin Scott Thomas, has four other children and had two husbands both killed in the Fleet Air Arm. The disadvantage of the glamorous twosome was that they kept disappearing. On one occasion Sissy was gone for three quarters of an hour. Where had she got to? Had some furious hairy miner dragged her into his house to give her a piece of his mind?! It turned out a miner had invited her in. 'Come in, love. You're so pretty. It's freezing out there. You know you're wasting your time. Have a Polo and let me make you a cup of tea.'

Halfway through the campaign Jamie Oakes – who was a friend of Exeter MP John Hannam – rang me up. Jamie explained that his father had been a pit owner in the East Midlands and that he knew the psyche of the British miner inside out as he had been brought up amongst them.

He lived in a quite grand house in Derbyshire and spoke with quite a grand accent. I had my doubts! He arrived in a spanking new top-of-the-range Mercedes and was wearing an ankle-length black overcoat with an astrakhan collar. We gathered round to see what we could learn.

He strode confidently up the path to a house on an unadopted road which had to be occupied by a miner as there was a German Shepherd tethered to the fence. Gingerly he manoeuvred around the growling dog and knocked on the front door. It was clear that the front door was not the usual entrance and he was summoned to the back. We could not see what happened but we could hear.

Jamie berated the miners for their selfish demands which were so damaging to the country. 'Do you not realise how lucky you are in comparison to the conditions that existed in my father's days? Do you not know you are the highest-paid industrial workers in the country?' (It turned out halfway through the campaign that they were not.) The harangue continued as Jamie retreated backwards around the side of the house while the occupier, wearing a stained purple T-shirt and sporting a moth-eaten pair of bedroom slippers, pushed him backwards until he fell over the garden gate. Luckily for Jamie, the dog's chain saved him from a mauling. Terry Laver and Malcolm Templer, the two printers from Yeovil, could not contain themselves. Poor Mr Oakes dusted himself down, climbed back into his Mercedes and was never seen again.

Malcolm and Terry had never been north of Bristol. It took them three days to find Pontefract. The first house Terry called on was answered by a large lady. Terry asked her politely if she might consider voting Tory. She rounded on him, 'Not bloody likely! I work!' Terry grabbed her by the shoulders and shouted back, 'What do you think I do, mother?' As the husband hove into view, I told Terry to beat it.

The young Conservatives had devised an effective poster campaign. Late at night they would park Sissy's Mini Cooper at the end of a terrace. One climbed on the roof and another hoisted themselves on to the first's shoulders. They then stuck large blue posters – proclaiming 'We Needham in Pontefract' – thirty feet up on most of the gable ends throughout the constituency. It was almost impossible for anyone to get them down.

We thought our public meetings would be packed. How wrong we were. We laid out hundreds of chairs in the assembly halls of the local comprehensive schools. The best attendance was fifteen. Six of those were our own supporters on the top table and the rest were local Labour party members who had been sent along to heckle plus one local councillor to ask me tricky local questions.

The public will only go to a meeting if they think there's going to be a contest. Joe Harper, the local MP, did not even need to appear until the last five days of the campaign. He was helping out in marginals elsewhere. He arrived like visiting royalty, dressed immaculately in a pinstripe suit and silk tie. There was no need for him to lower himself to debate with the thirty-two-year-old in a blue jean jacket and matching trousers. The result confirmed his judgement. Joe Harper, Labour, 34,409, 74.79 per cent. Richard Needham, Conservative, 10,605, 23.05%. B. Lavery, Workers' Revolutionary Party, 991, 2.15 per cent. When the count was over Comrade Lavery gave us the benefit of a ten-minute rant until someone shouted, 'They have finished counting and you lost.' Lenin still had a long way to go in the Yorkshire coalfields!

We came away from the campaign with a much greater understanding what a political career would involve. Even in solid-Labour Pontefract, the Conservative parliamentary candidate and his wife were expected to know the answer to every question, although Sissy, when stumped on the doorstep by some irate teacher, could always swerve away with 'Hang on a moment – I'll just get my husband!'

There is no topic, event or issue that the aspiring MP, however remote his chances, can avoid having a view on. Conservative Central Office produces a Campaign Guide at every election, which for three weeks replaces the Bible. It covers every eventuality. After three weeks, no page remained unturned.

We both realised that from then on our lives would change forever. For the next twenty-three years we were to become public property. This was particularly hard for Sissy to accept as, up to then, she had had no exposure to public life. Her eyes were opened as to the grime and the grit that hung over the coal mining areas. It was a far cry from rural Somerset and a long way from her upbringing in Hamburg.

In 1848, at the time of a revolution across Europe that aimed at overturning the monarchical conservative settlement agreed at the Congress of Vienna in 1815, Alphonse de Lamartine, the French philosopher, claimed that 'the people are always right'.

I'm not too sure that was true in February 1974. Ted Heath was a humourless, awkward man who found it difficult to empathise, but he had little option than to call an election when confronted by left-wing dominated trade unions supported by a conniving Labour Party determined to bring the government down.

The question 'who runs the country' was a perfectly legitimate one. The miners were being used, mainly willingly, to destroy the government's economic programme. What was it supposed to do? Cave in to the miners, continue the three-day week? Limp on, in Norman Tebbit's famous phrase, 'in office but not in power'? Heath was right to ask the question. He fought a lacklustre campaign, though nowhere near as gormless and crass as Theresa May's in May 2017.

He was undone by a surge in the Liberal vote. The Liberal Party stood on a platform of 'a plague on both your houses', which was a cop-out alternative for those who didn't know what to do. The Liberals were led by Jeremy Thorpe who – as Heath knew – was about to be exposed and discredited over an attempt he had orchestrated to murder a former gay lover. If that had emerged in the campaign, the result might have been very different.

Heath hung on for a few days after the election. He had received more votes than Labour but four fewer seats. But when he could find no reliable partners he resigned. Jim Prior told me some years later that on the evening after the result, Heath had sat in Wilton's restaurant and consumed four dozen oysters at one sitting as he tried to find a way to hang on.

As for the miners, it turned out a pyrrhic victory. It proved that to take them on required careful preparation with huge coal stocks stored at the power stations to stop them defeating the government when they went on strike. Margaret Thatcher and Nigel Lawson didn't make the same mistake twice. In November 1973, the British Cabinet appointed an American industrial psychologist to try to understand why and what motivated the British miner. His report explained that when a man constantly and repeatedly lets down his wife by staying away and coming home late without ever bothering to let her know in advance, and then tries to comfort her with the well-worn excuse 'I'll make it up to you one day, darling,' he shouldn't be surprised to open the door one day to find she is no longer there.

The second most powerful emotion after love is revenge, and it was revenge that drove the miners to confrontation after decades of hardship and toil. The Coal Board may have been their nominal boss and their industry owned by the state, but they trusted neither any more than they had trusted the previous private owners.

Could Theory Y have made a difference? Could and should the pits have been turned into self-managed collectives with a central supervisory board of unions and managers allocating capital resources and agreeing wages across the industry. It might have worked for a while – increasing productivity and promoting innovation – but the coal industry, even in 1974, was facing imminent, irreversible, inevitable decline. Coal was yesterday's fuel source and was soon to be replaced by nuclear, natural gas and hydro, and later on solar, wind power and batteries. It would take Margaret Thatcher to break the power of the miners, reduce the subsidies and introduce competition.

Pontefract still just about loyally and regularly votes back a Labour MP but there are no miners among the voters. The Prince of Wales colliery – that employed two thousand men in 1974 and produced one-and-a-half million tons of a coal a year – closed in 2002 after 140 years with six hundred redundancies.

CHAPTER 12

Gravesend –
Almost but Not Quite

IT WAS TIME for me to move on – and quickly, as it was a certainty that Wilson would seek to increase his wafer-thin majority by calling another election soon, just as he had in 1966. I started applying for safer seats. Rochdale – which was a three-way marginal, but in reality, under Cyril Smith, a safe Liberal seat – offered me an interview. But before I could travel to Lancashire, I had a call from Bill McNeil, the chairman of the Gravesend Conservative Association and CEO of Berry Wiggins, asking if I would like to apply to replace the former Conservative MP Roger White, who had lost in the February election. White was an unprepossessing small man who called himself – rather bizarrely – 'the little white man'. He had not done much between 1970 and 1974 and was persuaded to stand down by Bill. Paul Bristol, the founder of the Monday Club and chairman of Berry Wiggins, had suggested me, which, considering our bumpy previous relationship, was a generous act. The seat was highly marginal and for decades had gone to whichever party had formed the government. I did not really want to win it. It was too far from my businesses and from Yeovil, where the children were starting school. I had not got the factories sorted out sufficiently to hand them over to my partner, Dick Rogerson, and the move would have put an intolerable strain on my marriage.

I gambled that if I could spend six months to a year and work really hard, I could get a good enough result in Gravesend to then find a safe seat in the West Country. I did not mention this plan to the selection committee! I was shooed in as the candidate. The new Labour MP was John Ovenden, who was almost as much of a nonentity as Roger White.

From April to September of 1974 I rushed around the constituency. I visited schools, mosques, the Isle of Grain power station, and all the major employers who would let me in. Some were scared of trade union reaction. The Kleenex plant managers appeared to be locked in their offices and it was the shop stewards who allowed me round while grilling me on the wickedness of Tory capitalism. Theory Y was not much in evidence. 'Us' and 'them' were institutionalised. There was a private dining room for the board of directors. There was a reserved parking space for the chairman's Bentley. I blamed the Labour Council for every pothole, and took up every local issue in the *Gravesend Reporter* and on Radio Kent. As the months went by it started to dawn on me – to my horror – that I might actually win.

The national campaign was fought around who best could unite the country after the disastrous winter. Both main parties had difficulties. How could Heath and the Conservatives hope to work together with the unions after their humiliating rejection in February? How could Harold Wilson show he was not a puppet of the all-powerful trade union barons? Inflation was running at 20 per cent, destroying people's savings, and a recession loomed. The country was disillusioned, scared and disbelieving. Both sides offered a social contract. Ted Heath wanted everyone in the tent; Harold Wilson was content with just his trade union supporters.

Jim Prior once asked Moss Evans of the Transport and General Workers' Union how differently he treated the two parties. 'Six months,' he replied. He would accept six months longer pay restraint from a Labour government before taking the lads out!

The Liberals rather strangely believed that they could be either returned in such numbers to form a government in their own right or lead a minority administration. They ended up with thirteen seats!

There was no way in the time available that I could do anything other than try to achieve a credible result by increasing my share of the vote. I had been selected in April, the election was called in September. A charming lawyer who was later to become a judge, Seddon Cripps, and his wife, Anne, offered us a bed for the duration of the campaign. I persuaded Sissy she should play a major part in our publicity. Our slogan was 'For your family's future vote Needham'. We promised to reduce the rates by removing teachers' salaries from local government and transferring their cost to the National Exchequer. We capped mortgages at 9.5 per cent for the duration of the next parliament. Neither were really affordable but housing costs were a big issue in North Kent and a judicious bribe seemed the only way to go!

My campaign did not start well. The first night involved two wine-and-cheese party fundraisers in the most prosperous area of the constituency,

Higham. Unfortunately, the first overran and I received the following note after attending the second.

Dear Richard Needham,

Please find the enclosed headline [in fact the clipping had not been enclosed] which could just as well have described the affair at our house last night. You came late, went early and said little or nothing whilst you were here. If the purpose of these whistle stop visits is to put heart into your supporters and get them out canvassing for you then last night's effort was a failure. I am not alone in thinking so. Gravesend will not be won like this.

Yours sincerely,
Ailsa Wright

In July, commuting back from the Cripps' house at the weekend before the start of the campaign in my 'new' second hand Jaguar XJ6, I was flagged down at the end of the A30 dual carriageway into Yeovil. I pulled over, got out of the car and walked back towards the police car because the driver had his window down. He immediately accused me of driving at over 120 mph. I retorted that this was nonsense – the most I had been doing was between 80 and 90. I had a problem, though. My speedometer was broken. I was driving using the rev counter, which had never exceeded the yellow warning level. I was charged on the spot with driving dangerously, driving without due care and attention, and exceeding the speed limit. Dangerous driving is a criminal offence and the last event I needed was to be faced with a court case in the middle of an election campaign. Patrick Moule, my solicitor, advised me to go for trial by jury as the justices invariably were on the side of the law.

The case was heard at Southampton Assizes and presided over by Judge McCreary, a crusty old Ulsterman, who had a reputation for supporting the police, right or wrong. The police evidence claimed that when they latched on to my tail outside Sherborne, they had been approximately three quarters of a mile behind and that they had closed up to a couple of hundred yards at the end of the dual carriageway three miles later. If I had indeed been travelling at 125 mph, they would have had to travel at 175 mph to catch me. I had my engine checked. At 125 mph the needle on the rev counter would have been through the yellow, through the red and resting at the far edge of the dial.

None of this concerned the learned judge. 'Don't bother me with statistics, Mr Moule,' he told Patrick. The fact that I was a Member of the Institute of Advanced Motorists made it possible that I would have been more prepared to take risks and be overconfident. When it was divulged that I was in politics, the judge winked knowingly at the jury and told them that they should take the word of a politician with care! In the witness box the policeman giving evidence had morphed from being the driver to the observer. Only later did we discover why they had changed places.

The judge invited the jury to find me guilty. The jury took twenty minutes to find me not guilty of dangerous driving or driving without due care and attention but guilty of exceeding the speed limit. The next day I made an official complaint against the police for knowingly 'gilding the lily' and committing perjury. The Somerset police appointed a detective inspector from Dorset to investigate. His only concern was to try and brush it all off with the minimum of fuss.

What transpired was that the officious driver – on seeing a youngish man in an expensive car – was determined to teach me a lesson. He accused me of dangerous driving as soon as I approached him. The observer knew perfectly well what speed I had been driving. When the case escalated to the Crown Court, he told his colleague that he would not perjure himself but he would agree to change places.

I received a formal apology. Throughout much of my public life I have been looked after, in Northern Ireland and in Wiltshire, by the bravest, kindest, most loyal of men and women, who have put their lives on the line for me. They became and remain my friends. But at every level in the service there remains a small number of officers, from chief constable to constable, who have a twisted and vengeful attitude towards the public in general and cause the most appalling misery and heartbreak to innocent men and women. It is the poor and the most vulnerable who have the most to fear from such people.

As a campaign team we knocked on doors from dawn to night. Sissy was on one side of the road with three or four helpers, leapfrogging each other and ensuring she did not get caught up, and I was on the other side.

Dave King, a huge local builder with a bristling beard and a high-pitched laugh, provided us with an immaculate battle bus. Unfortunately, after the election, Dave – whose bills exceeded his bank deposits – departed for Vancouver where he lost his sight. Jock Williamson was the driver and announcer. He had been in the Cavalry when his tank rolled over and squashed his face. But he had a David Niven speaking voice and imparted an appealing and repeatable message or slogan every thirty seconds. In between, we played Tamla Motown tapes. One favourite track was aimed at John Ovenden, the MP: 'Hang on in there, baby' by Johnny Bristol.

The campaign wasn't without mishaps. On one occasion, we were on the Isle of Grain looking for a mobile home site. The team were in the back of the battle bus. Jock was delighting the neighbourhood with his David Niven impersonations and there was no one in sight. We stopped by a gang of British Gas maintenance men who told us to keep straight on and we'd come to the caravan site in a mile. A mile later we were in a salt marsh with the sea about two hundred yards in front of us. No sign of a caravan. We climbed out and tried to push the bus out of the bog. The wheels spun, and mud smothered Sissy and me from head to toe. She sprained her wrist. Somehow, we got the van round and as we retreated past the gasmen, a voice shouted out, 'You Tories are so desperate, you've taken to canvassing seagulls!'

There was a number of old-fashioned, well-packed public meetings run by schools and churches. I was keen to avoid them as far as possible. John Ovenden was much better prepared and confident. Luckily, I had the Liberal candidate Lou Cartier as backup. The first meeting was in a school and the audience universally hostile. The opening question was on euthanasia. 'I'll take that,' piped up Lou, who owned an expensive, small, frozen food wholesaler in Rochester. He was a reedy man with a weedy voice. 'This is a very important subject,' he squeaked and paused. 'Yes,' shouted a voice from the back, 'because you're getting old.' That was the end of Liberal Lou, who we nicknamed 'Champion of the Few – keeps his prices hidden down amongst his ices.'

It was my turn next. A dreaded question on education. I was first on and I began by stating that we would do nothing without consulting the teachers. Fatally I paused after 'nothing'. 'Like you always do' came ringing down from the back of the hall. I survived, but it was my first really terrifying test in the cockpit of politics.

For Sissy, the snake pit was more a never-ending battle of juggling the children, who were going to a day school in Yeovil, with travelling to Gravesend at weekends where she canvassed all day, and was abused on the doorstep and saw me abused. She had to remember helpers' names and she was required to say 'a few words' when necessary. On one occasion she had to stand in for me. She learned her lines by heart and delivered them faultlessly, but she was terrified and I promised she would never have to do it again (inevitably another politician's broken promise!). To the faithful in marginal seats the candidate and his wife are their champions; their minor, minor royals, to be cosseted and shown off to their friends.

Sissy has spent a lifetime explaining to disgruntled supporters that I really did not mean what I had just told them. I did. Most Labour wives never went near their husbands' constituencies. For most Tory wives, absence was not an option. In my case, Sissy really was the other half.

There was the odd alarming moment. The boys from the factory narrowly avoided punch-ups with Labour-supporting dockers who were trying to rip down our posters as we did the same to theirs. One night my elderly mother, who had come over from Italy to help and was nothing if not brave, disappeared into a huge council estate in Northfleet nickname Colditz. She was eventually found by Debbie Idiens in front of a fish and chip van, asking the driver if he could help her identify the streets on the canvas cards she been handed. Behind her stood a line of increasingly irritated housewives in curlers and slippers waiting for their 'tea'.

We press-ganged the sixth-form girls from Cobham, a smart, private girls' school, to hand out 'bribery' housing leaflets on the local high streets and at the railway stations wearing T-shirts emblazoned with the slogan 'We Need Him in Gravesend'.

Our plan was to cover the constituency with window posters and car stickers. We aimed to build a momentum that would convince the voters that Needham was the winner. Wherever we found a Conservative, we put up a poster with double sided tape in their porch. We were extremely successful among the postmen, who were convinced that on stickers alone we were well ahead.

Unlike in Pontefract, shadow ministers were constant visitors and they were very often more of a nuisance than a help. They needed picking up, watering and delivering to a venue where the audience consisted entirely of party workers who would have been better employed elsewhere. A final rally on the day before polling brought Ted Heath to town. With him were Sara Morrison (who I would encounter again years later at GEC) and

William Waldegrave. William was already a golden boy. At twenty-seven he was five years younger than me and already destined for the top. He came from a very grand aristocratic background. He had won the Newcastle scholarship at Eton. He had been president of the Oxford Union, and then gone to Harvard University on a Kennedy scholarship. He had been elected as a prize fellow of All Souls College. In 1971, he joined the Conservative Research Department before Lord Rothschild took him off to the Think Tank, and now he was the leader of the opposition's personal assistant. What possible chance would I have against such a genius when I arrived at Westminster?

I told Ted Heath I thought we could scrape home in Gravesend while praying that we wouldn't. The results were John Ovenden 29,569. Richard Needham 27,264. Lou Cartier 10,244. Nationally Labour gained twenty-one seats. The Conservatives had lost twenty and the Liberals two. Harold Wilson had failed to enthuse the country as he had done in 1966. Labour was a weak government tied to the bootlaces of the union barons.

I had done creditably. Ovenden's majority had increased by eight hundred votes, but my share of the vote had also increased and I had been noticed in Central Office. Now I had to find a way to the centre of power, attach myself to a patron and get on the heels of William Waldegrave!

CHAPTER 13

In the Corridors of Power

I N FEBRUARY 1975, as soon as Margaret Thatcher became leader and Jim Prior had been appointed shadow employment secretary, I wrote to Prior, asking him if I could help. I sent him my CV, which had failed to interest any safe constituency, and the synopsis of my Theory Y analysis, which I had sent to James Douglas at the Research Department. I was phoned by his secretary. Would I go and see him in his Shadow Cabinet office in the House of Commons the following day?

The shadow cabinet corridor was a line of rabbit hutches on either side of a narrow corridor. Losing power is a humiliating experience. Gone are the private secretaries, the ministerial cars and drivers, and the spacious offices in the department and behind the Speaker's chair. Jim's office was the last one on the right – he was opposite Airey Neave, the shadow Northern Ireland spokesman. Jim sat behind a small desk in a small chair with room for two other small chairs. Opposite the desk was a window facing a blank wall. He was like a whale in a goldfish bowl. He looked miserable. 'I am a farmer,' he started off. 'I know nothing about industrial relations. She's put me here to fall flat on my face. I read your paper and I agree with every word of it. But whether Margaret and the right wing of the Tory party are into Theory Y I very much doubt. Most of them are after revenge.'

Sitting with him was Robbie Gilbert, his assistant from the research department, who is a canny, prickly Scot with acute political sensitivity. Jim asked me what time I had available and what I could do to assist in writing speeches, organising meetings and answering correspondence. It was the opportunity I had craved. Jim was clearly my sort of Tory. He was a 'big beast' even if he was on the wrong side of the party because of his closeness to Ted. I needed a mentor, and reform of industrial relations was what most excited me. The downside was that there was no money and I had to fund myself as his assistant.

In early 1975, the country was at its lowest point for a century. In late 1974, the Hudson Institute published a report entitled 'The United Kingdom in the 1980s' by James Bellini. It was a dreadful prognosis.

> That the outlook for Britain is sombre few will now deny ... a virtually unanimous agreement exists that the country is in its worst economic situation since the War and perhaps the Great Depression. A universal sense that the economic crisis is linked to a severe deterioration in the country's social and political health. Popular confidence in the competence of the government is very low.

Peter Jenkins of the *Guardian* wrote, 'We face an internal crisis with the lack of trust born of long and persistent national failure.'

Britain's per capita GDP in 1972 was already behind all its major European neighbours except Italy, and even she was approaching *Il sorpasso*. Our economy was still dominated by the manufacturing sector, with 44 per cent of the total. But our productivity growth was abysmal, our investment ratios inadequate. We were wrecked by industrial action. In 1972, one hundred million days were lost through strikes compared to 200,000 in Germany. In 1975, British Leyland lost the contract to supply Hong Kong with taxis to Toyota.

If the Labour Party was seen to be in thrall to the unions, the Tories were seen to be too antagonistic. The country had already given its verdict – that it preferred appeasement – in the first election of 1974. The Labour and trade union leaders' constant refrain was that another Tory government would lead to another three-day week. Only Labour could be trusted to work together with the unions to keep the lights on and the trains running.

The Conservative party and the shadow cabinet were divided into doves and hawks, although the nomenclature changed when Margaret accused Jim Prior and Ian Gilmour of being wet. The 'wets' were mainly older members of Heath's former cabinet. They included William Whitelaw, John Peyton, Peter Carrington, Christopher Soames and Francis Pym. Most of them – some with extreme distinction – had fought in the war.

They had seen and witnessed the privations and sufferings that ordinary people had had to contend with. They had an instinctive bond with working people and understood their loyalties to their class and their trade union. They wanted the party's industrial relations policy to avoid giving the impression of taking the unions head on, as had happened in the early 70s and which had offered an easy target for Labour to frighten the voters. A step-by-step approach allowed them to propose reforms to limit actions that the union members themselves found egregious, such as wildcat strikes, bullying pickets, dictatorial closed-shop agreements and inter-union disputes. The public wanted these outrages addressed but they didn't want a full-scale attack on trade union rights.

The more gung-ho approach of Geoffrey Howe, Keith Joseph, John Biffen and John Nott might have had greater intellectual cohesion but it would have given Labour a much easier target. Margaret Thatcher tended to take the side of the 'drys' but, as was often the case, her pragmatism and caution held her back. She was a wonderful combination of Theory X and Theory Y.

In 1977, John Peyton had organised a meeting with most of the shadow cabinet and the TUC under Len Murray. They had agreed to a pre-meeting at Margaret's house. Keith Joseph arrived late in a state of high excitement. What was the point of such a discussion? It would achieve nothing and the TUC would leak the meeting, making the opposition appear scared and weak. Margaret Thatcher put her hand on his arm. 'Keith, have you had anything to eat? You need something to eat to allow you to calm down. I'll get you something.' She beetled off, coming back five minutes later with a plate of sandwiches and a cup of coffee. 'There you are, Keith. Get that down you and you'll feel much better.' It is difficult to argue with your boss through a mouthful of sliced Hovis brown.

Between 1975 and 1979, a shadow cabinet committee under Geoffrey Howe produced a number of papers that aimed to circumvent the unions' ability to destroy another Tory government. Pragmatism, at least to start with, led the way. It was decided to avoid at all costs any direct imposition of a statutory wages and incomes policy, which would inevitably lead to a direct confrontation between the two sides. The tool to control inflationary wage increases was to be monetary policy. It worked. But when coupled with an oil-backed currency, its costs on manufacturing were disastrous for many sectors. Geoffrey Howe and his colleagues were highly intelligent, well educated men but they had very little experience or knowledge of industry and business.

One of the most worrying and remarkable aspects of British democracy – and still the case to a great extent today – is the level of resources available to an opposition to research, test out and check out the practicalities, the problems and the effectiveness of their proposals. David Howell, who helped to write the 1970 manifesto, recalls going in to see the cabinet secretary with his shiny programme filled with scintillating new ideas and staggering out two hours later realising that not one of them was without a fatal flaw.

The job I was given by Jim Prior was to infiltrate the unions. I managed to get myself on to a trade union recognition course run by an engaging Welshman called Ron Edwards at Henley Staff College. The great union leaders addressed us on how crucial they were to maintaining the rights of the working class against the hard-faced capitalist masters, who would otherwise screw their members for every penny.

The reality, however, was that the trade unions were out of control. Many of the leaders were former communists who believed in workers' control and wholesale nationalisation. Confrontation with the bosses was what they were there for. The shop stewards were the storm troopers to take on the foremen. The old ditty 'The working class can kiss my arse, they've made me foreman at long last' had been turned on its head as power had passed to the militants.

Demarcation disputes were rife and almost as widespread between the craft unions and the manual unions as between employers and workers. The railway unions had splendid head offices built to match those of the railway companies. Sidney Weighell, the general secretary of the NUR, showed Jim Prior and me round his boardroom, which had been built in the eighteen eighties to rival the GWR offices in Euston Road opposite. He sat at the end of the board table on a raised chair which resembled a throne. The offices were in the incongruously named Unity House. Sidney spent most of his life fighting it out with Ray Buckton, general secretary of ASLEF (the rail drivers' union), who was an alleged Special Branch informer. He had started life as a groundsman on a large country estate. Buckton was determined to maintain the differentials between the drivers and the railwaymen. 'The guard is the man who sits in the van, the van at the back of the train. The driver up front thinks the guard is a c**t, and the guard thinks the driver the same.'

Buckton lived in a nice house in Edgware, North London, owned by the union. His wife worked for the ASTMS (Association of Scientific, Technical and Managerial Staffs) union that was run by Clive Jenkins. Jenkins had built the largest white-collar union in the country. Under his leadership it had grown from 65,000 to half a million members in fifteen years. He was the only self-proclaimed millionaire on the TUC. He amassed a fortune from buying property, collecting antiques, writing books and making after-dinner speeches. But the rules governing trade union finances were opaque and open to abuse. Jenkins was the nearest the TUC had to a Mafia boss. Some thought him agreeable; others found him a ruthless, unprincipled, devious and a self-serving bully. He was a friend of Robert Maxwell's.

He was a member of the National Heritage Memorial fund and came over to Northern Ireland under its chairman, Lord Charteris, in 1986 to look at potential investments. I gave them a slap-up dinner at Stormont house and Jenkins spent the evening telling us Labour would win the 1987 election. I bet him a case of claret they would not. Soon afterwards for unexplained reason he disappeared to Tasmania and I never received the claret! There are those who thought he was lucky to avoid having his collar felt by the constabulary. If he had known about Theory X he would have welcomed it.

My frequent visits to Henley Staff College brought me a wide range of union acquaintances. Mark Young, general secretary of BALPA (the British Airline Pilots Association), asked me to give the after-dinner address at his conference, hardly a hotbed of Marxism. Later I became their parliamentary representative, taking over from Norman Tebbit. Tim Rice, who came from Kilkeel, my hometown in Northern Ireland, and was general secretary of EESA (the Electrical Engineering Staff Association), invited me to his country mansion to tell his members what a Tory government would do for them.

Many of the unions had bought large manor houses that offered spacious and relaxed accommodation for the brothers and occasionally sisters to undergo training courses in collective-bargaining, picketing, secondary action and other helpful methods of disrupting production.

There was one often-repeated anecdote much beloved by trade union negotiators. There had been a lengthy strike at Ford's Halewood plant in the early 70s, when the unions were trying to break the Heath government's pay cap. There were twelve union representatives and six from the employers' side round the table. They had explored every possible avenue to break the pay freeze. Halfway through another deadlocked session a young man in a pinstripe suit arrived and opened his briefcase. 'I know you think us chaps in head office in London have been ignoring you, but we have been sweating blood to find a way round the impasse. We think we have found a solution. The hourly paid workers receive no additional benefits (Theory X!) and unfortunately, about a hundred die every year. So we propose offering all the living free life insurance. For them it would be equivalent to another 3 per cent on the basic pay when their time comes. All in all, the package would rise to 7.5 per cent, which is well above the government's guidelines and is consistent with your demands.' This offer was greeted with silence. After a time, a loud banging was heard from under the table. 'Hang on, Chairman,' said Bob Wright the union convenor to Tony Piers, personnel director on the other side. 'I hear someone knocking.' He leant over. 'What do you want?' he said, pressing his ear to the table. He looked up at Tony and said, 'He wants to know if you can make it retrospective.' The strike continued.

In 1978 I went to Barnsley to meet Arthur Scargill. He sat behind a huge mahogany desk in a huge office. A bay window behind him had lowered blinds. All you could see of him was a silhouette. On his desk was a model of a sputnik. His outer office was manned by a smart, good-looking personal assistant. The walls were covered in hanging files that contained the case notes of all his members, past and present, who were in receipt of injury and other benefits. There were thousands of them.

He told me he didn't fear a Tory government because he knew his goal. His job was to represent the miners. To gain on their behalf every benefit, every perk, every penny he could screw out of the owners – the government, in this case. He was not interested in market conditions, profitability, productivity or the price charged to the customer. If the price was too high then it was up to the government to subsidise the difference. There was in his mind a clear demarcation. He was responsible for the terms and conditions, the pensions, and any compensation for injury or illness; the Coal Board was responsible for everything else. In his view, the miners' loyalty was to each other and to their pits, and what they cared about was being properly paid for their efforts. The Coal Board bought their time and their labour. It was 'us and them', dialectical materialism in action, and a constant battle for advantage between the two sides. It was irrelevant that the pits belonged to the government and therefore the nation. The relationship was based on conflict not common purpose. It was Theory X at its most brutal. Any improvement in productivity or any benefits arising from new technology or investment had to be recognised in the miners' pay packets, which were what they cared about. He distrusted worker-directors in any form as the wily owners would compromise worker-representatives in order to increase profits.

It did not matter that wage inflation was impoverishing the poor and the needy. What mattered was maintaining the power and authority of the National Union of Mineworkers. His members, particularly in Yorkshire, adored him. This attitude ran throughout the trade union movement. Dog eat dog. The craft unions must preserve their differentials. If a light bulb needed changing a member of the EEPTU must be summoned. The hierarchy and pecking order must be preserved. No wonder the Americans, the Japanese, the Germans and the French were rushing past us.

Meanwhile we continued in our efforts to infiltrate the unions. We had a quarterly breakfast meeting with some of the most senior industrial relations directors in the country to gauge what they believed was happening amongst the workforce and how we should be presenting our policies to their staff.

We had lunch parties for the industrial correspondents in Jim Prior's flat with the cooking done by his wife, Jane. Barney Heyhoe, his deputy, provided the wine and I did the 'pouring' and 'waiting'. Almost without exception, the correspondents were on the side of the unions, whichever paper they worked for. By the pudding they were invariably well away. One of their number was Mick Costello, who wrote for the *Morning Star*, which had a readership of around fifty thousand. Within one hour of the lunches ending, a report of what was discussed must have been on the relevant desk in the Kremlin. I still don't know why we invited him. They all stuck together like peas in a pod and covered for each other by sharing any titbits if any one of them could not attend.

We set up a Conservative trade union group in Central Office where some members of the staff had already joined a branch of ASTMS. It was run by Andrew Rowe (later MP for Mid-Kent and my parliamentary private secretary) together with John Bowis, who also went on to become a distinguished MP and MEP. They made constant trouble, questioning the rulebook, challenging the accounts and running candidates for union elections in the local branches.

But we needed funds to broaden our membership. I was deputed, along with Richard Ryder, Margaret Thatcher's private secretary, to go to see Alistair McAlpine, the party treasurer. We were summoned to breakfast at 7.30 one winter morning in Alistair's suite in the Dorchester, which his family owned. Richard is incredibly discreet, incredibly polite, incredibly hard-working and, at that time, was rather short of money. He had been suggested to Margaret Thatcher by Bill Deedes of the *Daily Telegraph* as one of their up-and-coming young journalists. He had rearranged her private office and employed Matthew Parris as her correspondence secretary. He came to the breakfast wearing his father's threadbare overcoat, which hung on him like a sack. Food and pay were not part of his agenda. He was a skeletal tribute to the Theory Y principle of money not being a motivator!

We were invited into the palatial McAlpine sitting room and sat down while white-uniformed waiters covered in gold buttons served us tea, coffee and biscuits, which we took to be the breakfast. A few moments later Alistair appeared from his boudoir, encased in a magnificent kimono-style dressing gown, looking every inch an emperor. At the same time, at the other end of the room, the door opened and two huge trolleys appeared, covered with massive silver salvers. Richard looked as if he might be sick.

The salvers were lifted and we were invited to choose between the Full English, kedgeree, kippers or kidneys, or all four if we wished. Richard turned green. Alistair's salver concealed twenty rashers of bacon and half a loaf of fried sliced brown bread, which he devoured. Richard fiddled with a biscuit.

We were invited to state our case. It was soon clear that Alistair had little or no interest in the Conservative trade unionists. What he wanted to talk about was Margaret Thatcher's absence at the opera. Alistair was a great patron of the arts and he was worried that she should be seen as a supporter and avid frequenter of the theatre. Richard was tasked with finding spaces in her diary. We left with the promise that he would find funds for our trade union campaign in return for Margaret becoming a habitué of the Royal Opera House.

We returned to Westminster to report the outcome. Richard showed me into the Leader's office. It was the first time I had met her. He introduced me as the recently adopted candidate for Chippenham. 'You look ghastly,' she said. 'I have just returned from a family holiday to Indonesia and contracted a virus infection in my liver, which has turned me pale yellow,' I told her. 'What on earth persuaded you to go there?' she demanded. I explained that my wife had been brought up in Java and my parents-in-law had asked us all to stay with them. 'If I'd been the chairman of your association, I should have forbidden your going,' she glowered. Not much evidence of Theory Y in our opening encounter!

I believe that the measured approach pursued by Jim Prior and his colleagues between 1974 and 1979 went a considerable way towards calming the understandable concerns about how the unions would react to a new Tory government. By concentrating on the most shocking use of trade union militancy, the abuse of the 'closed shop' by unions such as Slade (a print Union), the internecine fight over membership, the flying pickets and the threats of unnecessary industrial action, the Tories were able to mine a rich seam of public outrage.

By the use of measured language laying out a moderate step-by-step approach to trade union reform, the Tories were able to draw the sting out of the Labour government's claim that the return of the Conservatives would lead to chaos. Too often we experienced chaos under Jim Callaghan.

By getting to know the union leaders and understanding their different agendas we could exacerbate the differences between the Labour government and their union paymasters. There was a degree of arrogance that led some of the big union leaders to believe that they had enough power to dictate terms to any government, who sooner or later would roll over to their demands. They were soon to discover that this was no longer the case.

CHAPTER 14

Across the Starting Line

I HAD RASHLY believed that working as Jim Prior's personal assistant would count on my CV when safe seats came up. I was wrong – I was still failing to make the shortlist. I went into Central Office to see Doreen Hudson, who was still in charge of administering candidate selection. She showed me the filing cabinet in which the CVs of prospective candidates were stored. They were all produced to a similar format on photocopied A4 white paper. They were all incredibly boring. I asked if I could produce my own CV – she had no objections.

I designed and printed an immaculate résumé on blue paper that included a fulsome explanation of my talents and experiences, and a fetching picture of the family in the right-hand top corner. When the selection committee was confronted with a pile of 'possibles', mine was the only one printed on blue paper with a photograph. My problems were over. I was spoilt for choice.

First Ludlow contacted me but Sissy and I decided it was a bit too far from London. Then the Wirral, where Selwyn Lloyd had stood down and brought about a by-election. I was down to the last three but in the end I pulled out as it was also too far away. I was then interviewed for Carshalton in South London but they didn't want what they supposed was a former 'toff'. Bristol West was a seat I thought I could win, with my West Country background, but I was pipped to the post by the William Waldegrave, who had even closer connections.

Each time I was invited for interview, I spent a day or two in the constituency. I would visit the editor of the local newspaper and get as much background as I could on the competing local candidates. There were invariably two or three who fancied their chances; equally invariably, they would at one time or another have upset one or another member of the selection committee. I would find out the local issues and research the accomplishments of the selectors so I could flatter them during the interview. I would try and find some family connection, however distant, that I could bring up.

After several months I ended up in the last three both at Sevenoaks in Kent and Chippenham in Wiltshire. The final interviews, in front of the whole of the two associations, were a week apart, with Chippenham first. Chippenham was a Liberal marginal with a majority of under two thousand. Sevenoaks was rock solid. But Chippenham was in the West Country, much nearer home, although I would still have had to move if I won the nomination. I knew I was in with a good chance because I had already knocked out Chris Patten and Peter Brooke. My two opponents were the Conservative leader of Bristol City Council – a decent, uncharismatic, urban Tory – and John Browne – a smarmy, smooth, superficially charming former Grenadier, who went on to become MP for Winchester, disappeared to Florida and was fortunate to avoid further investigation before standing for UKIP in Cornwall and subsequently North Devon.

I gave the two hundred or so members my version of a Theory Y, Tory-led industrial revolution. Chippenham, despite its rural image, had some big industrial plants, such as Harris's in Calne, Westinghouse in Chippenham and Linolite in Malmesbury, all now long-since vanished. My speech went over their heads. Then I talked about what I wanted to do locally and how I had already grasped the difficulties that people living in rural areas faced. Finally, I proclaimed that I would defeat the Liberals with Sissy's help. Most of the men had their eyes glued on her.

After an agonising wait – with all six of us, candidates and their wives, sitting icily in a draughty anteroom in the town hall – I was elected on the first ballot. The following day Colonel Hugh Brassey, the president of the association and a distinguished former soldier who wrote delightful sonnets, took us for lunch at The Old Bell in Sutton Benger. We had lobster, which had not travelled the hundred or so miles from the nearest port fast enough, and we spent the rest of the week in bed with food poisoning.

The sitting MP Daniel Awdry, an upright and pleasant local solicitor who was even to the 'left' of me, had decided to stand down out of the frustration of being in opposition. But once I arrived, he regretted it, and worked harder in the last two-and-a-half years of his tenure than he had in the previous twelve. This made it difficult for me to gain a foothold or build up any personal support as all the publicity and attention still focused on him. It was frustrating and worrying.

The Liberal candidate Ronnie Banks, who had fought the previous two elections in Chippenham, had become an established local politician, whose views were very much on the right of his party and included being anti-EU. He had also fought three other elections in Croydon. He was personable, clubbable and an effective campaigner. He promoted himself as Dan's natural local successor in a seat that had always had a strong Liberal vote.

In 1977, once I had won the nomination, we had taken a huge gamble and moved to the northern boundary of the constituency. My parents-in-law had helped with the financing. At one stage in the campaign, with Ronnie Banks and his posters rampant, it felt as if we had taken a risk too far.

As happens in most elections, the national campaign comes down to a slanging match between the two main parties. The 1979 election was no different. This offends a large number of voters who cry 'a plague on both your houses'. The Liberals do all they can to capitalise on this discomfort by promoting different policies in different parts of the country depending on local grievances. In Chippenham, where my majority was only 1,750, they determined to squeeze the Labour vote as a 'wasted' vote – which it was. They didn't have to squeeze very hard to win.

The Jeremy Thorpe affair, which had done them such damage in the middle 70s, quietly faded in the public's mind as the campaign progressed. I found it hard to project my image as even though I had been candidate for nearly three years, I had been marginalised by the sitting member hogging the limelight. The difficulty of projecting a strong image was made harder during the election campaign by the media having to give all candidates equal airtime.

As we moved nearer to polling day, the constituency became a sea of Liberal orange. The local Conservative organisation had creaked from the start, but it was now on the verge of collapse and rebellion. The agent Jim Forsyth – a good, brave man, who was missing a leg due to the impact of a German torpedo in 1940 – repaired to the Constitutional Club for most of the day, leaving all admin tasks to his admirable secretary, Mary

Pullen. She became completely submerged by elderly supporters who rather than doing anything useful, spent their days making tea, collecting canvas returns which no one knew what to do with and bemoaning the inadequacies of the campaign.

The chairman John McNair, who had political ambitions of his own and was a senior executive at Rolls-Royce, disappeared for most of the four weeks on an 'urgent' business trip. The formidable Marjorie Hall, a farmer's wife, came to the rescue. Due to the enormous efforts of her and her team, all our election addresses were stuffed and delivered, although how many got read and what effect they had on those reading them, I have little idea.

I decided to run my own separate campaign. I brought together all those who had been with me in Gravesend and Pontefract, and produced really good local leaflets that ignored Central Office's output – which overwhelmingly dealt with countering the Labour Party and was useless for fighting Liberals. We knocked on doors from 9.30 to 12.30, from 2 until 5, and from 6 to 9. We visited factories and offices, walking in unannounced and uninvited. We stood outside schools, kissing mums and hugging babies.

Billy Harding came up from Yeovil with some of his mates from a scrap metal background and brought the stakes and the flag boards. Billy was an acolyte of mine from my time as a county councillor in Yeovil. He could best be described as a market trader, and he was always in some sort of trouble – whether financial, medical or mental. He somehow managed to remain just on the right side of the law. Billy and his mates plastered every road with Needham posters, every street corner with Needham banners – and took an active dislike to those of the opposition.

It was enough. The majority went from 1,749 to 4,697 in Chippenham – and the Labour government was out. Chippenham was still a Liberal marginal but by the time of the next election, I would be the sitting member, and I would have four years to organise the seat as I wanted. However, any ideas for gaining promotion or making a big splash in Westminster would have to be delayed as I would need to concentrate on securing my base.

I had made it! What happened then? Nothing. Silence. I rang up my friends: they were as unsure as I. I tried to reach any number of MP colleagues I might know. (Colleague is a euphemism that covers those you love and those you hate.) They were on holiday. Finally, at the end of the first week, an envelope arrived by special delivery stamped 'Secret'. It was the 'Whip', an A4 sheet that would dominate our lives for the next four years and that ordered me when to vote. The first Whip was a request, twice underlined, to attend the election of the Speaker the following Wednesday. Members would then be sworn in over the following two days.

At last I found a local MP colleague to take me round the House of Commons. The first port of call was the Post Office. I was presented with two huge sacks of mail, but had nowhere to put them and nowhere to work from. Even four hundred years after the overthrow of the monarchy, the British people still have pitifully little idea of how parliament works. Although most of them despise politicians, they still believe that their local MP can solve almost any problem.

At first, like most new members, I was lost and bewildered. We had decided that Sissy would be my full-time secretary, but she was as lost as me. She spent two days a week in London in a shared office and our Indonesian au pair looked after the children. It was a stressful, difficult time, particularly for our youngest, Christina, who was only two at the time. Robert and Andrew, who were thirteen and ten, also missed out because neither of us could make sufficient time for them.

Sissy's office was a fifteen-minute walk from mine and she had to carry numerous files, often in the pouring rain, on a journey that took in an underground tunnel and several security checks. She shared it with six others. The noise of clattering typewriters, ringing phones, MPs giving dictation and a lack of air conditioning made working conditions more than taxing. The only advantage of the set-up for a newcomer like Sissy was that there were other more experienced secretaries to ask for advice.

Perhaps, if we had known, Sissy might have stayed out of it, but on balance we felt that being together and being able to share the constituency workload was more important to our marriage than being separated. We had read too many stories of marriage breakdowns because of the impositions of parliamentary life. Now it is impossible for wives to work for their husbands – a Theory X imposition that can only lead to more strain on many MPs relationships.

My sponsor Jim Prior had disappeared in a ministerial limo and, although I had a few acquaintances, I had not any real soulmates. I was allocated a pigeonhole office in the upper ministerial corridor above the House of Lords to share with Michael Colvin. Michael had married well to a beautiful daughter of Lord Cayzer of the British and Commonwealth shipping line. He came from a throwback Tory past. Eton and the Grenadier Guards. He was privileged, rich, good-looking – everything that on paper ought to assist you to the top in the Tory party. But he spoke through his nose, which made him sound like a super toff, and he was. He was right-wing: more Theory X than Theory Y, in an old-fashioned way, and he was not a performer of any stature in the House. He was very nice and very genuine, but he was not going to help me up the ladder. (In an appalling tragedy, Michael and his wife were burnt to death during a terrible storm in 2000 that raged through their beautiful house in Tangley near Andover.)

I needed mates on to whose coat-tails I could cling and I found four, who all shared an office: Chris Patten, William Waldegrave, Tristan Garel-Jones and John Patten. They had all had apparatchik careers before being elected in 1979. Chris had been director of the Conservative Research Department, William had worked at Number 10 for Ted Heath, Tristan had been personal assistant to Peter Thorneycroft when he was chairman of the party and John Patten, a don at Hertford College, had been organising other Conservative dons in Oxford. They were considered the cream of the 1979 Tory intake and one of them – probably Chris Patten – was tipped to be prime minister. There had been a fifth member but he had problems with his armpits and was moved out. They were looking for a replacement, and after much discussion chose me.

As soon as Chris, William, Tristan and John had been elected, they had established an influential dining group of twelve like-thinking new MPs called the Blue Chips. Blue signifying the colour of their blood rather than their party. This was pretentious, particularly as most of the members were – at best – middle-middle class. We were all around the same age, early to mid-thirties. We were all 'wets' – at least until we were offered promotion – and we all had becoming a member of the Cabinet as the least of our ambitions. The five of us became known as the politburo of the Blue Chips. I was the last one in, the last to become a parliamentary private secretary, the last to become a parliamentary undersecretary, the last to become a minister of state, the last to become a privy counsellor, and the only one not to be ennobled (I had to be content with a knighthood) and not to make it into the Cabinet.

Soon the office started to suffer depletions. John Patten was the first to go – he became a minister in the Northern Ireland Office under Jim Prior. He was quickly followed by William Waldegrave, who went to the Department of Education on Mrs Thatcher's instructions, to 'keep an eye' on Keith Joseph. Tristan joined the whips' office in 1982 and, when Chris went to Northern Ireland in 1983, I was alone, left behind in the office.

The 1979 election had been a triumph for the 'dries', who on the whole were Theory X monetarists. Although the manifesto had been bland and cautious, Margaret Thatcher was determined to bring down inflation by cutting the money supply, decreasing public expenditure, lowering taxes – particularly for the better off – and reducing the power of the unions. By 1981 the economy was hurting. The big increases in oil prices at the end of 1979 had sent the world into recession. The British economy faced a further double whammy. The arrival of North Sea oil had led to the value of the pound soaring, putting huge pressures on 44 per cent of the economy still based on manufacturing. The government's action – increasing VAT to 15 per cent while reducing higher tax rates – had also increased inflation and reduced consumption. Unemployment was up to 3 million and the deficit was ballooning.

Although many of the senior civil servants in the Treasury were from the north of England and came from relatively humble backgrounds, such as Sir Terry Burns, they were all monetarists. The Treasury ministerial team was made up of barristers and a journalist (Nigel Lawson). They were ill informed about or uninterested in manufacturing. They were free traders to a man. Their successors are now the Brexiteers. They believed in free markets and untrammelled competition, even if our main mercantilist competitors did everything in their power to protect their own industries and markets. Privately Jim Prior pointed out that they would have found managing a whelk store challenging.

The 1981 budget cried out for a financial Keynesian stimulus in the face of an economic blizzard. Geoffrey Howe did the opposite. All of us in the Blue Chips did what we could to support the minority of 'wets' in the cabinet to reduce the consequences of this destructive monetarist policy. We wrote a pamphlet called 'Changing Gear', which was a heavily disguised criticism of the effects of government cuts on the poor and on British industry. I helped draft the CBI's budget submission, sitting in the back of the millionaire industrialist Sir Emmanuel Kaye's Rolls Royce with a blanket over my knees. It didn't help. Lansing Bagnall, his company that built forklift trucks, was sold to the Germans. CBI chairman, Sir Terry Beckett, claimed he would start a bare-knuckle fight with the prime minister and the chancellor but he failed to land a punch.

The service side of the economy started to pick up sooner than people expected. The stock market boomed and the City was delighted. The fat cats in the square mile, sitting at their lunch tables puffing on their cigars, claimed a good shock was what industry needed. In Keith Joseph's phrase, 'we were separating the lean meat from the fat'. In one sense he was right – only the fittest survive – but the shock killed whole swathes of British manufacturing, such as machine tools, shipbuilding, chemicals, power generation, the automotive industry, much of steel and a host of component manufacturers. It was a disaster that has left Britain with the smallest percentage in manufacturing of all the G7 countries with the exception of the US. Forty years later, when 70 per cent of our remaining manufacturing industry is foreign owned and admittedly a much smaller part of our economy, the Tory 'dries' seem destined to repeat the 'experiment' through a nonsensical Brexit which will drive many inward investors out.

I had not gone into politics to take money from the poor to benefit the rich. But this was precisely what the government was proposing in the budget of 1981. It was culling benefits on the spurious assumption that people would be forced back into work. But there wasn't any work. Unemployment was three million and rising.

There were two particular proposals that I found obnoxious. One was to stop the supplementary benefit for men on strike once their unemployment allowance had run out. The argument was that while the state should provide for the family it had no obligation to a striker who has voluntarily withdrawn his labour. The reality was that the members of the striker's family would share whatever little was available.

Since Elizabethan times there had been a principle enshrined in welfare support that said, 'Take not out on the women and the children the faults of the father.' Any cut in the man's benefit would lead to serious distress, bitter opposition and an even greater determination by the families to support their menfolk.

The second proposal was to reduce unemployment benefit by 5 per cent. Unemployment benefit was part of the National Insurance scheme, and most people believed that it was an insurance policy into which they had paid in the form of contributions from their weekly or monthly pay packet to assist them in times of difficulty. 'Oh no,' said the Treasury. 'It is a pay-as-you-go scheme. There is no pot of money to back up the unemployment contributions. National Insurance is no different from income tax and we need to cut the outgoings.'

The savings from the cut would amount to £60 million. But at the same time the Treasury had introduced the taxation of benefits which would save £650 million a year. It was too much for me and several other sensible Tory 'wets'. We put down an amendment to oppose the government. We lost by 283 votes to 291. My cards were well and truly marked.

Tristan Garel-Jones wrote me a nice letter from the whips' office. 'That was the best speech you've ever made. I'm not happy to have been working against you. Perhaps we can talk it over when it's all over [sic]. You're a good man, T.' Chris Patten wrote in a similar vein that I was 'a brave bugger'. He could have added 'daft' but didn't.

Looking back, I do not regret that I behaved as I did. What the right-wing, doctrinaire, Theory X monetarists were doing was downright wrong.

I felt that my immediate promotion hopes had been dashed and, worse still, this feeling was confirmed, in a backhanded sort of way, at a reception in Downing Street. Sissy and I somehow became separated. I was chatting to some mates when suddenly I felt a hard tug on my sleeve. I turned to face the prime minister dragging Sissy close behind. She had found Sissy on her own and exclaimed, 'Where is that terrible husband of yours? Let's find him.' Having reunited Sissy with me, she glared and said, 'Don't you dare leave your wife by herself, and by the way, are you voting with the government for a change tonight?'

Nick Budgen was a right-wing, waspish, amusing, clever lawyer who had been persuaded to become a whip in between insurrections against government policy. He told me that I needed a serious role and suggested me for the Public Accounts Committee (PAC), the blue riband of select committees. It is Parliament's oldest and its function is to oversee the effectiveness and value for money of all government expenditure. Its members are supposed to be astute forensic investigators with a business background – something that most of them do not have. The chairman was Joel Barnett, a formidable former chief secretary to the treasury, best known for the Barnett formula for distributing government funding across the countries of the UK. The PAC's reports were presented by the comptroller and auditor general, Sir Gordon Downey. His reputation for discovering waste and incompetence was legendary. As the PAC was the only committee that took evidence from civil servants rather than ministers, it was looked upon with fear by the senior mandarins. Civil servants hated being called in front of it, not least because many of its inquiries dealt with events that had taken place years earlier. It is always easy to be wise afterwards and retired civil servants' reputations could be trashed by their successors.

There were several occasions when I was told 'Minister, we cannot authorise this public expenditure as it would lead to a PAC investigation and you would be excluded from giving evidence.' The PAC staff are responsible to Parliament and they are excellent but they are few in number and therefore can only scratch the surface of total government expenditure. This scrutiny has become even less effective as more and more services are contracted out.

I huddled up to Joel Barnett who used to feed me lines of questioning that he wanted explored. It required several hours of background reading each week. The Ministry of Defence was the most often in the dock. The price of missile systems always seemed out of control. The legendary Sir Frank Cooper was the ministry's defender. Every time when I thought I had an unanswerable argument of time wasting and delay, he would wriggle out, in desperation falling back on reasons of national security for not replying.

Sitting next to me was Robert Maclennan MP, who was known as Bob and who represented the Caithness constituency. Perhaps because he lived so far away, he was often late, never appeared to have much time to read his papers and most of the questions he asked were mainly irrelevant or ill informed. He stayed on the committee for twenty years. He was a junior Labour minister for four years before deserting to the SDP and then to the Liberals. He ended up a life peer and a privy counsellor.

There were too many on the Public Accounts Committee like him, although they were counterbalanced by men such as Sir Peter Hordern, who once on to the scent of waste was impossible to budge. Too many of the chairmen have used the PAC as a tool to boost their own ego and importance. The result is that many imaginative and innovative schemes never see the light of day because of civil servants' fear of being dragged in front of the committee.

Parliament should consider expanding the PAC's remit in three ways. It should call before it former ministers responsible for the implementation of policy when it is clear ministers have played a major role in that policy's introduction. It should question the civil servants responsible for the execution of government plans at the time rather than only questioning their successors. At the moment, the committee focuses on value for money criteria based on economy, efficiency and effectiveness. This remit should be broadened to include structure, competence and productivity.

For many years it has been obvious that Britain has been poorly and inefficiently governed. The recent pandemic has thrown up just how serious our shortcomings are.

CHAPTER 15

Japan – The Sun Rises

I HAD LONG followed the rise of Japan and its revolutionary system of industrial relations based on quality circles. Everyone worked as a team to satisfy the customer with the most exciting and innovative products. Long gone was the Japanese reputation for cheap tinny copies of Western designs. Workers trusted the management and everyone was involved in all discussions that affected them.

New products were vigorously tested before being launched. Quality was everything. The workforce was paid a stable wage that took into account people's ages and responsibilities. There was no piecework. No Theory X. It was a Theory Y paradise adopted by over 150,000,000 people – or was it?

In 1980, at a reception given by the Japanese embassy, I made friends with Wateru Aso, the MITI (Ministry of International Trade and Industry) attaché. MITI was the powerful department responsible for coordinating and implementing the Japanese government's industrial and overseas investment strategy.

Aso was a Keynesian 'wet' and was horrified by the monetarist policies of Margaret Thatcher and Geoffrey Howe. He wrote a critique of the 1981 budget, which included his own proposals for it. I circulated it around the Blue Chips and it became known, not very originally, as the 'Aso' plan. Much of it was incorporated into our pamphlet 'Changing Gear'. Years later Aso became the elected governor of Fukuoka, one of the greatest cities in Japan. It was a pity he couldn't have become chancellor of the exchequer.

It occurred to me that we might replicate the concept of the 1963 Königswinter conference that I had attended with Japan. But there were formidable difficulties. Japan was little known, and its image and the reputation of its people was still blighted in the eyes of most British people by its behaviour in the Second World War. Who would sponsor and pay for the conference? Who would pick the participants? Who would organise it and act as secretary? I was just a newly elected backbencher, out of the mainstream of government supporters, and I had never been to Japan.

In the House of Commons, Japanese issues were under the vice-like grip of Julian Ridsdale, MP for Harwich and a nephew of Stanley Baldwin. Julian had been a military attaché at the British embassy in Tokyo at the outbreak of the Second World War. This posting had given him significant authority with the Japanese embassy and led to them still treating him as their contact point with MPs of all parties. They supplied him enough funds every year to enable him to invite whoever he liked – usually three or four from each side of the House – to go on a week-long jolly around Japan. He chose those he owed or from whom he wanted some favour. He was also happy to accept the nominations of the whips. They weren't particularly interested in Japan, but took the opportunity to reward some loyal backbenchers who had taken part in debates or who had asked planted questions at the whips' bequest. There was no structure to the visits; no outcome and no follow-up. I managed to persuade Julian to include me on one, although I did not fit his loyalty criteria.

The Foreign Office, who privately agreed that the visits were an expensive waste of time, did not want to be involved. Fortunately for me, the Japanese government, under pressure from Japanese industry, had decided that they should put more effort into tackling the European market, and the UK was the most obvious place to start, not least because of the language. In 1981 the Gaimusho (Japanese Foreign Office) had sent over to the embassy a young diplomat, who had spent the previous three years in Washington as a lobbyist promoting closer relations with the US, to undertake this role. His name was Yukio Satoh. Aso was moved aside and I was taken under Yukio's wing. He asked me to produce a list of names of those who might form the core of the new Anglo-Japanese wisemen's group, and he would do likewise. We decided to call it the Anglo-Japanese 20th Century Group.

As a young MP, it is crucial to get to know the movers and shakers outside the narrow House of Commons hothouse. It is particularly vital to get in with the highflyers in the Civil Service, the Treasury, the Foreign Office and big business. At the time I did not know any of them and had no route to them. Yukio provided it. He used the wonderful facilities of the Japanese ambassadorial residence and their even more spectacular cooks to invite a wide cross section of the up-and-coming. The first two I provided were Chris Patten and Nigel Forman. Nigel had beaten me for the nomination and become member for Carshalton. (He was supposed to have also been a link for MI6.) Yukio delivered Terry Burns and Alan Budd, who later became permanent secretaries at the treasury.

We soon had the outline of the group we wanted but we still had to deal with the redoubtable Sir Julian and gain the backing of Number 10. Sir Julian, after a lengthy rearguard action, finally agreed to support my idea but we were forced to go to Japan for two days to get the agreement of the general secretary of the Liberal Democratic Party (LDP), a Havana cigar-chomping heavyweight called Aso (a different Aso to my friend with the same name at the MITI). He listened patiently whilst Julian rambled on and then suddenly leapt from his chair and said, 'Ridsdale-san, you are the past; this young man is the future.' We had done it!

At the meeting was a dapper colleague of Aso's called Wateru Hiraizumi, who was a foreign affairs specialist. He turned out to be a right-wing friend of Julian Amery, Churchill's son-in-law, and attended conspiratorial conferences at the Villa D'Este outside Milan. We discovered later that he owned 150 French handmade suits. His wife was the daughter of the founder of Kajima, one of Japan's largest construction companies. He was also vice chairman of the LDP. At the end of the meeting he pulled me aside and said he had a budget to invite two rising star members of parliament to come to Japan for ten days with their partners as guests of the Party. He asked me to put forward another couple to accompany Sissy and me. 'By the way, please send a photograph of the wives.'

My first recommendation was Tristan and Catali Garel-Jones. However, Hiraizumi wanted a blonde and Catali was Spanish; next I suggested Michael and Sandra Howard. They passed muster and so the four of us set off for our first proper visit to Japan. We toured the country and although we were at different ends of the party, we became close friends. There were a number of embarrassing incidents. Michael did not appear to have socks without holes and everywhere we went we had to take our shoes off. I was unable to move backwards on my knees without knocking down the surrounding paper screens at a tea ceremony – not once but twice.

All went well until Hiraizumi invited us to a cocktail party at his huge house in the middle of Tokyo. Halfway through the evening, I realised that Sissy and Sandra had disappeared. I grabbed Michael and we set off to find them. They were in his study. He was sitting in a large armchair with Sissy on one arm and Sandra on the other. Their eyes were on stalks – Hiraizumi had a famous collection of pornographic woodcuts which he was proudly displaying.

At dinner after the cocktail party Hiraizumi told us the following story. His father had been cabinet secretary when the Japanese war cabinet met on 5 December 1941 to decide on whether to attack the United States. One of the arguments revolved around a second track on the Trans-Siberian Railway. Japan was suffering an ever-tightening economic blockade from the United States and the United Kingdom. Japan had to decide how and whether she could break this blockade and open up the markets in Europe, or whether she should submit to the humiliating terms demanded by the United States. The Japanese government came to the conclusion, after a lengthy debate, that Germany would defeat Russia in the winter and spring of 1941/2, and that after their successes in China, the Japanese army could knock over the Dutch and British possessions in East and South East Asia, possibly including Australia and India, thereby joining up with Germany in the Caucasus. This would give Japan access to the rich, German-dominated European markets. Their industries would receive all the raw materials and oil they required from the captured colonial possessions. For this to be successful they would need to destroy the American fleet at Pearl Harbour and drive the Americans into isolationism and neutrality. But most importantly, they would need a second track on the Trans-Siberian Railway to move their goods from Japan into western markets. The outcome of this meeting became apparent when, on 7 December 1941, Yamamoto launched waves of his bombers on to the US fleet.

Hiraizumi then went over to his desk, unlocked a drawer and pulled out several sheets of paper, which were the original minutes of that war cabinet meeting, torn out by his father and kept by him. He claimed that because of the American stranglehold, Japan had no alternative, however risky their decision.

It still took three years to get the first Anglo-Japan conference up and running. The first one was held in London in 1984 and the Japanese delegation included Dr Toyoda of Toyota; Dr Sekimoto, chairman of NEC; Akio Morita, founder of Sony; Saji of Suntory; and Dr Mukaibo, boss of the Japanese nuclear industry. Our side was as distinguished as we could make it but hardly compared to the Japanese heavyweights.

We had a lengthy meeting with the prime minister at which she gave an undertaking that Britain would be a safe and profitable base for the operations in Europe and that we would be reliable partners for the Japanese as they expanded in the European Union. As a result, billions of pounds worth of Japanese money has been invested in the UK – but as we are now leaving the EU so inevitably Japanese investment will decline. Margaret Thatcher became a great advocate for Japan after she had overcome her initial reticence – she was persuaded by Cecil Parkinson and David Young that anything chaired by Jim Prior and organised by Richard Needham was not all bad.

The formal sessions of the first few conferences were awkward and stilted. The Japanese came with long prepared statements that they handed out in advance and then proceeded to read out in badly broken English. The danger was that the British hogged the subsequent debate while the Japanese looked on clutching their simultaneous-translation headsets.

There was a memorable incident. We had arranged a tour of Blenheim Palace, where we were having dinner on the Saturday night of the conference. The guide was a rather grand, loud, opinionated lady who talked at the Japanese as if they were slightly slow, deaf children who were lucky to be allowed into such wonderful surroundings. I kept whispering to her to speak normally but she glared at me and continued to declaim about Marlborough's military victories in a posh and condescending diatribe. At the end of the tour Keizo Saji, the owner of Suntory and one of the world's richest men, said in halting, broken English, 'Excuse me, can I ask something? I know England is in a very bad way and your taxes are very high. This place must be very expensive to look after. How much do you want for it?' The bossy guide looked aghast and spluttered, 'I'll have to ask his Grace about that.' Saji winked at me.

As the years went by the Japanese relaxed, their English improved and real dialogue and debate became possible. I did not notice any of our side becoming more fluent in Japanese. However, we did have two Japanese speakers. In 1939, the British government had realised that we faced a possible war with Japan and they set about trying to recruit potential young interpreters who could be used to interrogate captured prisoners of war. They decided to concentrate on grammar school boys who had parents working in the Far East. Fifteen students were taken on and sent to Greenwich to learn Japanese. After the outbreak of war and having finished their studies, they were then sent over to Singapore but with typical bureaucratic incompetence, they were all placed on the same ship. It was sunk going through the Mediterranean and only a small number survived. Two of them, Sir Peter Parker and Professor Ron Dore, became founder members of our group and were able to teach the rest of us how the Japanese mind worked.

So, were the Japanese a nation of Theory Y practitioners? Hardly. Japan is a homogeneous beehive that is changing ever so slowly. The Japanese do not by and large welcome immigrants because there is nowhere for them to go. Japanese men often describe themselves as workaholics living in rabbit hutches. Western cynics claim Japanese make small things as there is nowhere to put large things. Japanese people are small for the same reason and they are clean and tidy because of the past dangers of dirt and disease.

Like a beehive they work on behalf of the interests of the hive. Until recent times the emperor played the role of Queen Bee. They are deferential and obedient. They rarely question orders from above. Most will work phenomenally hard for the common good.

They remain a male-dominated society, partly because their language discriminates against women in any argument with men.

This is changing as the strength that comes from being part of the beehive is being slowly undermined by others who are more flexible, more questioning, more innovative, more prepared to think outside the box. As Japan's population withers by the decade they are having to face existential threats that will challenge their culture and their rigidities. This is made harder by their unquestioning Confucian respect for their elders, who are not always their betters. Nevertheless, their ability to work together under a common umbrella of high educational achievement, joint problem-solving, attention to process and detail, sharing the spoils and trusting each other other's motives have made them one of the world's miracle economies.

For over thirty years the Group has had a major impact through its recommendations on Anglo-Japanese cooperation. In 2005 the emperor of Japan presented me with the Order of the Rising Sun Gold and Silver Star. This took place at a private investiture in the ambassador's residence. I was allowed to bring sixteen family members and friends. The pony tailed Ambassador Nogami (whose wife Geraldine came from county Roscommon and according to Nogami, insisted on referring to Ulster as the six counties) read out the royal citation in ancient Japanese from a parchment scroll against the backdrop of both countries' flags. It was followed by a sumptuous sixteen-course dinner, washed down with sake and the finest claret. We had come a long way since 1945.

However, before that could take place, permission from the Queen had to be asked. Privy Counsellors are not allowed to hold foreign orders without royal approval. The ruling goes back to the first Queen Elizabeth who, when asked by Sir Francis Walsingham whether he could receive some foreign honour, replied, 'I will not have my dogs wearing other men's collars.' She passed me.

Some of the younger Japanese Diet members have gone on to greater things. Yukio Hatoyama, the grandson of the founder of Bridgestone Tyres, became prime minister, even if only for a few months. He was one of my closest friends on the Japanese side of the group. I arranged for him to spend a few days with me in Belfast in 1987, and he came – against the advice of the Japanese Embassy who claimed it was unsafe for him to go. He was fearless.

One day in 1990 I had a request from a young student, Paul Carter, who had just enrolled in the JET (Japanese Exchange and Teaching) programme. Additionally, he wanted to study the Japanese political system while he was there. I suggested he got hold of Yukio Hatoyama when he arrived. Two months later Paul wrote to me to tell me that he been taken on by Yukio as his political aide – the first Briton to fill that role to a Japanese political leader.

Some fourteen years later, in 2004, Paul rang me to say that Yukio, his wife and several MPs from Yukio's newly formed breakaway party were in London and wanted to see me. I suggested that Paul bring them down to our wood in Wiltshire – as it was spring, we could have a barbecue and look for butterflies, which I knew that Yukio collected. When they arrived we went around the wood with a butterfly net and to his and our enormous surprise and pleasure we found a white Admiral, which he declared also lived in Hokkaido in northern Japan.

Yukio is extremely shy, very good looking, vague and a mystic. His new party was a chaotic mix of former disgruntled LDP members and other parliamentary malcontents. The only point of agreement was their opposition to the corrupt and cynical party bosses that had been in power since the end of the war.

During the lunch I asked Yukio and his colleagues what they would do when he became prime minister. There was a long pause and then a hesitant 'I have no idea'. His wife – who had spent much of her time in California, had a broad American accent, and who wore leopard print shoes and a miniskirt – immediately intervened. 'Of course you know what you're going to do.' Another pause. 'No, I don't. I've no idea.'

Sure enough, once he had become prime minister, he found it impossible to bring together his squabbling colleagues, and after eight months he was out. For all that, he remains the nicest, kindest, gutsiest, most honest and – unfortunately – most hopeless politician I know. Meanwhile after two years with Yukio, Paul had returned and gone on to Cambridge University to complete his Japanese studies. Although he would deny it, Paul has quite a lot in common with Yukio. Paul went on to gain a place on the Conservative parliamentary candidates list. In 1997 he stood, unsuccessfully, for election in Bradford West. He became a political advisor to Jeremy Hunt, then foreign secretary, who had also spent two years in Japan on the JET programme. Jeremy has become an eloquent and dedicated advocate of closer ties with Japan, to the extent that he once publicly described his Chinese wife, Lucia, as Japanese.

CHAPTER 16

The Not-So 'Jolly Abroad'

ONE OF THE perks of being a junior backbencher is the invitation to go on a 'jolly' – although sometimes the trips I was on turned out to be anything but. In early 1982, Tom Benyon, MP for Abingdon, invited me on a Palestinian Liberation Organisation tour around Jordan, the West Bank and East Jerusalem (paid for, no doubt, by the Saudis). Others on the mission included John Major, Dale Campbell-Savours, Peter Snape and Jack Aspinwall.

It was an eventful three days. In the middle of the first night we were woken up and bustled into a convoy of black Range Rovers. Hoods were pulled over our heads and we were driven around the centre of Beirut at high speed for about fifteen minutes before being deposited outside Yasser Arafat's office, which was next door to our hotel. The meeting took place in the chairman's office. None of the shelves of the mahogany bookcase had seen a duster and, instead of books, they displayed tarnished silver models of military hardware, donated by the arms suppliers to the Palestine Liberation Organization.

We sat on both sides of a long board table and Arafat's secretary brought in a tray filled with small glasses of frothing sweet tea. He was a short hunchback who had been with Arafat all his life. As he approached the table, his heel caught in one of the holes in the worn-out Persian carpet that covered the floor. The tray went flying across the table, parting company with the teacups on the way and spraying everyone with hot sticky tea. Arafat was mortified – he whipped off his keffiyeh and started to mop up displaying a blotchy balding pate covered in tufts of greying hair. Now we knew why he always wore his headsets.

After order was restored, a heated debate began on the failure of the Palestinians to recognise the state of Israel. The attack was led by Dale

Campbell-Savours and Peter Snape. Arafat who had been quite polite and amusing, suddenly snapped. 'Why do you think I should give up my one card, the recognition of the state of Israel, in front of a batch of unknown British backbench MPs?'

I decided to intervene to try to reduce the tension. 'Chairman, I am a half-Jewish Irish lord and I am most interested in hearing your position and learning more about your views.' Silence. Then a huge smile. 'How do I address a half-Jewish Irish lord?' he asked. 'On your knees,' the ever-humorous Snape shot out. More silence. Were we for the firing squad? Arafat then moved up the table and knelt in front of me.

The next day we went out in a convoy of cars from Beirut to Bethlehem to meet Elias Freij, a Palestinian Christian, and mayor of Bethlehem. After being held up for a long time by Israeli soldiers at the Jordan border, we suddenly found ourselves in an ambush. The convoy halted and we were trapped in a fire fight between stone-slinging Palestinian youths on one side and Israeli pistol-firing settlers on the other. Foolishly we got out of the cars to have a look before diving back into them again. I pushed Snape into the well of the back seat and told everyone to get down as an Israeli started kicking me into the car. I looked down and I saw Snape was lying on top of a female MI6 operator who was accompanying us. 'Typical bloody Tory toff giving out orders. Us working-class lads know when to get down and where to put our heads,' as he glanced up from a partly open cleavage. When we got to the mayor's office we all hit his brandy bottle. We had had a close shave, and a vivid lesson on the hatred and determination of both sides to state their claims to the land of Judea.

In the afternoon we visited the Church of the Nativity. Snape stayed behind with the mayor and the bottle of brandy. 'Once you have seen one stable, you've seen them all.' That evening in a hotel room Tom Benyon and I were discussing what we should say to the British ambassador to Israel who was giving us a reception the following day. John Major walked in and started to give us the benefit of his opinions. This rather annoyed Tom and me.

We saw John as a rather grey and unimaginative backbencher – not versed in the nuances of international diplomacy like we were. 'Shut up, Major,' I said. 'Look at the back of your head – you've got a bit missing!' This, it turned out, was not a career-enhancing comment. Not as serious as being taped by the paramilitaries calling Margaret Thatcher 'a cow' on my mobile phone, but nevertheless a mistake, particularly as John never ceases to remind Sissy of my concerns about the shape of his crown.

We came back shocked by the violence, the damage, the intransigence, the lack of any dialogue or structures to try and find common ground. The Balfour Declaration was no doubt right but the failure of the western powers to manage and implement its consequences and walk away has left the differences as unresolved now as they were on our visit thirty-six years ago. It was a foretaste of what I was to find in Northern Ireland, with which I was soon to become involved. Palestinian flags fly in nationalist West Belfast while Israeli ones flutter on the other side of the 'peace' walls. There are no Theory Y management supporters in Hamas and Hezbollah, and not enough in parts of the government of Israel.

When I returned from Beirut, a letter was waiting for me from the American ambassador, John J. Louis Jnr. It was an invitation to visit the United States for a month as a guest of the US government. The invitation came from a shadowy organisation called the International Communications Agency, which may or may not have had connections with the CIA. Apparently around forty Brits a year were invited, under the heading of the Junior World Leader Programme. The invitees were allowed to go anywhere they liked within America and could pick a subject around which to base their visit. They got free air travel, free hotels and $110-a-day spending money, which was adequate in 1982, but not over generous.

I decided I would use Theory Y in management as my theme. For each place I wanted to travel to, I was given a contact point, a very skeletal programme and allowed to get on with planning the visit myself. It was a brilliant and typically American concept. Its British equivalent programme was much smaller, run by the Foreign Office, highly organised, structured and controlled. The American government had the self-confidence that America would sell itself. All that was required was to put the guest on a plane and let them do what they wanted. The participants were all intelligent, motivated young people and the majority would return home overwhelmed by what they had found and seen.

I planned a schedule. London to Boston, including a detour to Needham, Massachusetts. Then to New Orleans, followed by Texarkana,

Texas (which is nearer to Chicago, Illinois than it is to San Antonio, Texas). San Francisco to Yosemite. Then Los Angeles then Cleveland, Ohio with a stopover in Detroit, and finally New York and home. Sissy, thanks to the generosity of British Airways, joined me in San Francisco.

I began in Boston with a professor at the Harvard Business School. Theory Y was still taught, but it was being side-lined by the explosion of new financial instruments and technologies that were revolutionising business practices, and generating huge fortunes and huge bankruptcies.

I caught a bus to Needham Town, Massachusetts. I met the board of select men and its chairman H. Philip Garrity Jnr. The town had been settled by persecuted and impoverished Puritan pilgrims from Suffolk in the seventeenth century. It had long lost its East Anglian connections and was now a prosperous suburb of Boston, not far from Route 128, which forms the backbone of one of the greatest IT explosions in the world economy. Needham Town's roots were strong Irish Catholic. There were few supporters of British policy in Northern Ireland. Like most Irish Americans, they had the very haziest understanding of the real issues. The escape of their ancestors, many during the time of the Famine, led to considerable sympathy for the IRA and financial backing for Sinn Féin.

I was surprised and pleased when four years later, in January 1989, I received the following letter:

TOWN OF NEEDHAM

MASSACHUSETTS

Office of
BOARD OF SELECTMEN

TELEPHONE
617-455-7512

January 30, 1989

Richard Needham, Member of Parliament
Westminster
London, England

Dear Mr. Needham:

Since your visit here some years ago, to the Town that bears the same name as your forbears, we have followed your career with great interest.

In your capacity as Minister of Environment for Northern Ireland, we note with interest your efforts in orderly and balanced development in that section of the country. Your sensitivity to the needs of the community as a whole without regard to those considerations that are so often devisive honors the name of Needham both as to yourself and to this Town.

It is then with pleasure that we recognize those efforts, commend your accomplishments and anticipate your positive contributions to peace in the future.

Sincerely,
BOARD OF SELECTMEN

HPG:kd

H. Phillip Gerrity, Jr.,
Chairman

Attest: Town Clerk

A True Copy

ATTEST:

Town Clerk of Needham, Mass.

The month passed in a whirlwind. America is both tasteful and tasteless, beautiful and hideous. Shopping malls along highways are identical where ever you are. There are downtowns that have the world's highest and most beautiful buildings. There are areas of conspicuous wealth alongside ghettos. Black kids lounging on street corners and unemployed families sitting on collapsing wooden porches staring morosely at passers-by. The contrast exists in every great city.

One of the highlights of the trip was to catch up with Joe Sullivan and his wife KK. In the fifteen years since my two-week course at the Harvard Business School in Jamaica, Joe had developed a highly successful corporate law business, with investments ranging from engineering components to electric toothbrushes. He arranged for us to meet with Frank Valenta, head of the United Steelworkers Union in Cleveland, a steel city going through hard times because of Japanese, German and even UK competition. Valenta was a 6'4" Italian-American, weighing in at 250 lbs, who did not like competition, did not like Limeys and wanted protectionism. My job was to try to get Frank to modify his position as any increase in tariffs would be very damaging to the steel industry in south Wales. Joe promised to back me up. He claimed he was a great supporter of free trade and he maintained that the US steelworkers were pampered and overpaid. It was high time they fessed up.

Valenta sat behind a desk that matched his size. He had the Stars and Stripes on one side and the flag of the US steelworkers on the other. 'What do you want?' he enquired brusquely as we sat in chairs well below his eye line. I explained why free trade helped everyone and that protection would lead to beggar-my-neighbour responses. He glowered, thumped the desk. 'How much do you pay your workers? $15 an hour,' he answered himself. '$15! that's not even the living wage. My members are on $25 and they are struggling to survive. My members work for money not peanuts. Your government must be subsidising your steel companies at that level or your workers must be starving.' I turned to Joe for help. There was a pause.

Joe replied, 'Sure Frank, now you put it like that I see you have a strong point.'

We were dispatched with bone-crunching handshakes.

'Why did you rat on me, Joe? You know they will all lose their jobs in the end.'

'He was too big to argue with,' said Joe. Ever afterwards, Joe became known as 'Sure Frank Sullivan'. Theory X still flourished in the US steel unions. A year later the unions' refusal to accept wage concessions led to US Steel phasing out its Cuyahoga works.

America is so friendly, so informal, so welcoming. Their teeth so shiny white, their handshakes so firm. They are so big. The men grab you with huge hands and the women in affectionate embraces. There is no noticeable social division by class or profession. Wealth is the largest differentiator. They talk endlessly about money: how much they've got and everybody else they know has got. How much everything is worth and what it costs. Perhaps they are Theory X after all, but they treat each other as equals. The chauffeur very often calls his boss by his Christian name. Money is the lubricant that makes the cogs go around but it is not the motivator. That remains ambition, power, promotion, leadership, involvement and enjoyment. It is such a refreshing 'can do', 'it will happen if you want it to' place. We returned home awestruck and motivated. It was pouring with rain as we left the terminal at London Heathrow.

CHAPTER 17

Securing the Base

Iɴ 1983, ᴍʏ parliamentary seat's name changed from Chippenham to North Wiltshire. It was a huge area – some thirty miles by thirty miles and with 76,000 voters. It should have had its boundaries redrawn years earlier to reflect a national average of 60,000 electors per seat.

It is claimed by pollsters that the sitting member can at most garner fifteen hundred personal supporters. My experience tells me that double that figure would be closer to the truth. Between 1979 and 1983 I had worked relentlessly to establish myself as a caring, hands-on, always available MP. My home number was in the telephone book and we handed it out during elections.

I held advice centres, advertised in the local newspapers, every weekend on Friday evening and Saturday mornings in the main towns, which were Chippenham, Calne, Corsham, Wootton Bassett, Malmesbury and Cricklade. They started at ten and were supposed to finish by one, but in reality, often went on much longer. Everyone was welcome, no appointment was necessary. Liz Sexton was my tireless, polite, calming assistant, who took down people's details and kept them plied with coffee and biscuits while they waited. From 1985 until I stood down in 1997, there was an armed Special Branch detective with her at these advice centres, but I cannot recall a single unpleasant or threatening incident.

At the end of the session I would go off down the High Street to talk to shoppers and then end up in the bar of the nearest Conservative Club or in one of the local pubs. The Conservative Clubs form the foundation of working-class Conservative support in any constituency. To be a member, you have to state that you are a Conservative voter but in reality, it is a mixed membership and very often the club chairman does not encourage too much political discussion. It took me two years before the Chippenham club accepted me as a member. At the interview, the chairman Maurice Cowley, asked me whether I was a Conservative. I replied I was, which was more than could be said of him!

At the advice centres, the range of constituents' concerns covered every aspect of human activity, many of them tragic and sad. Some of them were funny yet serious, as the attached letter – one of the first I received as a newly elected MP – relates.

Dear Mr Needham,

I bought this property [in Cricklade] in July 1978. As yet it does not boast a bathroom or toilet. I am incidentally a registered disabled person suffering from a damaged spine. I started to restore the property. The rates promptly shot up by almost 100%. I drive to Cirencester, a return journey of 18 miles, several times a week to use the public baths there. For toilet purposes, I have been using the public toilet at the High Street opposite my home. Without any warning whatsoever this public toilet was closed. There was no announcement in the papers or anywhere else. Not very efficient. I saw no indication anywhere as to when it was intended to reopen it. In desperation I phoned the District Council. I spoke to 2 people who stated they should have been told of the toilet closure but hadn't. In fact, the first time they found it had been closed was when they themselves had tried to enter it as part of their duties, having motored all the way here from Chippenham at the rate payer's expense. What a way to run a Council!

I know you must be up to your ears in other matters affecting the country and the free World as well as our little town. However, I hope you might find the time to do something about this very serious problem.

Yours sincerely,
Paul Bowen

As a new MP there is no induction, no training and nowhere to turn for advice. I quickly learnt that the key to solving such problems and gaining the credit was to ring up the officials of the local authority and act as a go-between. Sissy then had to follow up.

Most cases did not require me to take sides and some, like planning controversies, I kept out of. However, when I found something intolerable or damaging, I would champion the cause. My only ultimate remedy was to call for an adjournment debate on the floor of the House of Commons at the end of the day's business. My main method of gaining publicity was holding a Monday morning press conference in the Conservative offices, which the local journalists of the *Chippenham News*, *Wiltshire Gazette*, *Bath Evening Chronicle* and *Bristol Evening Post* would attend. As my exposure grew, so did demands for my involvement. Every week I had stories to feed to the local press that they would not have known about without my passing them on. It could be a possible factory closure or expansion, a neighbourhood dispute, a claim of abuse, the police being heavy handed, or the hunt having rampaged through someone's garden. I learnt to keep the hunt at a distance, despite their offers of help. David Eccles, my distinguished predecessor, claimed that every time the Beaufort chased a fox through one of his villages and mistakenly came across a cat, he lost at least two votes. I do not oppose hunting but there are certain aspects of it that I find extremely distasteful.

Wherever possible, I also tried to reach the uncommitted. I addressed Round Tables, Rotary Clubs, Chambers of Commerce and sixth forms. I visited factories and offices, hospitals and further education colleges. I did post office rounds at five in the morning. I went to the ambulance and fire stations. Whenever possible, I took a photographer and issued a press release. Not many a week went by without me appearing in the local papers and doing an interview with the local radio. Every eighteen-year-old got a personal letter on House of Commons notepaper, personally topped and tailed, encouraging them to vote. Similarly, those who moved house or moved into the constituency received a welcoming letter.

I also spent as much time as I could at Party fundraising events, usually wine and cheese parties, where saying 'a few words' often ended in some unguarded comment that upset one or other of the faithful. Sissy then had to clean up by reassuring them that her views were in accordance with theirs rather than mine.

The misunderstanding of an MP's role often leads to confusion and conflict. Local councillors feel left out because the public may know who their MP is but they have not a clue who represents them at local government level. Too often local MPs weigh in behind any lobby, knowing that they have no responsibility for its outcome, with the intention of embarrassing political opponents.

There have always been demands for more politicians who have had successful previous careers in business and management. And that if they were paid more it would attract a better class of candidate, essentially a Theory X argument.

By and large, businesspeople do not make successful politicians. Often they are dictatorial, secretive and inarticulate. They are used to getting their own way and believe if it is good for their company, it must be good for the country too. Many of them have Theory X mentalities and believe that money is a major motivator. There are exceptions, like Michael Heseltine and Stanley Baldwin, but they are few. Archie Norman was phenomenally successful at running Asda but disappeared without trace as soon as he became an MP. He looked wonderful but was a poor debater who had his ego pricked every time he spoke. John Davies, former director of the CBI, had suffered a similar fate two decades previously.

Being an MP or a minister is a Theory Y profession. You need to trust people, listen to them in confidence, find compromise where you can, represent their concerns while holding fast to your own convictions and beliefs. You need patience, certainty, dedication and ruthlessness, but you don't have to have been a middle manager, a marketing executive or city financier to have these attributes.

In recent years a plethora of special advisers and outside political apprentices straight from university have gone directly into parliament. They often come from similar cultural backgrounds and love the life of plotting and intrigue. What the House needs is a mix of all sorts. It is not the crowded conditions of work or the lack of money that is putting off bright young professionals; it is the danger of family intrusion, constant personal attacks through social media and the tabloid press, and risk of exposure for some minor, long-past discretion. Currently weak leadership and constant changes of ministerial posts – not for reasons of good governance but for internal party balance – lead to uncertainty and disillusionment.

By the spring of 1983, Margaret Thatcher's reputation had soared as a result of the Falklands victory. She had triumphed over the 'wets' in the cabinet. The economy was firing up, even though a huge chunk of British manufacturing had been wiped out in the process. Unemployment was coming down, as was inflation. The Labour party was in confusion. Everything was in place for a thumping victory. But was it for me?

Although I had increased the majority in 1979, Chippenham was still a target seat for the Alliance. The two Davids, Steel and Owen, were an attractive pair. The Labour vote was being squeezed in the west of England and the Alliance party in Chippenham had a thrusting, young, some thought clever candidate in Chris Graham. He was a BBC current affairs producer, so was well briefed and articulate. He had moved home into the constituency. He infuriated me by carrying around a tape recorder with the BBC logo stuck on the side. One of his closest supporters was Hugh Pym (now the BBC News health editor), the son of a Malmesbury GP and a Liberal county councillor mother. Pym continued on the BBC tradition of impartiality by himself standing as a Liberal Democrat candidate for Chippenham at a later election.

As the campaign progressed and the vitriolic abuse ramped up, Graham produced the old Alliance Liberal mantra. 'We are the nice guys. Everyone is fed up with yahoo-boo politics. Vote for us and for a reasoned centre way, which will keep at bay the lunatics on the fringes of the two main parties.' The whole constituency was awash with orange dayglo posters. My heart was racing. Fortunately, I had Billy Harding, my supporter from my days in Yeovil, to help. Within a few days North Wiltshire was a carpet of blue and the orange flood had all but disappeared.

We had some party figures come to address the faithful. The North Wiltshire members are an enigmatic, taciturn bunch and difficult to rouse to an enthusiastic pitch. Jim Prior said it was like talking to a field of Norfolk heifers and even Michael Heseltine found it impossible to shift them off their backsides. The old Wiltshire adage is 'sometimes they sits and they thinks and other times they just sits'.

On the day, the orange wave was halted at the tideline and I was re-elected with a majority of 7,232.

CHAPTER 18

Ulster Beckons

IT WAS 'MAKE up your mind' time. I had to decide whether to continue as a vocal left-wing Tory rebel, like Julian Critchley, and be the darling of liberal media, or to do what I had gone into politics for, which was to become a member of the government and change things. Jim Prior had indicated that after the election he would go on for another year in Northern Ireland and then retire. If I was to get off the back benches, I had to find a sponsor. Jim was the obvious candidate as I had worked for him in the 1970s, and Northern Ireland was where my family had originated. But Jim had his ministerial team in place and Fred Sylvester had been his faithful parliamentary private secretary for the previous Parliament. I bit the bullet. I told Fred I wanted his job and it was time he gave up. Fred was quiet, unassuming and modest. He enjoyed working for Jim. He seemed surprised to be told to go by me, but went.

The ministerial team under Prior included Nick Scott, who was in charge of security. He had been flagged as a future prime minister – but charming though he was, he never had the mojo or the parliamentary skills to get beyond minister of state. He died early from dementia in 2005 after loyally serving a prime minister he despised. Chris Patten covered environment and health. Adam Butler, the son of Rab Butler, was the finance and industry minister, and Rodney Elton, followed by Charlie Lyell, were the obligatory peers. Their main function was to stay in the Province at weekends while House of Commons ministers returned to their constituencies.

Fred had been quite a laid-back PPS and had concentrated his efforts on trying to persuade right-wing unionist colleagues to support Jim's legislative program for a devolved assembly. The PM had once described Northern Ireland as being 'as British as Finchley' – which was not obvious to the people of West Belfast. Her PPS was Ian Gow, a shrewd, white-velvet-drinking, right-wing plotter who did all he could to encourage a cabal of his like-minded colleagues to undermine Jim's attempts to bring back power-sharing self-government to Stormont.

I decided that I would take a more hands-on approach to persuading doubting MPs to support the government's power sharing initiative. I took groups of four or five backbench Tory MPs on two-day tours of Northern Ireland so they could see for themselves the differences between Finchley and Belfast. We had a jam-packed itinerary. On day one, police and army briefings, then a lengthy tour of Belfast, up the Shankill and down the Falls, followed by a dinner at Stormont House with local community and business leaders. Finally, we had a nightcap in the form of joining an RUC patrol through some possible trouble-spot. The following day we went out west to the more nationalist and republican areas, where we often had fractious debates about the behaviour of the army and the RUC. We then took the evening shuttle back to London. I also spent a lot of time with the Northern Irish MPs and asked them to guide these groups around their constituencies so that they felt involved and consulted.

First, though, I had to expand my own knowledge and understanding. In September 1983 I flew over to Belfast with Jim and Jane Prior in an RAF Hawker Siddeley 125 that was specially camouflaged to protect against IRA rockets.

I cadged a lift up to Derry with Chris Patten in his armoured police car with an armed escort for the launch of one of Geoffrey Howe's enterprise zones, which gave investors grants and tax rebates. Ten miles before we reached the City we changed into an armoured monster and trundled up to the Guildhall guarded by the police, who were being guarded by the army.

Lunch was a grand affair. Everyone was present: John Hume, the MP; Bishop Edward Daly, famous as the priest who had intervened to stop the shooting on Bloody Sunday; Bishop Mehaffey of the Church of Ireland; the mayor in his robes; the councillors; the businessmen; the media. No one went unrepresented except for Sinn Féin and the IRA.

I had arranged in advance that I would go down to the Bogside after the event to meet a constituent, David Richardson, who came from Malmesbury and was a bookbinder. He had been enticed to go to Derry to work in youth and community workshops, teaching the young unemployed the secrets of vellum. A straightforward, moustached

Englishman, who enjoyed his pint in the Rose and Crown, he now found himself teaching the children of republicanism how to rebind the books of Londonderry, that had been bequeathed to the residents by their former colonial masters.

For some reason I never discovered, David had been taken on by Paddy 'Bogside' Doherty – one of the early leaders of the Civil Rights Movement. One of the challenges that faced me in my early days as PPS was to find roots in the nationalist community that I could cultivate and call on when confronted with official briefings from the NIO. David Richardson presented me with my first introduction to Irish nationalism.

I had been told that as a PPS I was not a security risk so after an inedible lunch and numerous speeches, I was picked up by a government car service vehicle and taken into the Bogside. I was wearing a tie with the Derry City emblem on it which I had been given at the lunch. I was scared as we approached the huge mural emblazoned with the slogan 'You are now entering Free Derry'. Paddy was standing there waiting for me and as I got out, he fixed me with his piercing blue eyes, stuck his finger into my chest and greeted me with, 'That skeleton represents what you and your kind have done to the people of this city for hundreds of years'. I trembled. This was definitely not Finchley.

The following afternoon, surrounded by policemen, Chris and I toured Belfast city centre. Except for the vicinity of the City Hall where Marks & Spencer had held its ground, the streets were pockmarked with bombed-out gap sites. The great Victorian buildings were empty above ground level and plastered with crumbling estate agents' 'to let' signs. The facias above the shops were gaudy and ugly. Every hundred yards or so there were checkpoints and barbed-wire-festooned gates. Every bus, car and delivery vehicle was searched before it could pass. We were overtaken by an army patrol of unsmiling, helmeted young soldiers, their guns pointing towards the navels of the shoppers. It did not look or feel like a place to take your children to see Father Christmas!

Meanwhile my tours started gaining traction so I began to broaden the guest list. The most demanding visit was an outing to Derry with Sir Julian Amery and Sir John Biggs-Davison. Julian had asked me to pick him up from his house in Eaton Square and take him to the airport, but I did not realise that this arrangement would require me to pack his smalls into a battered leather holdall while he drank half a bottle of good claret with his breakfast.

I had warned Paddy Doherty that he would be receiving high-ranking Tory grandees and he had grumbled. Before meeting Paddy's team, we had lunch with the Honourable Irish Society. The Society was founded by the City of London to raise the finance to plant settlers in the north-west of Ireland – hence the London prefix to Derry. By the 1980s, most of its wealth and power had long since gone, but it still had a wonderful Georgian house next to the cathedral and right by the army barracks within the walls of the city.

Its secretary, Peter Campbell, brother-in-law to the Duke of Abercorn, gave us a spectacular lunch while Sir Julian and Sir John reminisced about the Empire. After brandies, and with large Havana cigars clamped between John's and Julian's teeth, we travelled down Shipquay Street to discover how the other half lived.

Paddy had arranged a slide presentation of the work he was doing with the local young unemployed, who were in attendance. Many of them had pink Mohican hairstyles, rings in their ears and high-laced Doc Martens. They looked in astonishment at the cigar-smoke-shrouded, Astrakhan-coated grandees before them. Paddy invited us guests to sit down while the punks lined the wall at the back of the room.

As the slideshow unfolded, Julian decided that he would prefer to be facing the enemy rather than having his back to them. He swivelled his chair around and stared at the mob while sucking on his cigar. The mob stared back. Paddy continued with his presentation, which grew progressively more anti-British as the slides moved from one bombed-out building to the next. The RUC constable standing by the door looked increasingly nervous. Mercifully both sides seemed so shocked by the appearance of the other that no words were spoken.

As soon as Paddy had finished, I suggested we take a short tour of one or two of the sites themselves and visit the city walls. Paddy set off with Julian on one side and John on the other. Julian, who had been parachuted in to help Tito's partisans in the Second World War, could recognise a fellow resistance fighter when he saw one. He immediately started to question Paddy about his part in the Troubles in the early 70s. Paddy whispered to me that if he had known who I was bringing, he would have organised a different sort of reception, and then explained to Julian how the Walker monument had been blown up. (Walker conducted himself heroically during the siege of Derry in 1689 and his statue dominating the skyline over the Bogside had long been a source of irritation to the nationalist community.) 'There,' Paddy said as we got to the wall, 'Walker was blown up and he fell down the slope without dislodging a roof tile or breaking a window. The monument landed within six inches of where it was expected to. Who says Paddies can't do a proper job?' Julian, who had spent much time ambushing Germans in Serbia, looked on admiringly. Within minutes they were friends swapping jokes and stories. On the way back Julian said with a twinkle, 'We should have locked you up years ago.' I said I was sure the Germans would have liked to have done the same or worse to him. As far as I am aware, the remains of the statue are still in a D of E store!

We used to meet as advisors and ministers for prayer meetings in the secretary of state's office when we were all together in Belfast. One morning in the summer of 1984, Jim Prior said he was unexpectedly going home that night to his newly acquired farm in Hampshire, where he would be unreachable. He had intended to open a new housing association scheme in Strabane the next day but the IRA had got wind of it and were planning to blow him up. This was also the first day of one of my tours which included, among others, Nick Budgen and John Oaksey. Oaksey, a famous jockey and race commentator, was a neighbour and a friend. He had become involved in negotiating the return of the famous racehorse Shergar, which had been kidnapped by the IRA in 1983 and disappeared without trace. He wanted to understand more about Northern Ireland 'on the ground'.

That night we went out on a patrol in an RUC armoured Land Rover around the notorious Divis flats in West Belfast. John and I sat in the back alongside a young policewoman. As we toured the rubbish-strewn open spaces at the bottom of the flats there was suddenly a shout of 'slam'. At that moment the officer in the front passenger seat pulled a lever and metal shutters clattered down across the steel-meshed windows of the Land Rover, leaving a slit for the driver to peer through. There was an almighty crash and something large hit the roof and bounced down on to the tarmac behind us. The policewoman lifted up the shutter. 'It's only a fridge,' she explained. 'They must have thought we were coming to collect for the jumble sale.'

When we got back, I received an urgent message to contact Sir Ewart Bell, head of the Northern Ireland Civil Service. 'You're going up to Londonderry on one of your tours tomorrow,' he began. 'The secretary of state was due to open a new housing association project in Strabane and, as he has been called back to London on urgent business, he wondered if you could pop down and stand in for him. It's a lunchtime engagement – it will only take an hour or two – and then you can return to Derry and pick up your colleagues.'

I could not let on that I knew why the secretary of state was going home and why I was replacing him. When I got out, I told John Oaksey that we would be going up to Derry together in the morning. I explained that I would leave him with the city council clerk and his officials while I went off to Strabane – and that it was possible that I would not be coming back! I told him the background. 'I am coming with you, Needham,' he replied. 'If we go, we go together.' I told him that he definitely wasn't coming with me.

Desperately we tried to think of a way out. We couldn't tell Sir Ewart because Jim had breached the Secrecy Act by informing us of the planned attack. I phoned the private office and got hold of Jim's principal private secretary, the extravagantly bow-tied Noel Cornick.

'Could I have a word with the secretary of state?' I asked.

'No, he's unobtainable.'

'Well, if he rings in will you tell him I'm going to Strabane in his place tomorrow.'

'What's wrong with that?'

'Well nothing, of course. Just please tell him should he ring in.'

At 8 o'clock the next morning, Noel rang me back to tell me that Jim Prior had rung in and I was not to go as he would go himself at a later date. It turned out that the NIO had been suggesting that I should act as a replacement at some of his more hazardous events!

Our first stop the next morning was at a multi-million-pound recreation centre in Shantallow, the northern part of the city. We were taken round by the city clerk, Colm Geary, a Southern Irish man of infinite patience and charm. As we stood looking down over the balcony at a number of muscular young men pounding up the swimming pool, one looked up. It was Martin McGuinness. Apparently the facilities were used by the IRA as a keep-fit centre. Colm suggested we move on.

As we were climbing back into our car, a large man wearing a Sinn Féin T-shirt appeared and ran over to us. He greeted John Oaksey with a hug and asked about John's family and mother. He had been in the British Army and at some period had become closely involved with the Oaksey family. They then proceeded to talk about horses for ten minutes. The

Sinn Féin supporter complained that he had always followed Oaksey's tips but had never had a winner. Nick Budgen was sitting in the back, dying to say something. I hissed at him to keep quiet. The last thing we needed was a braying Home Counties English barrister's voice entering the conversation. If there is one thing that unites the English and the Irish it is racing, which is why an enlightened English government would have made John Oaksey secretary of state.

In the autumn of 1984, Jim Prior stood down and my version of Needham's tours came to an end. They were continued by Kenneth Carlisle MP, the PPS to the new secretary of state, Douglas Hurd. They had been a success for me personally and – to a lesser extent – politically. I had gained a reputation in Westminster for doing something slightly daring and different. In Northern Ireland, local politicians, particularly unionists, felt more involved.

By the end of my year's parliamentary secretaryship, I had accompanied over thirty MPs, business people and journalists on these tours. Most returned better informed and often a little chastened. Did the visits change the deeply rooted prejudices, particularly of the right-wing Conservative MPs? I doubt it. They did, however, give the participants a better feel for what might be done and some understanding of how, even at the bleakest of times, many people in the Province had got on with their lives untouched by the Troubles.

CHAPTER 19

A Security Leak?

MEANWHILE, AN ATTEMPT to get agreement on Prior's bill to reintroduce a power-sharing assembly on to the statute book was running into trouble. Jim was always walking a tightrope. The prime minister was not really interested or supportive, and she didn't trust the Irish. The Irish wanted some sort of involvement in the internal affairs of Northern Ireland, which was anathema to the unionists. The Tory right wing adopted integration as their solution and had learnt nothing since the battles over Home Rule a hundred years earlier. The unionists refused to take part as long as the Republic laid claim to the North in clause 4 of their constitution.

To help, in 1983, the Irish government decided to send over an experienced diplomat with a large expense account so that he could wine and dine the Tory rebels, and explain its policy. He set up shop in the Garrick Club. Richard Ryan was married to a Korean. He was a distinguished poet, a bon viveur who was well versed in the ways of the world, an intellectual and was most things that Northern Ireland unionists are not. Scratch him hard and he was a nationalist with a long-abiding, probably inherited, dislike of the Brits. He acted as a back channel to and from the Irish government to the Northern Ireland Office, the Home Office, the Foreign Office and the Ministry of Defence. He was extremely successful at a price borne by the Irish taxpayer.

But sometimes things went wrong. On occasions I was tasked by Jim Prior or one of the other ministers to pass on their views, which were not always in complete agreement with those of the Foreign Office. The FCO had a reputation for being 'green'. Some officials believed the sooner we could get rid of the Ulster problem and hand it over to the Irish, the better. It was a thorn in their side. Large resources were required to explain to the Americans and Europeans why we were not old-fashioned colonialists hanging on to a relic of our imperial past. Why was there such discrimination in favour of Protestants over Catholics? They were always on the defensive. Foreign Office officials seconded to the Northern Ireland Office spent much time either in London or in the safety of North Down, far away from the flashpoints and the sectarian interfaces, working out ways of dealing with loyalist intransigence. Many of them wished Northern Ireland could be towed out into the Atlantic and sunk.

I faithfully passed on to Ryan what I had been told to – that which concerned the secretary of state and his ministers as being too bright 'green' to be acceptable. One day I was summoned by Jim Prior to his office, which had once been that of the first lord of the admiralty, Winston Churchill. Behind the secretary of state's desk was a map showing the positions of the fleet at the outbreak of war in 1914. The windows looked out over Horse Guards Parade. It reeked of history. Prior sat at Churchill's desk. Alongside him was the permanent secretary of the Northern Ireland Office, the imposing, hawk-nosed Sir Robert Andrew. I stood to attention. 'Was I aware that I'd been passing on sensitive information to the Irish government? That I could well be in breach of the Official Secrets Act' asked Sir Robert. I trembled.

'No. What information?'

'We are not allowed to divulge that. This is an official warning for you to be much more careful in future.'

'I have only passed on what I have been asked to pass on. How do you know what I said?'

'Oh, the Irish government have complained.'

I was dismissed.

I rang Ryan and berated him for dropping me in it. 'Oh my goodness,' he said. 'I know what has happened.' After our last lunch of grouse and claret, Richard had – not surprisingly – felt unwell and, instead of writing out the details of our conversation and sending it over to Dublin in the diplomatic bag, he sent it on the cypher. 'What cypher?' I demanded. 'Probably a British Army code that we've been using since 1921,' came the reply.

It dawned. Someone had read the contents and passed them on. One of the rules of international diplomacy is supposed to be that a country does not spy on its friends and allies. This clearly was not happening with Dublin.

It would have blown over had I not compounded my misdemeanour by repeating the story under the Chatham House Rule during a drunken evening at the annual British Irish Association dinner in Oxford in front of Tim Pat Coogan, a deeply republican journalist and author. He delighted in spreading the news that Britain spied on all and sundry on the front page of the *Irish Press*, thereby gaining me another stinging rebuke for indiscretion.

As everyone who mattered knew what was going on, it was ridiculous. I have always believed that secrecy is too often used by civil servants and ministers as a way of covering their backsides and hiding their mistakes. I dislike secrecy and so-called confidentiality. The people have a right to know and the general presumption should be for transparency and openness. As one civil servant jokingly said to me, 'There's no point having a secret if you can't share it!' My belief and my behaviour have got me into trouble throughout my public life. But I have never said or done anything that has put someone's life in danger or under threat, and I have always respected confidentiality when asked.

I believe that involving people, consulting them, asking their opinions and, wherever possible, sharing views, options and alternatives is the way to conduct government business. It is also Theory Y. As 1983 ground into 1984, it was clear that Jim Prior's efforts to bring a political and peaceful settlement to the Irish impasse was sinking deeper and deeper into the Ulster bog. As soon as one side was showing a glimmer of interest, the other would walk out. As soon as both sides showed flexibility, some terrible terrorist outrage would send all factions scurrying back to their burrows. The Irish government and Garret Fitzgerald did their best to find some common ground, but their proposals were too much for the unionists to stomach. In the wings, De Valera's protégé Charlie Haughey waited. His lifelong mantra was to promote a united Ireland in the belief that 'England's misfortune is Ireland's opportunity' – which he proceeded to follow by taking the Argentinian side during the Falklands War, therefore ensuring a tidal wave of British fury.

The Reagan administration was supportive and balanced, if somewhat disinterested, but Democrat-controlled Irish America was universally hostile, and the situation in Northern Ireland was used by the party as a political tool for garnering votes and too often raising dollars for the IRA. The simple slogan 'Brits out' was sufficient and they made not the slightest effort to try to understand the sectarian horrors in Northern Ireland that they were doing so much to exacerbate.

The Province was in paralysis. Northern Ireland was dominated by warlords: the British government, the IRA, the UDA, the army, with the Irish and American governments on the sidelines. For much of the time the Queen's writ did not run.

During 1983 I read the contemporary books on the Troubles but found that whatever perspective they were written from, they offered no way out. Everything had been tried. Padraig O'Malley's book *The Uncivil Wars*, based on a series of interviews with the major protagonists, summed it up:

> Indeed, the story of Ireland today North and South is the story of endemic division, symptomatic of the larger illness, a creeping paralysis of will choking off political dialogue at every turn, it's debilitating contagiousness more pervasive because of the seemingly irreconcilable divisions between the two parts of Ireland and within Northern Ireland. Thus, the opening months of 1983, were very definitely not the best of times.

Attempts were made by well-meaning groups to bring all sides together. One such effort was a weekend in Airlie, Virginia, in 1985. It was a gathering of the movers and shakers: business, politics, government, academia and all shades of opinion – American, Irish and British. Even the unionists, including Peter Robinson and Sammy Wilson of the Democratic Unionist Party, came.

Most of the weekend passed – unsurprisingly – in an alcoholic fog. I remember Professor John A. Murphy of University College Cork battering Ken Maginnis around the head, like a grey squirrel attacking a grizzly bear. Afterwards Murphy became a sophisticated advocate of the unionist case in the south, so sometimes conferences do help to alter perceptions. The Irish ambassador played the piano while Peter Robinson and John Hume sang 'We Shall Overcome', the hymn of the 1960s civil rights marchers. Seamus Mallon was bitter about the police and army.

Chris Patten represented the authority and intelligence of government, which covered up for a lack of both in much of the NIO. Journalist Bruce Arnold gave a learned treatise on how the British establishment needed Northern Ireland as a strategic flank from any Russian attack across the northern Atlantic. This was too much for me and I interrupted to say that as a member of the British establishment and a member of Pratt's Club (aptly named) — where the cream of the establishment met nightly to discuss affairs of state — I had never once heard this argument. As far as I was aware there were only two proponents of such a view: Enoch Powell and Sinn Féin. One was no longer a member of the British establishment and the other was unlikely to become one. It was another seven years before Peter Brooke finally put to rest the nonsense about Britain's selfish or strategic interest in Northern Ireland.

The difficulty with such conferences is that everyone agrees about the problem but no one agrees about the solutions. The solutions can never be discussed without causing a row that ruins the conference.

At the inconclusive end of the discussions, I travelled to Washington. Some time before I had been invited by Neil Livingstone to have dinner in the Watergate with some of his associates. Neil was a gravelly voiced, bald, sinister-looking former CIA agent who wrote books on how to kill terrorists without being found out. He ran a PR company called Global Options and his wife was assistant secretary to the army in the Reagan administration. I had met Neil at a trilateral conference at Wilton Park in Sussex, comprising Japanese, American and British participants a couple of years earlier.

The dinner was in their apartment. A number of tall, clean-shaven men in their late thirties and early forties, all with crewcuts arrived, one of them with what I thought was a tennis racket. It turned out to be an Uzi submachine gun in its case, which he proceeded to point out of the window to prove that he could shoot down the President's helicopter as it flew overhead. The conversation was bizarre, with a flow of ideas that became ever more outrageous and ridiculous as the drinks flowed. I ended up having a blazing row with the man with the machine gun. Still recovering from three sleepless nights with the Irish, one large gin and tonic was enough to get me going. I remembered nothing about the rest of the evening.

Some years later I saw a picture of Colonel Ollie North on the news and I had a vague recollection of having seen him before. I mentioned it to Neil. 'Oh yeah, that's the man you were so rude to at dinner!' North was convicted for his part in the Iran-Contra Affair. He was a member of the staff of the National Security Council. He was the president of the National Rifle Association from 2018–19. If these were the men that held power under Reagan, it makes one shudder to think what those who advised Trump while he was in office were proposing!

In Northern Ireland, as 1984 dragged on, power drained from the secretary of state and his ministers. Everyone knew he was leaving and that politically, nothing was going to happen. Jim told me that he would do everything to try and get me promoted before he left, but he was told by Number 10 that there was only to be a minor reshuffle and I would not be part of it. But as an indication that I was high on the list for advancement, I was asked to second the Queen's speech at the Opening of Parliament in November 1984. My predecessors included Jim Prior, Ken Clarke and Kenneth Baker. I almost did not get this opportunity because of the IRA bomb that detonated at the Grand Hotel in Brighton on 12 October. The bomb had been planted two months before – if it had gone off two hours earlier than it did, I would have gone with it as I was dining with friends, at the next-door table to the Wakehams.

The occasion was the first time I had addressed a packed and expectant House and I knew that it might be the only time. I had to get it right. The night before the Queen's speech there is always a dinner in Downing Street where the prime minister addresses her ministers and the chief secretary to the cabinet reads out the speech with about as much gusto as the Queen herself would muster on the morrow. Everyone pays in advance for their own dinner. I had sent a copy of my speech to Downing Street so that the prime minister would be briefed. Alastair Goodlad, a Blue-Chip whip, told me to take out my best joke because Sir Paul Bryan, the proposer, was going to speak first and he needed the joke more than I did. The prime minister remarked that my views on Enoch Powell were as biting as any she could recall. I could not make out whether this indicated approval or otherwise. For once in my life I ate little and drank less.

At 2.45 p.m. the following day, 6 November 1984, I was in my place on the distant backbenches, knowing that on this occasion I would catch the Speaker's eye. I had hoped to speak without notes but my nerves got the better of me, and it was wiser to feel comfortable and perform confidently than to be too clever and forget some of the best lines – or worse still, dry up completely.

I called Alastair's bluff and began by remarking that I spoke on behalf of the junior ranks of the backbenches, and that in such circumstances many of us felt like amateurs in comparison with the professionalism of the front benches. However, we could comfort ourselves with the knowledge that whereas the Ark was built by amateurs it was professionals who built the *Titanic*! The remainder of my speech was listened to on both sides of the house with sympathy and support.

Afterwards Jim Prior took me to the tea room and showed me off as a proud housemaster would his star pupil at the end of the school play. Sometimes the House has its rewards and the praise of one's peers is the greatest that the Commons has to offer.

CHAPTER 20

A Sideways Move

In November 1984, William Waldegrave asked me if I would become Patrick Jenkin's parliamentary private secretary. Patrick was secretary of state for the environment. He was a considerate, civilised man who spent a political lifetime serving the Party and doing whatever he was asked to with enormous application and determination. Unlike his dangerous son, Sir Bernard, who has divided the Party and threatens to ruin the country through his advocacy of Brexit regardless, Patrick was a Theory Y manager. He had been made responsible for abolishing the Greater London Council after the 1983 election, and had been duffed up by Jack Cunningham and Jack Straw in the House of Commons, and Ken Livingstone outside it. He needed someone to help him through what everyone thought would be his final year in the government.

As a way of getting to know each other, I suggested that Patrick and his wife Monica and Sissy and I should go for a weekend to Cornwall. We stayed at the Budock Vean Hotel on the Helford River, where he was surprised by the recognition and admiration he received from the guests. His morale picked up.

We spent a couple of hours at the Helford oyster beds, which were run by Len Hodges, who I had known since I was a child. Len explained how his business was being destroyed by flakes of Tributyltin anti-fouling paint falling off the bottom of yachts. This caused havoc with his oysters, mutating their shape and preventing the spread of new spats (colonies). Tributyltin has been described as one of the most harmful substances knowingly introduced into the marine environment. The ICI factory on Merseyside that made it lobbied hard for its retention, supported by famous yachtsmen like Ted Heath.

Len gave us all a dozen of his finest local delicacies. We took them home and Patrick was violently sick all night but his resolve was unaffected – he had been horrified by the misshapen oysters – and the substance was banned. In gratitude, Len Hodges told me I could pick up any wild oysters and mussels that I could find in perpetuity on his riverbed concessions. Unfortunately, two years later he disappeared off to Cyprus with his girlfriend, and I was threatened with being arrested for theft by the new managers when they caught me taking up Len's offer.

There were two big issues facing the Department of the Environment: the introduction of the poll tax and the never-ending struggle to get local authorities to control their spending. The Treasury, under Nigel Lawson, were in formidable mood and determined to cut as hard as they could, particularly in housing. With his reputation already dented, the secretary of state was between a rock and a hard place. Kenneth Baker was nominally in charge of the preparations for introducing the poll tax but once he realised its potential for calamity, the details were left to William Waldegrave, parliamentary undersecretary at the Department.

As so often is the case, the devil is in the detail, and it was the detail of how to collect the charge that was never properly addressed. The real problem lay in an unthought-through manifesto promise that now could not be abandoned. The prime minister had been sold on the principle by a slick presentation from William and Kenneth, which did not dwell on the mechanics. The other bugbear was, as always, the Treasury. They never believed in the politics of the tax and they were determined to reduce further the Treasury subvention to local government. So, the tax was set at an individual level, which led to riots and the loss of Tory Scotland. The result was a controversial new tax which was inadequately funded by central government. The outcome: political disaster, followed by a U-turn, which in the end cost the Treasury twice as much as they would have paid had they not cut the government contribution. So, the tax turned out to be financially uncollectable and politically unacceptable. I learnt enough never to introduce it into Northern Ireland when I became minister for the environment there.

I helped Patrick to write his speeches and prepare answers to parliamentary questions. I organised backbenchers to support him in debates and statements, but I spoke little on the floor of the House. I had one devastating setback when I forgot a supplementary question I had intended to ask following the murder of nine policemen in Newry and was left sinking to my seat in total confusion. It shattered my self-confidence for several months and not even friends reminding me that Churchill had once dried up in a major debate could console me. I was not Churchill!

At the end of November 1984, I took the train to Brighton to see John Wakeham, the chief whip and a close friend of Jim Prior's. He was still in hospital because of the injuries he had suffered the night of the bombing. His wife, Roberta, had slipped away to her death, lying alongside him, crushed by the falling masonry. His legs had been terribly badly injured and it was far from certain at the time I saw him whether he would ever walk again. At his bedside, he told me as he recuperated, that he was recovering because he had drunk a tremendous amount of water, something his consultant had instructed him to do shortly after his arrival in intensive care. Others who could not died. His bravery saw him through to a full recovery. I left with a clear signal that it would not be long before I would be back in Northern Ireland.

The prime minister allocated one of her most charming, long-serving and dedicated private secretaries to become John's personal assistant. A year or so later, to everyone's delight, they married.

The following summer, my family and I went on holiday to Brittany with the Pattens, where I attempted to teach Chris to waterski. This experience was like pulling a tethered seal at high speed just below the surface of the water. After two seawater enemas, he decided to try a different sport. We all knew the government reshuffle was due early in September, and what the moves for us were likely to be. What we did not know was that Chris had left the wrong telephone number with his private office for where we were staying. After two weeks in Brittany we left to spend the final week of our holiday in Cornwall while the Pattens remained in France.

Sure enough, while we were in Cornwall, the reshuffle was announced on the afternoon of Monday 3 September. I huddled with my family around the phone, waiting for a call from Downing Street that never came. The first call that did come was at 7 o'clock the next morning. It was the BBC asking me to comment on the announcement that Tom King was to be the secretary of state for Northern Ireland. As Tom was a neighbour of mine and had started his political career in Chippenham, I was able to give him glowing references, although disappointment at not hearing about my own fate was itching at the lining of my stomach. The next caller was

Patrick Jenkin to tell me he had been sacked, and how nicely the prime minister had fired him. He now had no idea what he was going to do. I asked him if he had been able to put in a word for me. There was a pause then, 'I'm terribly sorry,' he said. 'I was so keen to stop her getting rid of George Young that I completely forgot about you!'

The third call was from Chris Patten's private office in Belfast. Number 10 had been trying to get hold of him but no one could find out where he was. One of Chris's permanent secretaries, Maurice Hayes, had heard my interview with the BBC on Tom King and cleverly construed that I would probably have the right number. I had. But I had been trying to phone him and there was no reply. It was not until later that I discovered a similar family drama to mine had played itself out on the other side of the Channel. Chris could not understand why he had not heard from Number 10 and, in the end, decided to take his family out for the day. It was only later that evening that Number 10 finally tracked him down.

After another anxious night, the call I had been waiting for arrived. I was to phone the prime minister at noon. From a callbox in Manaccan, overlooking the Helford River where I had been brought up, I telephoned Number 10. Unfortunately, the prime minister had had to leave for Birmingham but her private secretary on foreign affairs, Charles Powell, informed me that I was to succeed my best friend as a minister in the Northern Ireland office. I heard later that he was reported to have said that if Tasmania had been available, it would have more sense to send me there! I went to have my hair cut and we set off for home.

A day later, another call. 'Minister, this is your private secretary Aileen Porter. I wish to make arrangements for you to come to the Province as quickly as possible.' It did not take long for the family to start accusing me of 'ministerialitis' at the first hint of any pomposity. As my eight-year-old daughter remarked, parliamentary undersecretary in Northern Ireland is hardly the Cabinet.

Having Tom King as boss had one immense advantage. Because his home was so close to mine, I could catch a lift with him from Lyneham, the nearby RAF airfield, when he flew to Belfast at the start of each week. Usually travel was the curse of an England-based minister working in Ulster but not for me. The following Monday, 10 September 1985, I was on my way. It never occurred to me that it would be nearly seven years later that I would take my last plane back to Lyneham. As soon as we touched down at Short's private airport in Belfast, Tom and I sped off in different directions. Aileen and I sat in the back of my car with two armed RUC escorts in the front. Issues of security would go on to dominate and occasionally haunt mine and my family's lives.

One of the escorts asked Aileen to move over as he wanted to brief me. 'To put it bluntly, Minister, I'm the man who shoots the man who shoots you. In other words, I can't get my gun out until he's got his out!'

I was the biggest-spending minister in the Northern Ireland government, responsible for health and social services, environment, local government, housing, transport and, bizarrely, construction rackets and social security fraud. After 1989, I swapped health and social services to become minister of the economy.

I was effectively two ministers with separate departments. I had two private offices in different buildings, employing most of the Northern Ireland Civil Service. My principal private secretary had to decide how I divided my time between my offices in Parliament Buildings and Dundonald House. I was the face of the government for the delivery of most public services. Quite quickly I became a well known face on television and voice on local radio. I travelled around the Province visiting councils, hospitals (including Belfast City, the most expensive new hospital in Europe, largely because of terrorist-inspired kickbacks), shops, offices, charities, building sites, social security offices and, after 1989, factories. I spent three to four days a week in Northern Ireland, flying over early on Monday mornings and returning home late on a Thursday evening. Sometimes I had to go backwards and forwards mid-week if the Whips wanted me in Westminster. I also had an impressive office in Old Admiralty Buildings looking over Horse Guards Parade, and a dingy office in the basement of the House of Commons which I hardly visited.

In Belfast I stayed at Stormont House. The old speaker's home had been converted into a guest house, where ministers and visiting, London-based NIO civil servants had bedrooms, sized according to rank. There was also a section where the security services had their offices. There was a singing chef, called Frank McIlmurray, who claimed he was related, and a family team, led by Larys together with her daughters, who kept the place clean and tidy. The décor was worthy of a two-star seaside hotel. The food was plentiful, if lacking in imagination. The place was always bustling.

During my first weekend back in Gloucestershire, we were visited at our home by Inspector Bristow of Gloucester Special Branch. He explained that, although we lived in Gloucestershire, my safety would be primarily the responsibility of the Wiltshire police as I was member of parliament for Chippenham. The house would be secured by the Home Office and the Met. He had a large number of political targets, including several royals, living on his patch and his budget was extremely tight. If I was to be shot at home, his chief constable would not be too happy but the blame could be passed elsewhere. On the other hand, his colleague, the Wiltshire chief constable would have his job on the line if I was knocked over in Chippenham. Wiltshire Special Branch provided me with armed cover while I was on duty but they were supposed to turn back at the Gloucester border and not enter my property. I was not sure whether the IRA was aware of these arrangements. The system of county police forces in England can make the fight against terrorism more difficult. Collaboration between forces was often poor, procedures were frequently different, equipment was not always compatible, objectives not always the same.

Bristow then proceeded to tour the house. One of his first suggestions was that we should place bars on the downstairs windows. But on reflection he advised against it, as the IRA would attach timing devices to the bars which would blow through the windows and cut Sissy in half. This was not much of a reassurance to a young mother with three children. I saw no evidence that Theory Y played any part in Gloucestershire police training manuals!

The Home Office nominated a company to install the alarms, which turned out to be more effective at barricading us in than keeping the terrorists out. On one occasion we had a fire in the flat at the top of the house. It burnt through the electric cables and plunged everything into darkness, thereby making it impossible to ring out and impossible for the fire engine to get in. It was fortunate that, fumbling around in the dark, Sissy found an override key to the front gate to let in the firemen with their hoses.

Later, when the threat was deemed to be lower, the system was revised and privatised. The first alarm call was answered by a call centre in Cardiff, from where it was routed to Birmingham, and then to the police in Cheltenham, who rang Cirencester, who then informed the local bobby. He used to come round most Sunday mornings on his bicycle for coffee to see if we were okay. One day when he rang the bell, I asked him to identify himself. 'Don't play silly buggers with me,' came the retort. I asked him what he would do if he really thought we were being attacked. He said he would wait and see!

Several years later Bristow rang me up to tell me he had been on a Home Office-sponsored course about the IRA. He had not appreciated how well educated they were. He was concerned that they might have a better idea of famous political targets living locally than he had. And he asked me whether I could give him the names of any prominent local personalities who had Irish connections.

I asked him whether he knew Sir Crispin Tickell, our former ambassador at the UN who was now a master of an Oxford College and one of the world's leading experts on the environment. He was also a confidant of Mrs Thatcher, and a Dublin landlord. The inspector looked incredulous. 'What does this man do?' he asked. I repeated Crispin's shortened CV. 'Excuse me,' said the Inspector, 'but how can Mr Tickell do all this and run a pub in Dublin?'

There were disturbing times, such as when Alistair McAlpine, a former Conservative party treasurer, had his house blown up. We were told that all openings in our home should be closed and bolted. We had a cat flap in the washroom, under our daughter's bedroom. It was the ideal place for the IRA to insert a bomb and it was only a few feet from our heating fuel tank. To move the cat flap elsewhere was, for a variety of reasons, impossible. In any event, the advice was to block it up. Should we get rid of my daughter's cat or explain to her why she could no longer sleep in her beloved bedroom? In the end, after much heart searching, we decided to do nothing.

There were comical moments. I was once invited by the bishop of Bristol to a village church wine and cheese buffet, only to find him green faced at the time of my arrival. Apparently, the sniffer dog had cocked his leg repeatedly against the trestle tables, snuffling at the sandwiches rather than sniffing out the explosives.

Security was not so intrusive or suffocating as it was for the secretary of state, Tom King, or the security ministers, such as Nick Scott, John Cope and John Stanley. Stanley found the risks hardest to handle and stories abounded about his instructions to keep the roads clear for his passing. He once held up the secretary of state's convoy at a roundabout outside Aldergrove as he was being driven to the airport. The strange part was that the public had no idea who he was.

I always felt reassured to have armed policemen protecting me wherever I went. Those who lived under constant threat were, among others, local unionist MPs, senior councillors, RUC officers and builders who worked on police stations. They had to be on constant alert for ambushes or bombs taped under their cars.

It was worse for the wives. Sitting at home, not knowing where their men were and not knowing if their homes might be subject to sudden surprise attack. Sissy was once phoned in the middle of the day by a police officer who told her to stay inside and lock all the doors – an armoured response unit with sniffer dogs was on its way. It later turned out that the local publican had seen a man with a gun – which turned out to be a fishing rod – nearby.

On a number of other occasions our home address was discovered concealed on and in the bodies of IRA scouts sent out to reconnoitre targets (such as Ian Gow) for assassination. In the eyes of the IRA we were legitimate targets. We had to be sensible with our precautions and get on with our lives. Given how protected ministers and their families were, it was probably more likely that we'd be run over than killed.

CHAPTER 21

Ulster During the 1980s

B RITISH POLICY ON Northern Ireland was cross-party and with the exception of a few fringe mavericks such as Jeremy Corbyn, had followed exactly the same lines for years. There were three strands: security, political and economic/social. Northern Ireland was ruled directly from Westminster by British ministers.

There were minimal powers delegated to local politicians. Security and political policy was enforced by English ministers who, for the most part, were ignorant of Ireland and its history. Political and security programmes were administered by English officials from the Home Office, the Ministry of Defence and the Foreign Office. By and large, they were neutral, and they did not favour one side of the community over the other but they often operated in secretive silos with their own agendas. They accepted there was no security solution and that without a security solution, there would be no political solution. They relied on the local population to reject paramilitaries and terror as economic prosperity isolated the terrorists in the violent swamps they occupied.

The secretary of state was supposed to be the emperor but, in reality, he was constrained by warlords on every side. These included the RUC (Royal Ulster Constabulary), who reported to the chief constable, and the Army, who reported to the secretary of state for defence. International political relationships were determined by the Foreign Office, and the Roman Catholic church, which reported to Rome. Health was a branch of the Department of Health and Social Security in London. The budget was determined by the Treasury in London.

The only areas of real discretion were housing, planning, industry, transport, tourism and environment. These were administered by the Northern Ireland Civil Service, and the junior minister in charge of these delegated powers was me. The silos were exaggerated by the so-called necessity for 'security'. Loose words could cost lives. This mantra led to cover-up, cock-up and a culture of blame. In the case of the army and the police, Queen's Regulations applied. Theory X management reigned supreme. No one could be trusted, orders had to be obeyed, and challenging superiors' judgements or decisions was tantamount to insubordination.

During my first week, I asked if I could go up to Derry to see Paddy Doherty to discuss his inner-city initiatives. Ministers were warned they should avoid Paddy as having connections. Of course he had connections – Eileen, his wife, had been looking after the McGuinness family whenever Martin was in prison, and Paddy and his ten children were all strong republican sympathisers. This did not stop Paddy having eclectic taste in the people he worked with. In his efforts to support the deprived of Derry, he became close friends with the Prince of Wales and worked hand in hand with Glenn Barr, the well known loyalist.

How was it acceptable for me to visit him as parliamentary private secretary to the secretary of state one week and not as parliamentary undersecretary the next? In fact, there was another much more telling argument. According to the local superintendent of police (who travelled up to Londonderry every day from Bangor as it was too dangerous for him to live there), it would take five hundred of his men together with an army battalion to ensure my safety. These men would be required to guard the roads taking me there, so they would become easy targets for IRA snipers. Finally, the cost of mounting such operation would be entirely disproportionate. The superintendent had no idea who I was; nor did he much care what happened to me. All that concerned him was ensuring that if anything went wrong, he would not be blamed. Such behaviour handed victory to the terrorists without them having to lift a revolver. Ministers were cooped up, like frightened rabbits in their burrows, terrified of being seen by the public. So much for democratic accountability.

I was determined to get out and discover how other troubled places had changed their fortunes. Having considered visiting Beirut, we chose Naples as the best place to go. My sister-in-law's family came from there and her uncle, Gianni Ferrante, was the senior thoracic surgeon at the main Naples hospital. We found a brilliant, young, left-wing, Northern Irish, Italian-speaking civil servant called Douglas McIldoon. Together, we planned a visit to discover how the Neapolitans managed to attract so much more funding from Europe for their city than Belfast.

The British consul general was surprised to receive a ministerial visit from Northern Ireland. The posting was usually filled by a not-very-high-ranking official, near to retirement, whose major role was to help sailors stay out of the brothels when the Royal Navy came to call, and to find funds for penniless backpackers who had been waylaid in the city. He arranged a splendid lunch on the seafront and thirty Italians appeared. They proceeded to yell at each other for the next hour, at the end of which the enormous, grey-bearded Neapolitan who was sitting next to me picked me up and kissed me. He explained that at the table were representatives of the 'Commune', the city and the region. For the first time in their memory, they were being asked to give a presentation to a visiting dignitary on how Naples was governed. He explained that it had taken an hour of shouting to come to a common position. He gave me another kiss. The consul general beamed. Silos were not unique to Belfast! The presentation was seamless, sophisticated and all embracing. Naples was clearly the European city of the future.

That evening the mayor gave a reception and I asked him for a message to take back to Belfast. 'Naples', he said, 'is a city full of *caca*, but amongst the *caca* are some diamonds.' The issue for the city was how to reduce the shit and grow the diamonds. When I arrived back in Belfast a local reporter asked me how we had fared and what we had discovered at significant public expense. I told him that Belfast 'was a city full of shit and we had no effing diamonds'.

In the consul general's office were all the presentational plaques of the Royal Navy ships that had visited the Port over the previous fifty years. Amongst them was one from HMS *Kilmorey*. When the tiny minesweeper had been in Naples and what it had been doing there, no one seemed to know, and there was no record in the log. Captain the earl of Kilmorey appears to have used her as his personal yacht at some time in the 1960s!

As Chris Patten had departed, he had whispered in my ear that the key to the regeneration of Belfast rested on the river Lagan. By the early 1980s, the city was in trauma. The centre had been bombed relentlessly for ten years. Most new buildings were tasteless, cheap concrete and characterless. They reflected the mood of the people. The Lagan was dirty. There was no private housing in the city core. The hotels were few, their accommodation barely adequate, their service indifferent and their food often stodgy. With depressingly few exceptions, restaurants came and went. Confidence had drained away as barbed wire spread like ivy. Security checks delayed shoppers while armoured cars rumbled through the streets, the soldiers with blackened and unsmiling faces. The City Hall and the city fathers had had their powers castrated by the British government.

But there was a sliver of opportunity. The law demanded the publishing of a new city plan and the drafting of that plan allowed us a chance to fit all the jigsaw pieces together to give us a whole that we could then promote as the biggest series of opportunities for the city for over a century. We were determined to make the plan the vehicle on which the hopes and dreams of the citizens would ride. We had to find ways of capturing the public imagination. We faced considerable opposition. One contentious criticism came from the Bishop of Down and Connor, Cahal Daly. Research had shown that, small as Belfast is, very few of those living in West Belfast ever went near the city centre unless they worked there. He argued that to stop parts of the city becoming no-go ghettos as far as employment and investment was concerned, we should concentrate on a programme in West Belfast that would provide local jobs for local people.

I believed that such a plan could lead to disaster. Not only did the levels of lawlessness in that part of the city make success highly unlikely, but failure would reinforce isolation in what were already slums. We had to find alternatives that would create safe areas where both communities could mix and match. The tribes already lived apart and I could think of no way to attract private capital into districts that were without skills and were beset by intimidation and violence.

The political pressure on the Catholic church came partly from Gerry Adams' constant reiteration of the need for two thousand industrial jobs in his constituency, West Belfast – a bleat which he knew to be fatuous. What company would invest in a war zone! What we could prove was that 50 per cent of those in West Belfast who did have jobs worked in the city centre. What we had to do was provide thousands more to attract the alienated young and to provide work that they could do and be paid for. We also knew that the IRA would use their newly acquired horde of Libyan Semtex to stop us.

Laganside, Royal Avenue and Great Victoria Street would be the hub of our efforts to provide offices, shops, cinemas, culture and food. We had to create a quality of life that everyone from everywhere would enjoy.

When I arrived in 1985 there were small shoots of improvement. It all depended on imaginative leadership. Luckily for me the undersecretary in charge of urban regeneration at the Department of the Environment (DOE) was Gerry Loughran. He was one of the few Catholics at or near the top of the Northern Ireland Civil Service and the only one who has ever been permanent secretary of the Northern Ireland Civil Service. He is exceptionally able and can be exceptionally provocative. He and I started off with a ferocious row when I ordered the final paragraph of one of his draft press releases to be amended and he changed it back again and released it in its original form. Peace was brokered and for the next seven years Gerry was to be my right-hand man in almost every initiative that we promoted in Belfast. Moreover, those he had around him had humour, optimism and guile against which no obstacle stood a chance.

Shopping in central Belfast was a mess. With a few notable exceptions, the great retailers boycotted Belfast out of fear of the bomb and ignorance of the opportunities. Many of the old, established retailers and department stores had closed. Their frontages were boarded up, the offices above deserted. But there was one golden opportunity and it became known as CastleCourt. Could we get it off the ground?

It was an enormous project of 350,000 square feet of shops, 180,000 square feet of offices and parking for 1,600 cars. It would cost around sixty-five million to build and a further twenty million to fit out. But without an anchor tenant and without a government grant the project was doomed. There were other questions. Who would become the long-term investors once it was complete? Could CastleCourt compete with new edge-of-town developments? Could we entice the people of Belfast back to the city centre? Most worrying of all, what would the IRA do to CastleCourt?

As important to me was what it would look like. The first design more closely resembled a Victorian jail – far from sympathetic to the 'the beaux arts Grand Canyon' of graceful Victorian buildings that were also awaiting restoration along Royal Avenue. I was alarmed at the prospect of a three-hundred-metre-long, unadorned brick frontage. I was determined only to agree to a building of international significance, with the finest street furniture and street lighting. Ministers have little enough to be remembered for by history for what they do or do not do and I was absolutely determined that my legacy would not be wrecking an immense opportunity for Belfast. The development team would have to go back to the drawing board. I pledged to find another anchor tenant to replace

Selfridges, our first-choice – they had demanded a pitiful rent and a free fit-out.

I also requested that the building should be faced in glass. CastleCourt was to be the defining landmark of the city's new confidence. At a meeting with the planners this suggestion was greeted by silence, then disbelief, and then a fairly acrimonious discussion. 'Glass, Minister? You must be mad.'

'What will happen to all the shoppers when the IRA blow it up?' interjected a doubting Thomas.

'Should we build it out of concrete blocks?' I retorted. The shoppers would not differentiate much between being decapitated by flying glass or crushed to death by falling masonry. I was not to be budged. Roy Adams – who was managing director of BDP, one of the UK's most original architectural practices, and who was then in charge of their Belfast office – supported me. Within a few weeks we came up with a spectacular design.

The total development covered a massive eight and a half acres and, when completed, would create two thousand new jobs. Our secret fear was that the IRA would not let us finish the building without destroying the confidence of future tenants. During the three construction years from 1987 to 1990, we held our breath and, despite the best endeavours of the RUC and the builders, the IRA did what they could to destroy our 'diamond'. In all, during construction, there were four bomb attacks and an endless number of hoaxes, the last one just a week before we were due to open. The Department insisted on the most rigorous security monitoring. The car park was built like a fortress, but the fear of an uncontrolled fire before all the systems were in place was a constant worry.

We had also devised another strategy to try to neutralise the terrorist menace. Adams and his followers had criticised the project for introducing low-paid service jobs while the profits would find their way into the pockets of greedy English shop owners. We persuaded Debenhams, the anchor tenant, to take on 150 young trainee shop assistants from West Belfast, many of whom came from families with republican connections. We sent them over for training in their Liverpool store. Once they started work, the attitude in West Belfast changed. (Some witless Tory MP complained on the floor of the House we were giving in to terrorists by employing their children.) The only downside to the success of this neutralising plan was every time I was seen in the complex, there would be a coded bomb threat from the IRA within ten minutes. On the opening day in 1990, the winner of the free hamper as the first shopper through the door happened to be the mother of a Maze inmate.

We had CastleCourt up and running. We had at last the foundation stone on which to expand the city, east and west, north and south. By 1990 we had all the more major multiples setting up shop and more were in the pipeline. In 2017 CastleCourt had sixteen million visitors a year and the sales densities ranked in the top 10 per cent in the United Kingdom.

CastleCourt was big but it was not the big one. That was Laganside. Bob Crane, who was managing director of the *Belfast Telegraph*, asked me to meet and have dinner with a few of his senior managers and reporters during my first fortnight in Northern Ireland. His boardroom wall was covered with a massive painting of the city which so fascinated me that I failed to take in the erudite and subtly phrased briefing they were keen to register with their new apprentice minister. Through the centre of the tapestry ran a great silver sword – the Lagan – and yet on each bank there was nothing but dereliction, scrapyards and coal tips. The city had turned its back on a diamond and allowed it to become dirty, dark and smelly. Here was a chance to do something.

Up to the mid-80s, capital investment in the city had been paid almost entirely from the British exchequer. Now we had to market ourselves in competition with a hundred other cities (including Dublin and Glasgow) to persuade investors to pour their money into Belfast. We had schemes such as Urban Development Grants and we had funds for clearing sites and putting in basic services, but if Laganside was to succeed, the ratio would have to be at least five pounds of private investors' cash to each pound of government funds.

Gerry Loughran and his team started on a search for consultants to help us design and promote a scheme for the river. A group of us went to Baltimore and Boston to see how Jim Rowse and Steve Coyle, the legendary city strategists, had reworked their waterfronts. The Americans are so brash and so certain of success that nothing appears inconceivable to them, and, as a result, often nothing is. As many of those involved in Boston were of Irish extraction, they were happy to help. We soon realised that we would have to build one step at a time and that the key would be how we organised ourselves, how we marketed ourselves and how we could make a success of the first site. If that went well, we believed that the rest would follow.

After his involvement and success with CastleCourt, Roy Adams was an obvious choice as architect but we needed a Belfast equivalent to Boston's energetic Steve Coyle. Gerry came up with Peter Hunter, who I later discovered was the designer behind the redevelopment of Salford Quays outside Manchester.

I could not really believe that Gerry was serious when he introduced me to this bespectacled, shy, slightly dishevelled, unassuming, uncertain and uncharismatic man. Then Peter started to tell me what he proposed to do. Step-by-step he took me along the Lagan. There would be a weir here, a private housing estate alongside a river walkway there, a massive new theatre complex, an international hotel, a leisure island, a marina for seagoing boats, a working maritime museum, 200,000 square feet of office space, 100,000 square feet of speciality shopping, a riverside garden, a closed channel for canoeing, a gateway centre for schools and tourists, cinemas, bars, discos, restaurants and health clubs. The traffic would be redirected, and new rail and road bridges would be built. 'This, Minister,' he concluded, 'will make the Lagan one of the most attractive rivers in Europe and I'm sure, Minister, that together we can sell it to both investors and the dear people of Belfast!' The man was a genius.

And to turn Peter Hunter's and Roy Adams' remarkable plans into life we founded the Laganside Company. For the chairman we picked James, Duke of Abercorn. 'Jimmy the Duke', as he is occasionally irreverently referred to by his escort, was no patronising, patrician figurehead. He is a super salesman, a 6 foot 2, former Grenadier who exudes enthusiasm, optimism and energy. He also knows a lot of people around the place. Once he had taken up the challenge there was no suitable city not visited, no property developer left unassailed and no conference opportunity ducked. Wherever and whenever there was the sniff of something that could help our cause, James would be after it.

We launched Laganside officially on 10 March 1987. We claimed the plan would bring £280 million of investment into a 1.5 mile stretch of river. Sammy Wilson, the DUP Lord Mayor of Belfast, boycotted the launch. But various landowners, estate agents, bankers, builders, lawyers and accountants who could see the potential didn't.

Two months later we gave permission for new road and rail links, and we also disclosed the details of the new weir which would control the tide and hide the smell of the mudflats. Even the scrap metal men around the Abercorn basin began to accept we were in earnest, though some perversely continued to claim that scrap was a visitor attraction.

From 1989 onwards, when I became minister of economic development as well as of the environment, it became much easier to coordinate the activities of the Belfast Development Office and Industrial Development Board into focusing and inviting potential investment. The silos had gone!

But the new Belfast had to be used in a way that would improve the lot of all. Much of the city remained in trauma. Whole districts were in deep shock, depressed and undermined by violence, with rates of morbidity and unemployment that were unacceptable in a civilised country. What could we to do to bring economic and social freedoms to a people on the rack of terrorist tyranny?

I was starting to feel that I was making progress but I needed a mate. Someone I could unwind with, spell everything out to, without fear of it being repeated or leaked; someone who knew the local scene but was not wedded too closely to anyone or anything, and someone prepared to get stuck in and back me up.

Two years previously, in January 1986, I had been at the British Irish Association Conference in Oxford – an annual attempt to bring all sides together but boycotted by Sinn Féin and the DUP, thereby limited in its influence, and nicknamed by Chris Patten 'Toffs against terrorism'. I was propping up the bar when a shuffling, round, large-headed, bald, slightly waffly figure tugged at my elbow and said, 'I'm Hugh O'Neill. We were at school together. I was older than you, and always thought you were rather interesting, though I never fancied you!'

Hughie has a beautiful home outside Ballymena. He comes from a long and distinguished line of Anglo-Irish aristocrats. His Portuguese cousin Hugo is the O'Neill of the O'Neills, direct descendant of the line of the second earl of Tyrone who had led the flight of the earls with the first earl of Tyrconnell in the seventeenth century. His grandfather was the first speaker of the Northern Ireland Parliament and his father, Phelim O'Neill, was the leader for a short time of the Ulster Unionists and then founder of the Alliance Party. He had not lasted long with the unionists. After tolerating a three-hour meeting of the Unionist Council in his drawing room, he looked out of the French windows and exploded, 'One of my heifers has got more sense than all of you put together!'

Hugh had had a successful career as a 'debs' delight', which was surprising looking at him, although he must have looked very dashing in his National Service Irish Guards uniform and bearskin! He was at one time financial editor of the *Irish Times* and a feature writer on the *Financial Times*. He ran two very successful French restaurants on the Brompton Road near Harrods. By 1985 he was casting around for something else to do. He and his beautiful, chic wife, Sylvie, were not sure whether they should live on their wonderful farm at the foot of Slemish, among the Antrim hills, or move back permanently to London. I told him it was time to come home to Ulster and help. He had an inbred desire for public service – as all his family had over the centuries.

Northern Ireland Airports, which owned Aldergrove and Belfast City, needed a new chairman. The Department had put forward a worthy list of unimaginative, mainly Protestant, locals. I wanted Hughie. Gerry Loughran had a fit. Firstly, he had had to swallow the duke. Now here was another old Etonian toff mate of the minister's being put forward. I told him jokingly that there is no point having power if you can't share it with your friends. This led to a further explosion. But Hugh sailed through the interviews and went on to do a magnificent job in the most trying of times. He developed new routes that transformed travel to North America and Europe. He had style and taste. By the time he left, the International Airport at Aldergrove was ripe for privatisation.

A few years later the Northern Ireland Tourist Board chairmanship came up. At this time, no tourists came to Northern Ireland. Gerry Loughran did not object to Hughie's name going forward. Hugh established a working relationship with Bord Fáilte for an all-Ireland marketing campaign, which brought a massive increase in holiday visitors, particularly from the United States.

Hugh realised that good food would be key to any drive to attract tourists. At the time, Ulster food was basic. Although surrounded by sea, fish could only ever be procured with chips. Anything exotic – like oysters, lobsters or monkfish – was airfreighted to Hong Kong. Ulster plates were more typically piled high with overcooked slabs of beef, swimming in thick brown floury gravy, lumpy mashed potatoes, soggy cabbage, and carrots and peas as hard as bullets.

Hugh started the Taste of Ulster and reintroduced local, well cooked, uncomplicated and delicious specialities, such as grilled Loch Neagh eels and whole roast whiting. Hugh gave the best ten years of his life to making Northern Ireland an entertaining and interesting place, which was welcoming and attractive to visitors and where the food was reasonably priced and delicious. Despite all Hugh's efforts he never received any public recognition, which was disgraceful, and for which, I am afraid, I must share some of the blame.

CHAPTER 22

Making Belfast Work

IN JULY 1988 we launched the Making Belfast Work programme. We divided the city into blocks of several thousand electors and put a young bright, high-flying civil servant in charge of each one. The plan was that these team leaders could cut across the departmental silos, and articulate the wishes and needs of the local communities. It was Theory Y in action, with an annual £20 million budget per team, but some of the leaders could not let go of the umbilical cords that tied them to their sponsoring department and were scared of risk-taking that might lead to a failed project and a career black mark.

But the laggards were more than offset by the likes of Kate Kelly, who had cut her teeth in Watts County, Los Angeles, and achieved wonders for women's groups across Belfast. The Making Belfast Work Initiative was a vital part of our strategy to listen to and bring solutions to those who lived in paramilitary-dominated wards. It gave us direct access to voluntary groups and opportunities for those groups to wean their clients away from violence. The project brought us direct entry into every area of city life. Our objective was to encourage good and vilify evil. But it wasn't easy. The security forces and some of the departments felt that the action teams got in their way and as they saw it, undermined their tried-and-tested way of doing things.

The progress we made in improving the quality of life for many of the citizens was transformative. It was Theory Y in action. It brought the delivery of public services much closer to the communities in which they operated. Other than the odd good news story on BBC Business Breakfast, screened at six in the morning, the national media's grim coverage continued to flow. We needed to find a way to give Belfast an opportunity to celebrate what the city was, is and could become. We needed a celebration at which everyone could enjoy themselves, learn about one another, and be proud of themselves and the city in which they lived. We wanted to show the world there was another side to Belfast. We decided on a year-long party.

Billy Pinkerton, from the Belfast Development Office, had told me soon after I arrived that they were negotiating to bring the Tall Ships to Belfast. If this visit went ahead, then we would have the anchor for our year of celebration. Liverpool had its International Garden Festival, thought up by Michael Heseltine after the Toxteth riots. Dublin had celebrated its millennium in 1988, although no one seemed quite sure what had happened in 988. Glasgow was the European city of culture in 1990. Why shouldn't Belfast have a year to show off?

But if the venture was to succeed, we would have to embrace every aspect of the city's talents. We would have to attract international stars to play to the 'haves' but the 'have-nots' had also to be in the audience, and everyone had to work together to organise cultural, sporting, musical, commercial, historical, horticultural and religious spectacles. I wanted everyone to have a part. I also wanted it to be a party not for a day or a weekend or a month but for a year. From 1987 onwards, I told everybody that it was going to happen. We decided that 1991 would be the year, and the event would be known as the Best of Belfast.

I persuaded the slightly reluctant DoE officials to chip in £1.1 million towards the costs, on the understanding that every public pound was matched by a private donation. I got together an eclectic group of enthusiasts and believers, who also had quirky imaginations and strong views. We had a range of committees covering every aspect of the city's life. Because everyone was determined that the year was to succeed, it succeeded way beyond our hopes and expectations.

In all there were over four hundred events, starting with a Mozart concert. There was no triumphalism, no abuse – just people having fun. The highlight of the celebration was the arrival of the Tall Ships. Billy Pinkerton had twisted every arm and massaged every joint on the Tall Ships committee to persuade them to come. There were several doubters who, understandably, were worried about the safety of the crews and the image of their organisation should anything turn sour. The man most under pressure was the chairman of the Tall Ships committee, Lord Burnham. He was fortuitously a first cousin of my mother's and, as children, they used to spend Christmas together. So my mother was turned out. She complained bitterly that he was the most boring man she'd ever met and, anyway, he had broken her toys! Finally, though, she phoned him up and after half an hour reminiscing, he agreed to talk to me. 'It's completely mad,' he said. 'I can't think why anyone should want to go to Belfast, but for the sake of your grandfather Lionel, I can't stand in your way.' The Jewish side of my family had ridden to the rescue.

The Tall Ships are an awe-inspiring sight, but what was even more unforgettable was to see the thousands upon thousands of people spilling out of the Falls, the Shankill, the Ardoyne, Tigers Bay and East Belfast and all converging on the Pollock Dock. On 3 July the weather turned in our favour and for four wonderful days the people of Belfast forgot their troubles and came together in a seething mass of young and old, orange and green, rich and poor enjoying a unique family outing. The dock was open to all, and all came. A few of the RUC deserted their flak jackets and danced a jig to the Irish flute and whistle. Jimmy the Duke sailed off in *The Lord Nelson* with a group of disabled school children, leaving me with Hugh O'Neill, by that time chairman of the Tourist Board, complaining that the fast food outlets had more to do with Kentucky than Portaferry.

On the last evening Hugh organised a fireworks party that surpassed anything the city had ever seen before. The next day half a million people watched as the Tall Ships sailed away down Belfast Lough. On the Saturday those of us responsible for the organisation of the event mused over whether such an extraordinary congregation of the majority of Belfast people in one place, mingling together as if they were on a day out in Disneyland, held any long-term meaning. What we did not know was at that very moment the IRA were already plotting a final campaign to bring the city to its knees.

In 1991 there were other buds bursting into bloom. Northern Ireland has always been famous for its rose hybridisers. Dickson Roses of Newtownards remains one of the world's great rose growers, and one of the finest rose gardens in the world, the Sir Thomas and Lady Dixon Park, is in Belfast. The Rose Society of Northern Ireland had persuaded the Ninth World Rose Convention to hold their annual conference in Belfast during 1991.

Dickson had asked me to name a rose for the festival, hoping that I would choose a commercial and saleable floribunda. Instead, bored with the ubiquitous Chinatown, I saw a magnificent yellow hybrid tea rose, which was almost vulgar in its intensity, in the nursery. I picked it and named it Belfast Belle. 'Big, buxom and beautiful, just like Belfast,' I declared to a glum-faced Mr Dickson (yellow doesn't sell so well) and the accompanying press. I've never seen these roses in anyone else's garden but they are surviving splendidly in mine.

Having swallowed his disappointment, Mr Dickson asked for my help with something else. There was a famous and successful floribunda rose called Princess Michiko in honour of the Japanese Princess. Now that Emperor Hirohito had died, the princess had become empress. Could I find a way of securing the approval of the empress to have another rose named after her that was more saleable than Belfast Belle?

Luckily for me, that year there was a meeting of the Anglo-Japanese 2000 Group held at Turnberry in Scotland. One of the Japanese members at the meeting was Akio Morita, creator of the Sony Empire. I had tried many times to persuade him to build a factory in Northern Ireland but he always refused. He felt that if a small country could not live at peace with itself, he was not going to allow his staff to become entangled in an internal conflict about which he knew nothing.

My constant pleas for help, however, at least elicited sympathy for the difficulties we faced. He was chamberlain to the Japanese royal family, so I delicately broached the question of the rose. A few weeks later he called: he had spoken to the empress. She could not, of course, give formal approval to anything that bore her name as she wasn't in the business of advertising roses. Nevertheless, she would be very pleased to receive two dozen specimens to place in her rose garden if Mr Dickson would provide them.

Some three years later I went to lunch at the Imperial Palace with the then prime minister John Major after I had become minister of trade. I sat on the emperor's left. On my left was Akio Morita; the empress sat opposite. Halfway through the meal Morita gave me a nudge. I enquired if the empress recollected a small Irish company naming a rose after her. 'Oh yes,' she said, turning around. 'There they are, just outside the dining room window. I love them dearly and I can see them from many different parts of the palace.' We may not have obtained a factory from Sony but Dickson's had won the heart of the empress of Japan!

★

By the autumn of 1991, the Best of Belfast celebrations were attracting a wider audience, within and without the city. Investors were becoming a charging herd, scared of missing out on opportunities they had never before considered. If matters were going well for the city, they were not going nearly so well for Sinn Féin and the IRA. The IRA had been waging a vicious incendiary campaign for over a year, burning out shops in cities and town centres all across Northern Ireland. They employed women and girls as lookalike shoppers. Their mission was to slip hollowed-out cassettes filled with Semtex, and primed with a timer and detonator, into the pockets of dresses or to stuff them under seats of sofas and chairs in furniture stores. Late at night they exploded. By the time the fire brigade had been called and the keyholder turned up, the building would be incinerated.

A previous IRA campaign of throwing petrol bombs through windows had frightened most shopkeepers into fitting sliding metal shutters. These, the terrorists quickly realised, kept the fires burning inside while the firemen were marooned outside. For weeks that followed, while the assessors did their valuations, these blackened eyesores reminded all and sundry, particularly potential investors, that Northern Ireland remained far from normal.

As no insurance company would cover commercial properties for damage caused by paramilitary activity, the government was left to pick up the bills for the stock lost, and for the refurbishment and rebuilding. But the government did not pay out for any loss of profits while the shops were closed down and boarded up. The IRA were well aware of the knock-on effects their campaign was having on jobs and confidence. One outcome was that store staff had to stay long after closing time to search every item in case a bomb had been brought in during the day.

The IRA's largest triumph in the incendiary war was when they succeeded in burning down half of Sprucefield, the massive out-of-town shopping centre near Hillsborough. The incendiaries detonated in the early hours and with a force 8 south-westerly gale blowing, there was nothing any firefighter could do other than watch. The costs ran into tens of millions.

But even these calamities brought the occasional lighter moment. On a Monday morning in early January 1991, a week after the destruction at Sprucefield, I went into Marks & Spencer in Belfast city centre at the request of my son Andrew. Two Christmases before I had bought him a pair of black brogues there. He told me that they had developed a fault. To me, they looked as if he had been playing football with them for the previous twelve months. They certainly had never had any relationship with a shoe brush. 'I'm a poor student having to pay my poll tax, Dad. Please get me a credit.'

So, feeling ever-so-slightly guilty, I stepped on to the escalator to the first floor. As I reached the top, I could see an enormous kerfuffle. Staff were running in every direction. In the centre of the sales floor was a cluster of people all in a huddle. I was creeping towards the customer relations counter when an unmistakable voice roared, 'Dick, what are you doing here?' It was Sir Richard Greenbury, the chairman of Marks & Spencer. 'Look, Clinton,' he said, turning to Clinton Silver, his rather more diminutive deputy. 'Dick is coming to show solidarity with us after the fire at Sprucefield.' He came closer and pulled open my raincoat. 'He's got an M&S mac on, Clinton.' Then, after further investigation, 'He's wearing one of our blazers.' As this running commentary was conducted within hearing of the entire first floor, a small crowd had gathered. At that moment Rick noticed the plastic carrier bag I was trying to conceal. 'What have you got in there, Dick?' he blared as he grabbed it out of my hand. He pulled out one of Andy's dilapidated shoes. 'Oh, look at this, Clinton. Dick has come in for a return. What have you been doing with them? Do you live in a quarry? Have you never heard of shoe polish? You want your money back? You should be giving us money after what you've done to them and what's more, you have the cheek to bring them in here in a Tesco bag!'

Meanwhile a short woman wearing a violet mohair cap pulled down over her ears had pushed herself in between us and was following the incident intently. She poked my stomach and then, pointing upwards, said, 'Look at your big red nose, Mr Needham. The problem with you is that you drink too much!'

'That's right, missus,' declared Rick. 'That's one problem; the other is that if every customer we had wanted his money back after he wore a pair of shoes every day for a year in a quarry, we would be broke!'

With that I was dispatched with a push towards the customer relations counter, followed by a further stream of advice that I had better not try the same trick with the mac or the blazer. In spite of my uncomfortable encounter with them, Rick's and Clinton's presence in the store that day, together with their visit to the other M&S outlets, restored the confidence and morale of all the staff. They were friends in both need and deed.

I mounted a press campaign against Sinn Féin insisting they explain how such destruction could bring about a United Ireland. For once Gerry Adams was perhaps relieved that there was a government-imposed ban on the press reporting his public comments, for answer came there none.

The following November, the IRA decided that the moment had arrived for even greater spectaculars. The city was thronged with shoppers, many of whom had only recently picked up the courage to come back into the centre. November and December accounted for some 40 per cent of annual takings and late-night shopping was a big new attraction. The terrorist tactic was to leave hoax bombs night after night on the main approach arteries into the city. This paralysed the traffic, and caused frustration and annoyance, which the IRA knew would turn the customers away. By showing up the inability of the RUC and the army to keep the roads open, the IRA planned to crush the morale and self-confidence of the shopkeepers. Interspersed with the hoaxes was the odd real, big fertiliser bomb, which always caused enormous damage over a wide area, as the blasts curled around buildings, blowing in windows and doors, and scattering rubbish and debris in every direction.

Instantly I sensed that the IRA had decided to assault the very foundations on which we were trying to construct the restoration of Belfast's prosperity, normality and pride. If they could close down the city centre, day and night, the government would sustain a dreadful defeat, and the crusade to create an atmosphere in which both communities could work, drink, dance and sleep together would once more become a distant aspiration. The IRA had very clearly understood the dangers that our achievements posed for them. They now moved to restore the misery and confusion on which their power depended. Many in the NIO, the Army and the RUC appeared to have little realisation of just how dire the position was and what outcome would follow an IRA victory in shuttering up Belfast.

The secretary of state, the chief constable and the general officer commanding had regular meetings to discuss security, but ministers with other responsibilities were never invited. The absolute priority of the security forces was to avoid death and mutilations and so no corners could ever be cut. Any criticism of any existing procedure was met with irate disbelief that anybody unconnected with the army or police could offer a plausible alternative that might not further endanger the lives of police officers and soldiers. The very life of Belfast was bleeding away. The angry shopkeepers, many of whose businesses had been reduced to charcoal; the local and outside investors whose new buildings had been blasted; those who had received no recompense for the months when they earned no income; and the frustrated commuters – all turned to my Department and me for reassurance and explanation. But I was excluded from the security silo.

Fortunately for the people of Belfast, there was a lateral-thinking and fearless Brit who was deputy secretary for security in the NIO, John Ledlie. During his time in the Ministry of Defence he had been nicknamed 'Deadly Ledlie' and his time had come. I turned to him in rage and despair. We had to find ways of coordinating a response to the bombs and the hoaxes. We had to show that we could react more quickly to reassure the public, and we had to show that we could win.

Ledlie proposed a new, all-embracing security committee, chaired by me as minister of the environment, and consisting of the Belfast Coordinating Committee, the assistant chief constable for Belfast or a senior deputy, a colonel on the staff of the GOC, the head of the Belfast development office, the assistant secretary of the DoE in charge of roads in the city and members of the business community.

The army came more or less willingly, the RUC less so and even on occasion, not at all. It soon became clear that there were ways of diverting traffic around hoaxes which would lead to less disruption and that by bringing more bomb disposal officers into the city centre we could deal with incidents much more quickly. We instituted proper liaison between the traffic control centres in the city and the local RUC stations and army bases.

At the first meeting we made two startling discoveries. The immaculately uniformed RUC representative, with leather gloves and swagger stick, loftily informed us that, although he was well aware that the IRA were testing the city's defences and that bombs remained hidden and undetected in West Belfast, security cover was to be reduced because of restrictions on overtime and lack of manpower. We were also told that the police and army were considering closing off the city centre and searching everyone and everything that went into it. Such a double whammy would have produced cackles of delights from the IRA's Belfast active service units. Most of the efforts that we had put in to persuading senior RUC officers of the need and necessity to protect the social and economic leg of the government's strategy appeared to wither once the IRA attacks started. The security forces retreated to the comfort of their rule book.

We persevered. The overtime ban was overturned. The manpower problems were resolved and searches moved out to the west of the city. The flow of bombs diminished and the city started rumbling back to life.

Some bombs continued to explode with a deafening, jarring intensity. One lunchtime my office windows shook in their frames when an enormous device blew away Riverhouse in the High Street, over two miles from where I was sitting. Never before or since have I seen a room full of faces suddenly turn ashen. The fear for loss of life. The fear of shattered dreams and damaged aspirations. The stomach-churning fear for friends and family. After every explosion I would be down on the site as fast as I was able. The scenes were always horrible. Shards of glass everywhere, metal frames tilting out of windows, torn blinds blowing in the wind, a black hole five metres deep and twenty metres wide, where a car and its load had been parked. Sometimes the engine block would be discovered, embedded in a wall five storeys up. Often there would be a crowd standing around, watching the glaziers move in to sweep up and board up. Some would commiserate. Others would irritably challenge me on why the government was so impotent in defending their city and their jobs.

There were a few buildings that seemed always to take the brunt of the car bombs: the Europa Hotel and its neighbours the Grand Opera House and Windsor House. I promised that we would rebuild whatever was bombed and that in the case of ugly 1960s and 1970s buildings, we would do so using modern designs and modern materials. In a perverse way the IRA, I proclaimed, were doing the demolition work for us. But I knew that the reality was different. Money that would otherwise have gone to other budgets would have to be found to pay for the reconstruction work, with the result that spending on much-needed services would be curtailed. We could not tell the people of Ulster that not only had they to endure the bombing, but they would be penalised by paying for the aftermath as well.

The IRA capacity for perpetrating horror was limitless. In November 1991 they exploded a large bomb in a tunnel between the civilian and military wings of Musgrave Park Hospital. The explosion killed two people and wounded eighteen others, some dreadfully. I was the minister on duty and went straight to the scene. I was very, very angry. I told the television cameras that the men and women who had done this came from hell and that as surely as night follows day, they would return there. There was a huge public reaction to the bombing. The IRA was condemned, not least in its own communities.

By the first week of December the worst was over; by the end of the third week the city was thriving; and by the end of the January sales the shopkeepers had enjoyed one of their most lucrative seasons ever. The people of Belfast and its hinterland had not deserted their city. They had come back day by day, night by night, to work and enjoy themselves, despite the delays and disruption. They were not of a mind to surrender to the IRA. Within a month of my leaving the following April, I learnt that the six-month-old Belfast Coordinating Committee was to be disbanded. Sometimes I wondered whether the Italians were not making a better fist of running Sicily than some sections of the NIO were in Northern Ireland.

Over twenty years later I went to see 'Flash' McVeigh, who by then had become Sinn Féin chairman of the Belfast City Council's entertainment and culture committee. I was wanting him to support a massive new £120 million recreation and entertainment complex that would provide some nine hundred jobs in the city centre. 'We've never met,' he said. 'I was in the Maze when you were here. You used to get up our noses with all your claims about Belfast working. So we blew up Bedford House, Belfast's tallest office block, to teach you a lesson. I remember the look on your face when you appeared on the news that night.' I told him that I had just come from the bomb site where I had found my friend Hugh O'Neill sitting in a windowless office in an enormous Irish Guards overcoat, filling out his tax return. I told Flash that the building had been rebuilt at the expense of a new hospital. But he replied 'that's all behind us, and I can tell you those things now because we are all working for peace.'

The IRA didn't only blow up shopping centres and factories, they also tried to blow up ships.

John Parker, the chief executive of Harland and Wolff, had signed a cooperation agreement in 1989 with Kawasaki Heavy Industries (KHI) to build tankers. Part of the agreement was that the companies would share information on production methods. Teams of managers and supervisors from both sides travelled backwards and forwards between Belfast and Japan.

After several months John asked Dr Ohba, the president of KHI, to come to Belfast to see the fruits of the cooperation and to give a lecture. By coincidence, Dr Ohba was also a member of the Japanese side of the Anglo-Japanese 2000 Group so I had spent time with him at a number of conferences. He was squat and square with a mouthful of gold teeth. When he smiled, the sun came out. He also had a penchant for Margaret Thatcher, as did many of his colleagues. At every meeting of the group we were given the opportunity of meeting the prime minister. We sat in a circle around Margaret Thatcher and she asked questions of the Japanese participants. On occasion she would cross her legs and her skirt would ride up. She wore tight-fitting skirts and had very attractive knees. The middle-aged Japanese eyes goggled. She had, as President Mitterrand observed, 'La bouche de Marilyn Monroe et les yeux de Caligula.'

John Parker rang me up to say he would like to bring the chairman to see me in my London office on the way over to Belfast, where Dr Ohba was going to tour the yard and deliver his lecture. John had, over the years, become a friend. He came from a small farming background in the Mournes, not far from the Needham estates. He had worked his way up to the top of Harland & Wolff through a mixture of diligence and determination. He has a first-rate analytical and creative mind and gets on with everyone. He was the man you went to see with a problem and who gave you a solution rather than ten more problems. He was the Theory Y manager who gave credit to others rather than himself. He has deservedly had a stellar career both in the public and the private sectors.

All his talents were about to be tested. The meeting began at about ten o'clock and we were sipping coffee and exchanging pleasantries when a worried looking civil servant rushed in and gave John a note. John handed it to me. A bomb had been discovered on the *Fort Victoria*, a huge Navy supply ship that was being refitted in a dry dock. The yard was being evacuated.

John disappeared and came back giving me a thumbs up. He scribbled a note. 'Keep him talking while we sort it out.' Twenty minutes went by as Dr Ohba was encouraged to give us his life history. The civil servant returned with another note. The position had not changed. After a further twenty minutes John suggested taking Dr Ohba around Hyde Park so that Dr Ohba could have a smoke. While they were in the park the bomb went off and John was told that the ship was keeling over and about to sink (although I never understood how a ship could sink in a dry dock). John then developed an elaborate plan to keep the information from the chairman and allow the visit to the yard to go ahead uninterrupted. They flew to Belfast where Dr Ohba gave his lecture, toured the yard – where it was explained to him that flashing blue lights were a normal event – and returned to Japan none the wiser.

The job of running Harland & Wolff was unlike any other chief executive role in world shipbuilding. Unfortunately, despite all John's efforts and those of its owner, Theory Y pioneer Fred Olsen, Harland & Wolff never found a sufficiently profitable niche. The government turned down its request for support to build passenger liners, which with its history, it was ideally placed to undertake. The huge business in cruise liners went, with the government's backing, to German, French and Italian companies. Harland and Wolff finally went into administration in 2019.

Northern Ireland had a long and dark history of job discrimination. Each tribe employed their own. The shipyards and engineering works were overwhelmingly Protestant, as were the power stations. The linen mills, although mainly owned by Protestants, had a female Catholic workforce. As competition from the Far East bit, the factories started closing and unemployment soared on both sides. Because of the Troubles, attracting overseas or even local investment was a thankless task. It was made harder by a campaign run from America by Father McBride that attempted to introduce statutory quotas with the aim of redressing the imbalances. Local private sector management was overwhelmingly loyalist and the shrinking levers of economic power were held protectively by the unionist majority. The two main exceptions were the Northern Ireland Civil Service and the National Health Service, where Catholics were fairly represented. Up to the 1990s there had never been a Catholic head of the Civil Service or of the grant-giving Industrial Development Board. I changed that when I appointed John McGuckian to the chair of the IDB in 1991; that was followed after I left by the appointment of Sir Gerry Loughran as head of the Northern Ireland Civil Service in 2000.

In my first week I was invited to lunch by the board of the government-owned Transport Holding Company, which was responsible for trains, buses, airports and ports. The board was almost exclusively unionist. Pre-lunch drinks started at 12 o'clock in the Northern Ireland Railways directors' dining room and brandies were served at 2.45 p.m. Towards the end of the meal, the comfortably large Sir Miles Humphreys, the chairman of the railways, turned to me and said, 'Are you anything to do with the Kilmoreys from Kilkeel way?'

'Yes, I am the earl of Kilmorey,' I replied, pronouncing the name as it should be pronounced – Kilmurray.

'No, it's pronounced Kilmorey. Is that not right, Billy?' Sir Miles asked Sir Billy Hastings, owner of all the big hotels in Ulster.

'Yes,' said Billy, 'Kilmorey is the name.'

'No it is not,' I retorted.

'Don't come over here telling us how to pronounce your name,' came the response. Outside interference was not welcome! Unsurprisingly, 92 per cent of the employees of the railways were Protestants.

The government introduced a Fair Employment Act in 1988. It set out principles and practices that undermined 'custom and practice'. It cut out and made transparent all sorts of weird ways of institutionalising bias and discrimination. It introduced professional human resources methods throughout Northern Ireland business and over the years it succeeded in eroding religious discrimination at work. It introduced a Theory Y culture that has kept sectarianism out of the workplace. However, the fundamental problems remain. As long as the communities live apart and are educated apart, the sectarian culture ingrained in the psyche of the population will continue.

The failure of successive governments to force both sides to integrate Catholic and Protestant schools (92 per cent of children still go to segregated schools) leaves the possibility of a return to intercommunal violence an always-threatening possibility. The arrival of Brexit could, unfortunately, turn a possibility into a probability. Northern Ireland faces uncertain times both politically and economically. Civil servants are uncertain of their powers. A recent English Secretary of State didn't know that Nationalists don't vote for Loyalists and was in a state of paralysis in case she offended one side or the other.

Brexit poses a threat to the existence of the state of Northern Ireland. For sound reasons a considerable majority wishes to stay in the European Union. It may be that the rest of the world offers new and exciting opportunities to the English; it is not clear what Ulster offers to the rest of the world and why overseas companies would want to invest in a small, divided country with frail connections to its two largest trading blocs. We could be in danger of going back to the economic backwater of the

1970s, when Northern Ireland was the last point on the beach reached by the incoming tide and the first from which the tide retreated.

Looking to the future, Northern Ireland retains a jewel which can potentially grow into a diamond – Belfast. It can become one of the world's 'smartest' cities. Cities such as Belfast, Leeds and Bristol, and European equivalents such as Santander, are fast becoming the social and economic hubs of the future. Belfast is not too large and not too small. It is compact and its 500,000 population is a perfect size for an interconnected IOT service-based conurbation. It has the cultural, leisure and artistic facilities required for a modern, world-class urban centre. Two universities, international sporting facilities, restaurants, hotels, tourist attractions, theatres – it caters to a young, well-educated millennial workforce.

What it needs is leadership to introduce an IT infrastructure that can bring world-class products and services to its citizens, such as waste collection, traffic control, provision of social services, environmental improvements, all based on a fixed cable spine which public and private providers can tap into to provide cloud-based solutions. Its waterside parks offer ideal space for technology hubs and incubators. The city can provide 3-D infrastructure that can be shared by start-ups and existing small companies.

Power should be devolved from Stormont to the City Council and its officials. There should be an elected mayor supported by a power-sharing executive. Belfast already has tax advantages compared to the rest of the UK and comparable to the Republic. The way to reduce sectarian politics is to achieve social and economic success, based on common objectives and initiatives which benefit the whole community. Belfast may even get a world-leading recreational and entertainment centre. If the city succeeds, so does the Province. Smart initiatives can be developed across Northern Ireland. Derry in the north-west, with a catchment population of 250,000, can develop its own wired-up infrastructure and access to the world beyond Ireland.

When I became a minister in 1985, Belfast was like Minsk in Belarus. Now it has attractions that rival any European city of a similar size. If the DUP and Sinn Féin cannot come together to promote and introduce policies that are fit for the new world of technology, the country will become the failed statelet as it was once described by Gerry Adams. The young will leave and the pressure for a United Ireland, dreaded by the Republic, will intensify. The two main parties have a very stark choice: continue the distrust and the dislike of each other that has led to political and economic stalemate, or work for a future in which everyone has the chance to prosper and that will have umbilical links both to the Republic and Great Britain.

CHAPTER 23

Studying the Past

FOR BRITISH MINISTERS to be successful in Northern Ireland they have to be completely even-handed. They must understand why and how the country has come to its present position – how it is that the two communities have come to live apart in such a small place. They must have a love and affection for the cultures and the humour. They must concentrate on the good things and blank out the awful. It's not the fault of the people of Northern Ireland that they are where they are. It is a tectonic clash between the three different strands of Irishness: Anglo-Irish, Scots-Irish and Irish-Irish.

All three traditions have had their champions. It has been the misfortune of the Irish that too often the bad have won at the expense of the good. Daniel O'Connell, Charles Stewart Parnell, John Redmond, Joe Devlin, Michael Collins and John Hume were all men who strove to find, at some point in their careers, a Theory Y middle way to keep Ireland together and to bring harmony between Catholics and Protestants. But events – sometimes brought about by British governments, usually Conservative – betrayed them.

I believe that the following four men in particular must be largely held responsible for the chaos, division and civil war that have impoverished the island over the last hundred and fifty years. These four must take their place in the hall of infamy. They have made a divide deeper, bitterer, bloodier, more poisonous and infinitely harder to resolve.

Edward Carson (1854–1935)

One of the most powerful, persuasive and successful figures to divide Ireland was Edward Carson. His career involved risks that brought Great Britain to the edge of civil war and ended with civil war in Ireland. The divisions in Britain over Irish Home Rule led to convulsions that gave the Kaiser encouragement to invade Belgium in 1914, and almost prevented the United States from declaring war in 1917.

At the eye of the tempest was this haughty, complicated, obsessive and emotional man who fought for and lost almost everything he believed in. Much of what he stood for and advocated anticipated the rise of fascism in the 1930s, although he was more of a Margaret Thatcher (Ulster is as British as Finchley) or an Enoch Powell than he was a Mussolini. Many of the problems he grappled with were mirrored by the rise of nationalism across central Europe prior to the Great War. Carson was an Empire loyalist. His whole existence was predicated on the survival of the Empire. Without it he would've stayed a successful Dublin lawyer, a large fish in a relatively small pond. If Gladstone's Home Rule bill had been enacted, he could have sunk into relative political obscurity.

His personal life and circumstances drove his political imperative. He was raised in a privileged, isolated, middle-class family and as a child he had very little contact with Ireland 'beyond the pale', rather as well-to-do Protestant families in North Down viewed most of the Troubles from the safety of their living rooms. Carson's way up was to find a patron. A.J. Balfour – grandee, intellectual, and imperturbable and impenetrable chief secretary of Ireland in the 1890s – provided Carson's ladder to fortune. Balfour's policy of killing the Irish with kindness also involved killing off the malcontents. Carson's fearsome advocacy and courage fitted Balfour's purpose perfectly.

Carson married beneath him and so he had to make his own social connections. His early life and experiences reinforced his prejudices. His move to England made him into a social and legal star, but he could not drop the political baggage that drove and haunted him to take up positions that could never be held. As a consequence, he retreated from last ditch to last ditch becoming ever more bitter and depressed.

He was kept going by his court cases and his close relations with the aristocracy, particularly Lord and Lady Londonderry. His home life was often a mess, until he married for the second time, and some of his children a disaster. He refused a hereditary peerage to deny his son.

When at last he achieved real influence, his inability to see the other side, to compromise and negotiate, left John Redmond and the Irish Party isolated, his own party divided and the liberal government under Asquith hamstrung. As events passed him by, he was left no alternative than fall into the arms of Ulster, to endorse gunrunning and to threaten civil war.

He appeared to have little or no understanding of the damage he was doing to Britain's position in either the United States or Germany. The first he never visited, and he only went to the second to recuperate when overwhelmed by his annual hypochondria.

As he embraced Ulster so Ulster embraced him. By force of personality he brought together all sections of Protestant society from the big house to the urban hovel (a feat never attempted or achieved by Paisley). In September 1912, he tied them all together through the Solemn League and Covenant to fight so-called Home Rule and maintain Ulster's place in the Imperial Parliament, despite Asquith's Bill giving Ireland little more than glorified county council status.

In 1893 the Liberal Chancellor of the Exchequer, Sir William Harcourt, remarked to Carson that the Conservative Party had never yet taken up a cause without in the end betraying it. As the years slipped by, the Tories slipped away. The problems of Ireland required compromise and retreat. To Carson, retreat was defeat. He turned on his erstwhile friends and patrons with a raging venom which led him to isolation and depression. By 1922 his bolt was shot, his cause was lost. Breakaway Ulster was never more than a consolation. For the remainder of Carson's life Ireland drifted from bad to worse. In the North, bigotry and sectarianism became entrenched at every level of society. In the South, after the civil war, the Republic gradually turned into a petty, hate-filled, catholic-dominated, economic backwater, not unlike some former Slavonic provinces of the Austro-Hungarian Empire. The tragedy is that Carson – at certain key moments, with others – could have changed the course of history. He had the power, the oratory and the understanding to have found a way through, but he did not or he could not.

Éamon de Valera (1882–1975)

There are three main reasons for the terrible Irish migrations and divisions of the nineteenth and twentieth centuries. The first was the Famine and the British response: late, ineffectual, harsh and often incompetent. Following the failure by Pitt the Younger to give Catholics the vote after the Act of Union, the Famine made a split with Britain inevitable. However, the other two significant reasons were inflicted by Ireland on herself, one of them was the baleful influence of de Valera.

Although he can be held responsible for achieving real independence and sovereignty from Britain, in the scale of good versus bad, right versus wrong, enrichment versus impoverishment, he stands condemned before the Irish diaspora that he did so much to create. His behaviour at the signing of the 1921 Treaty led directly and inexorably to a dreadful Civil War. His virulent and public Anglophobia – which was in contrast to his private views about England – enraged Northern Protestants. His consistent and successful campaigns to take Ireland out of the Commonwealth, to achieve complete neutrality, caused bitter resentment in Britain and America.

His utter failure in the late 1940s and 1950s to turn his mind to economic growth and social reform resulted in the Republic becoming an irrelevant backwater. Tied as he was to the worst aspects of Catholicism, his social conservatism meant matters of equality and social advancement stagnated for a generation. His risible view of Ireland becoming some sort of Gaelic-speaking, pastoral idyll was epitomised in his 1943 St Patrick's Day broadcast when he described his ideal Ireland as 'the home of people who valued material wealth only as the basis of right living … a land whose countryside would be bright with cosy homesteads, whose fields and villages would be joyish with the sounds of industry with the romping of sturdy children, the contests of athletic youths and the laughter of comely maidens.' (*Éamon de Valera* by Ronan Fanning)

He completely failed to understand the religious and tribal hatred of the majority of the Northern Irish people towards his threats and his priest-dominated society. He wanted self-determination for the South but denied it for the North. There are those, such as Ronan Fanning, who say, 'Ah well, he may have had his bad points but only he could have brought the country together and embedded independence, neutrality and democracy into the new State.' But at what a price for the people North and South? When Ireland could and should have become another Switzerland, it was well on the way to becoming another Swaziland. It was he who created the chaos from which he was the only one capable of finding a solution. Finally, his tortuous relationship with the IRA, despite his misgivings and attempts at suppression, was a slippery slope to the terrible Troubles of the 1970s and 1980s.

Gerry Adams (b.1948)

I don't believe that anyone's character changes much for the better once they are over the age of fifteen. So, I suspect that Gerry Adams probably still is a bad man although he would have us believe that he underwent some sort of Damascene conversion at the time of the Good Friday Agreement. If he does not have blood on his hands, there is no shortage of it on his cuffs. He was once a senior IRA commander. The distance he has tried to place between Sinn Féin and the IRA is disingenuous, and membership of Sinn Féin and the IRA was often interchangeable. Adams is an intelligent man; sometimes witty in a bitter sort of way. But his mind is warped and many of his views continue to be ridiculous and dangerous. He claims a Marxist background in line with Jeremy Corbyn. That would be bad enough but, in reality, too often he has behaved like an early Mussolini.

Tim Pat Coogan, a Republican sympathiser, writes in his book *The Troubles* of how he tried to persuade Charles Haughey to meet Adams in 1986. 'Haughey was fully aware through his intelligence sources of Adams' importance in the Republican firmament. "He's the boss," he said simply.' Haughey wisely ignored Coogan's pleadings.

Adams came to peace because he and his movement were going nowhere. In the early 90s their share of the vote in the Republic was always tiny, and in the North it was declining. Every time the IRA shot a policeman, the UVF shot twice as many Catholics in retaliation. In the numbers game of murder, Adams and his partners were losing. In the 1992 general election, he had lost his West Belfast seat to the SDLP's Dr Joe Hendron, despite using every trick to try to retain it.

Adams needed a way out that would keep his Sinn Féin organisation intact while avoiding division that would lead to internal civil war. He had to show his followers that in some way the fight had been worthwhile, and he had to prise his men and women out of the prisons. His attempts to secure a United Ireland through violence have been a disastrous failure. Now that he has morphed into a benign grandfather figure, he has softened his image, particularly amongst the young. But he cannot escape his past nor his role in the disappearance of Jean McConville in December 1972, so gruesomely highlighted in Patrick Radden Keefe's book *Say Nothing*.

The cause of a United Ireland has been put back a century, if not forever, by his attempts to blast the unionist people into submission. In the history of Ireland, no man has done so much damage for so little purpose. There are film libraries full of news agency footage of Gerry Adams carrying coffins or watching them pass by. At last he's realised that sooner rather than later he might end up in one himself! On balance the people of Northern Ireland should be thankful for his transformation but no one should ignore his visceral hatred for the British and the loyalists. History will judge him harshly and the Almighty will send him down.

Ian Paisley (1926–2014)

At the end of the 1960s, the civil rights movement in Northern Ireland started demonstrations to address the grievances of the Catholic minority. Although there was some integration amongst the middle classes, the huge majority of people in Northern Ireland were brought up knowing nothing positive about each other. Every town and hamlet was either exclusively Protestant or Catholic, or there was a Unionist housing estate, a Unionist school and a Protestant church. The position was exactly mirrored in the nationalist community down the road. Each side despised the other. One felt oppressed and excluded, the other threatened by the prospect of a nationalist takeover of their culture and way of life.

Into this divided, embittered and economically backward community strode the Reverend Ian Paisley. Over the following thirty years he managed to do great damage to Northern Ireland by his extravagant, exaggerated, inflammatory – and sometimes seditious – rants about the horrors that were about to befall the Protestant people. He bashed and bullied his way to the top of unionist extremism by plucking on every nerve and every fear of the unionist people.

The greatest ally he possessed in maintaining the prejudice of his flock was the IRA. Without violence, I suspect, he knew that his war cries would soon appear irrelevant and arcane. By the time I came to know him he was sure of his position and of the strength of the support for him in the loyalist community. Although he was more relaxed than he had been, he still had a formidable rage and a formidable presence. As he grew older, he did start to mellow. He was always a dedicated constituency MP, a wonderful husband and a doting father, and in his last years he made a remarkable reconciliation with Martin McGuinness when he became first minister and McGuinness became his deputy. But his decades of inflammatory language and religious bigotry made the job of cross-community integration more difficult.

One of the last times that I saw him was at a reception in one of the Stormont dining rooms for Mencap, of which I was president. He bellowed at me across the room, 'Kilmorey' – he always called me by my Irish title in front of others – 'in all the misery and the treachery that you and your colleagues have brought to the decent, law-abiding people of

Ulster, there has been the occasional flash of sunlight through the ever-darkening clouds. One such occasion was the day you left us.'

'You don't really mean that, Ian, do you?' I replied.

'Oh, yes, I do,' he said. He then noticed that I had a glass of wine in my hand. 'It was you who was responsible for tempting the decent men of Ulster to abandon their bairns and take up the devil's buttermilk at the weekend!' (I had relaxed the licensing laws on Sundays.)

The hard men I have described fit the worst aspects of Douglas McGregor's Theory X. Their years in power revolved around fear, revenge, control of people and events, domination of outcomes, lack of trust, secrecy and the exercise of power to dominate others. If there is one trait they all share, it is cruelty.

CHAPTER 24

Brushes with Margaret

A S A PARLIAMENTARY under-secretary in the Northern Ireland Office my contacts with the prime minister were minimal, understandably. For Margaret Thatcher, Ulster was a running sore that did not feature very highly on her list of priorities. I had one near escape from a forensic interrogation when I was asked, with several other junior ministers, to a lunch in Downing Street in early 1988. In total there were eight of us: the prime minister; David Young, secretary of state for trade and industry; Willie Whitelaw (Leader in the House of Lords) who had come for the lunch; Ian Stewart, minister of state at the MOD; Colin Moynihan, minister for sport; Edwina Currie, the junior health minister; Ian Grist from the Welsh Office; and me.

The PM immediately started to savage Ian Stewart. 'What are you doing to tighten up spending in the defence department?' she demanded. 'There are too many top brass, endless duplication, no understanding of value for money, waste everywhere. You have to get a grip – and quickly.' Poor Ian had only been in the post a few months and a few months later he was moved on to take over from John Stanley in Northern Ireland. His attempted explanations were cut off mid-sentence and after a miserable quarter of an hour, the guns turned on Edwina. The prime minister had long had her eye on the NHS. 'It needs a thorough overhaul. Doctors are like lawyers: one of the last groups of closed shop professionals who always complain whenever radical changes need introducing. Some nurses are if anything, worse. Their organisation has become infiltrated by militants who are undermining nursing values and turning them into whingeing trade unionists'. Edwina was made of stern stuff and fought her corner. She supported the government's reforms but she pointed out the political pitfalls of introducing a market philosophy into healthcare. 'They have to learn like everyone else that no one owes them a living. If doctors and nurses do not perform, they should have a chance to go elsewhere,' declared the prime minister.

She then turned on little Colin Moynihan, former Olympic rowing cox. 'Why do we need a minister for sport?' she demanded.

'To deal with drugs,' he replied. This nonplussed her.

'Explain,' she rasped.

'Well, as you know, prime minister, drugs are endemic in sport. When there are governing bodies that need government money or subsidy, we can insist on internal rules and procedures that can eliminate drugtaking. We are being successful, particularly in sports such as athletics, but the biggest problem is snooker.'

'Snooker?' she asked incredulously. 'That dreadful game where everyone smokes and drinks and which Denis watches late at night in the flat? What drugs do they take?'

'Beta blockers, prime minister.'

'What are they?'

'They are designed to control blood pressure but they also slowdown the heartbeat so the snooker player does not jerk as he plays his shot. They are a widely abused drug among senior players.'

'I've never heard of them,' she reflected. Then, after a short pause, she continued, 'None of us round this table would ever have any need for them, would we, Willie?'

Willie blinked as he pushed his little pillbox under his napkin and boomed, 'Certainly not, prime minister.' She turned to me, but at that moment a lackey called her away, and I was spared.

By and large, prime ministers never know when to leave office. They are told that they are indispensable to their Party and to the country; that all their colleagues are pygmies by comparison, and that the opposition leader would wreck the country. As they go on, they build up frustrated enemies and envious rivals. Margaret Thatcher did not help herself as, although she was personally kind, she was an authoritarian and bossy Theory X-style manager. She wanted results, not affection. She frightened her subordinates. As a consequence, they did not always tell her the truth, and she began to lose touch with the public mood. By 1990, her abusive nature had lost her the confidence of her colleagues. Many of them had had enough, as had the country at large.

Meanwhile, in Northern Ireland, I was struggling with the problem of leaks. The RUC would often inform me that they had heard from a source that the IRA were aware of my schedule. Leaks usually came from someone at the venue inadvertently letting out that I was about to visit. The rules governing breaches of security meant that when one occurred the private secretary would ring up the event organisers and tell them that unfortunately the minister had suddenly been forced to change his schedule and undertake another engagement elsewhere. This tactic caused maximum annoyance – exactly what the IRA most wanted. In the autumn of 1990, I decided to turn the tables and from then on to tell the world that if a visit had to be aborted it was because our plans had been uncovered, and that to go ahead would put at risk everyone involved, not only me. I would then announce that I was extremely sorry to have to cancel after all the effort that had gone into planning the event, but that the blame lay not with me but with the men and women of violence. I felt that the benefit of making clear that it was the terrorists causing the cancellation outweighed the NIO's concerns about broadcasting how often the IRA knew exactly what we were doing.

The first occasion when we employed this new strategy was a long-scheduled get-together with Joyce McCartan at her fish and chip shop, The Gaslighter, on the Lower Ormeau Road. Joyce was one of the great ladies of Northern Ireland. A Protestant married to a Catholic, she had a large family and she lived and worked on one of the nastiest and most difficult streets in the city. The Lower Ormeau Road was in a constant state of tension. It is one of the most contested routes for the Orange Order on the Twelfth of July. There have been some sickening murders there, not least the shooting of five Catholics, cut down in Sean Graham's bookies, in February 1992. As always, Joyce was the first there to comfort and to calm. One of her sons, Gary, had been assassinated by the UVF in her kitchen some years earlier, but she abjured revenge and spent her life raising money to fund job creation schemes and improve the drab streets and houses in her 'village' by the Lagan. The terrorists were hard and vicious men who did nothing to help her plans for returning to normality but she was afraid of none of them and by the end of her life they were rightly scared of her.

Joyce had become a good friend to me and I tried, whenever I could, to help her efforts in cash or in kind. When word of my planned visit to her seeped out, probably from some volunteer in the shop talking to a customer, the RUC became nervous, aware that there was an active IRA unit in the area. I told Joyce the truth, and Joyce told the press, and the Provos (Provisional IRA) received a public roasting. Some in the NIO were not amused. This was another example of Needham breaking the rules of accepted procedure. The fact that the NIO knew that the IRA knew that I was going was itself 'confidential'. Such nonsense could be deployed as a reason for never venturing beyond the gates of Stormont Castle.

Meanwhile, quite separately, a note had been circulated, warning ministers that mobile phones were not secure. Under no circumstances should we divulge details, while using one, of what we were doing or of where we were going. Without giving me sight of it, my private office quite rightly read it and shredded it – there were some rules on security that were second nature to all of us after so many years. None of us would ever have dreamt of giving dates or times of visits on the phone. There was no mention in the note of the fact that equipment could be bought for a few pounds that would enable anyone to tape with crystal clarity any phone call on an analogue mobile. Nor was there any plan to provide ministers' offices with secure phones as there was no budget for such items.

At the beginning of November 1990 Mrs Thatcher faced a leadership challenge from Michael Heseltine. On 6 November I was returning from Newry in the early evening and I phoned home on my newly acquired government mobile. As always, my day had been hectic and full of interest. The only times when I could call home were the evenings or early in the morning. The arrival of the mobile was a godsend, or so I thought, as it enabled me to be in touch when I was in the car. During the course of my evening call, I told Sissy that I thought it was time for 'the Cow' to resign. I have to admit that had I realised I was being taped, I would have phrased it slightly differently!

Three days later I had completely forgotten this phone call when, as I was touring a factory in my constituency, there was an urgent summons from my private secretary, Norma Sinclair. She had been called by Andy Woods, the NIO press officer, a blunt and, as it turned out, not very supportive Yorkshireman. He told her there had been a call from *The Sunday Times*. The paper had received a tape of a conversation between Sissy and me in which I had said, 'It's time the Cow resigned.' They intended to publish under the headline 'Security breach puts Minister at risk' and they wanted my reaction! Andy's view was that my number was up. Dry-mouthed I drove home, telling Sissy on my car phone that something terrible had happened but that I could not tell her what it was.

When I got back, I rang Andy Woods. Naturally I tried to wriggle. I did not remember making the comment. He then played the tape down the line. There was no escape. After a panicky half an hour I got hold of Alastair Goodlad, the deputy chief whip. Alastair doesn't say anything when words have no purpose and so I stared at a noiseless handset for a good minute. 'You'll have to say sorry, old boy,' he finally said, and that was that.

An hour or so later a call came through from Number 11 Downing Street to warn me that the chief whip would like to talk to me. That evening he rang from his car phone. 'I will arrange for you to ring the PM and apologise,' he said, 'and that will be the end of the matter.' Not if she survives, I thought to myself. I would be happy to apologise for embarrassing her, I told him, but I could not say 'sorry' – that would make me a liar. 'I leave the exact words to you,' he replied, and hung up.

Another hour went by and the phone rang again. It was the prime minister, who said, 'If cow was the worst I have been called by my friends and my enemies, I should not have got as far as I have. Both of us, Richard, have jobs to get on with so let's do that.' Click. She had behaved magnanimously.

As they had proposed, *The Sunday Times* ran the front-page lead under the headline 'Minister apologises to PM for telephone insult' and then stated that the call had been secretly recorded by a paramilitary group using a radio scanner. The implications throughout the piece were that the tape came from the IRA. *The Sunday Times* claimed an agency had passed the tape on to them. The agency stated they had received it from the terrorists. But I doubt if they revealed all. Why should the agency give the tape to *The Sunday Times*? Surely, having been lucky enough to obtain such Danegeld, any agency would have expected some reward or auctioned the story to the highest bidder. If money changed hands, did any find its way back to the paramilitaries? None of the London media professionals in the BBC, ITV, in the broadsheets, the tabloids or the weeklies sought to enquire. Nor did anyone seem to care that *The Sunday Times* lead was potentially giving an enormous victory to the terrorists, if indeed, it was they who were responsible. They had succeeded in undermining a wounded prime minister and they had put in question the position of Northern Ireland's longest-serving minister. Well done *The Sunday Times*! It was left to a correspondent in the *Spectator* to point out that this invasion of privacy was perhaps one of the nastiest aspects of this self-serving repulsive piece of journalism.

Meanwhile another unpleasant side plot was developing. The security angle had not gone unnoticed by those in the NIO, not all of whom were my friends. Much of *The Sunday Times* article had dealt with the security lapse aspects, including a paragraph that read: 'This is the second time Needham has been intercepted in recent weeks. Security forces have confirmed that the opening of a community shop in south Belfast had to be cancelled last month when it became clear that terrorists were monitoring his movements.' *The Sunday Times* had neatly linked the earlier tabloid report on my cancelled visit to The Gaslighter – which had absolutely nothing to do with mobile phones – with the Margaret Thatcher story. A report by Chris Ryder appeared in Monday's *Daily Telegraph*, the gist of which was clear: Needham has always been a bit of a loudmouth. We have had to warn him on several occasions to keep quiet. Very dangerous these volatile ministers, you know. Some of us could not care less what happens to him but it's a bit rough on his escorts and secretary to get blown up because of his blathering.

This was nasty and a step too far. As I have remarked elsewhere, I had always tried to be open and to let some air into the corners of government where security could pass as a byword for cover-up and cock-up, but never had I been reprimanded or warned that something I had said or done might be a security breach. I had thought wrongly that the RUC might be looking for those who had criminally taped my conversation rather than having their reputations protected by anonymous briefers from within the NIO. I rang my solicitor who confirmed that the article was libellous and damaging to my reputation and advised me to sue. Then I discovered – as so often is the case – that nothing is quite as it seems.

I was advised that as a minister I needed the agreement of the solicitor general, Sir Nicholas Lyell, a trusted friend, and the attorney general, Sir Patrick Mayhew, to take legal action. I explained to the NIO in London that this was a private matter, as indeed the telephone call had been. Nothing is private when you are a minister, I was informed. I rang Lyell and explained. 'Very difficult,' he replied. 'Could be awkward if the case ever came to court.' I was incredulous. 'Well,' he said, 'the *Daily Telegraph* might claim that recent revelations about why you cancelled a visit to the Lower Ormeau were an indiscretion. They might ask you how you had known that the IRA had known you were coming, and in those circumstances, our security sources might be put at risk!' Never in my life had I heard such bunk. The real source from the Lower Ormeau was almost certainly one of Joyce McCartan's helpers telling customers that some bigwig was coming to open their new kitchen, and the IRA had put two and two together. 'Well, you can always resign if you feel so strongly,' Patrick Mayhew told me in the lobby. Perhaps I should have, but on balance I believed my going would have been another tick in the terrorists' ledger.

A compromise was agreed. I could write a letter to the *Daily Telegraph* in which I could state, with the authority of the secretary of state for Northern Ireland and his permanent secretary, that I had never been disciplined or spoken to about personal security lapses. The *Telegraph* lost the letter for a fortnight and I smelt another conspiracy, but after a phone call to Max Hastings, the editor, it appeared.

I realised that if I survived the weekend of 8 November, events would move on and my intervention would become a footnote in history. On Tuesday 13 November, in the following week, Geoffrey Howe (the recently resigned former chancellor) gave the speech of his life on the floor of the House of Commons. The next day, Wednesday, Michael Heseltine declared his candidacy for the leadership. I decided to support him in the first ballot as to have done otherwise after the telephone call would have been committing political suicide. Chris Patten asked me to join him in his office at 5.30 p.m. on Tuesday 20 November to hear the result of the first count at 6 p.m. The numbers were 204 for Margaret Thatcher and 152 for Michael Heseltine. It was not enough. I knew she was finished and I was better out of the way. I had long since arranged an Industrial Development Board inward-investment mission to Japan and Basil Feldman, one of the PM's closest supporters, had agreed to come selling with me. A friend of Margaret Thatcher's who had become a friend of mine, he was upset at what had happened between the PM and me, but he also knew that for Mrs Thatcher, the game was up. So, I phoned him and we agreed to go as soon as possible.

But first I had to decide who to support in the next round battle between Major, Heseltine and Hurd. More than anything else I wanted to keep Patten's chances alive of one day taking over the leadership of the party. I did not believe Heseltine could win – it would have been too divisive. If Major won, Patten's chance might have gone forever, so the politburo of the Blue Chips – Chris Patten, William Waldegrave, John Patten, Tristan Garel-Jones (for whom the decision was excruciating, as he was one of Major's closest friends) and I – campaigned for Hurd. A Hurd victory was the only outcome that would have allowed for a Patten–Major run-off later. I do not think any of us, including Douglas, believed that he would win but I owed it to my best political friend to try to keep the chink of opportunity open. Sometimes in politics a choice has to be made between friendship and ambition.

Ten days later, after Major had become PM, I was in a hotel suite in Kumamoto on the island of Kyushu in Japan when I learnt that Patten was to be chairman of the party following Major's reshuffle. There were no changes to the ministerial team at the Northern Ireland Office, except that my 'awkward' colleague, Brian Mawhinney, had been promoted to minister of state and given the responsibility for political affairs in the Province. This would give him even greater scope for promoting his own agenda and interfering with mine. Sure enough a few weeks later he criticised my comments following a terrorist attack in the centre of Belfast as being insensitive and inappropriate, which they were not.

When everyone else was running for cover Peter Brooke stood solidly behind me and backed me, even though there must have been several instances when I drove him to distraction. On one occasion the two permanent secretaries, Sir Kenneth Bloomfield and Sir John Blelloch, went to see him to demand that he reined me in. He asked me for lunch in his office; rather bizarrely there was an 'Ulster says NO' mug on his desk. We shared a plate of curled-up sandwiches and a warm bottle of hock, most of which he drank. After talking about cricket for three quarters of an hour, he said, 'Calm down a bit, old boy,' and then carried on with the cricket. I did. Peter is a wise owl who, in Wellington's words, puts himself on the other side of the hill and sees the world through the eyes of the enemy. He has not been given sufficient recognition for his contribution to peace, and he was always a rock on which I could rely.

The Cow Affair probably torpedoed any chance I had of getting into the Cabinet or the House of Lords, but politics is a risky business and if it hadn't been that banana skin, I'm sure I would have found another!

CHAPTER 25

Moving On

IN JULY 1990, some time before Margaret Thatcher stood down that November, there was a Downing Street reception. The prime minister saw me and scurried over. 'Richard, how long have you been in Belfast?'

'Five years prime minister.'

'That's a long time for a junior minister,' she said. 'You are a west country MP and you are a lapsed Irish earl. Where are your roots? Where do you belong?'

That was a very shrewd and penetrating question.

'Thirty-thousand feet over the Isle of Man in an RAF Hawker Siddeley 125,' I replied. It was a witty response but it didn't answer her question. Where did I belong? The longer I stayed in Belfast the more I felt my Anglo-Irish roots. I was responsible for so much of the economic and social activity in the Province that I became ever more committed. When Ireland play England at rugby I shout for Ireland and always will. On the other hand, by 1992, I had become increasingly tetchy and restless. I needed to move on. I had more in me than staying for longer as a Northern Ireland minister, however much I had enjoyed it. I was becoming too Theory X in my dealings with my staff. Not enough listening and too much shouting. It was time to go. The 1992 election would be the end date. But would John Major promote me? And would he win?

The prospects did not look good. The economy was just bumping out of recession. Unemployment had passed three million. Seventy-five thousand people had had their homes repossessed. National output had fallen and government borrowing had increased. The memory of the disastrous poll tax was still fresh in everyone's mind, despite the introduction of the replacement council tax, which was accompanied by a bigger Treasury subvention that helped soften the burden of local tax increases. The Tories were in danger of losing their one great advantage over Labour, their reputation for economic competence and their record of reducing taxes. Fortunately, in 1991, Labour had published spending proposals that would have cost an additional £35 billion and that allowed Chris Patten, then party chairman, to launch a penetrating counter-attack headlined 'Labour tax bombshell' and 'Labour's double whammy'. As I left Belfast – which I privately believed would be for the last time as a minister – I made it clear to the press that one day I would like to come back as their secretary of state.

I returned to my constituency for the 9 April election. North Wiltshire was no longer a marginal so we were expected to send helpers to neighbouring seats in Swindon and Bath. We needed to be careful as many of our elderly supporters, who had upper-class accents and a passion for hunting, did not go down well in the poorer parts of the neighbouring constituencies, which was where the help was needed.

For our election, Sissy and I assembled our own key supporters and turned the house into a bed and breakfast. Pat Sears, the association chairman, became our mother hen and planned our programmes from D-21 to D-1. She was known as 'The Commander'. As this was our fourth election, we had built a well-oiled machine. The Liberals had given up treating the seat as close and had chosen the leader of the group on the district council, Christine Napier, as their candidate. She was a humourless, do-gooding, Scottish former 'management development consultant', who was also chairman of the council finance committee. The Labour candidate, Christine Reid, was a local councillor, appealing, sparky, politically well-connected and fun, with family from County Armagh. She had little time for the Liberal Democrat candidate, and neither did I. Our slogan was 'Richard Needham, our Man for the 90s'. We campaigned on local issues, and on how Sissy and I worked as an accessible team to solve constituents' concerns.

I used one letter from Northern Ireland in my election literature. John Hume, who would go on to win the Nobel Peace Prize, had written, 'Richard Needham has been a truly outstanding minister of Northern Ireland and we thank the people of North Wiltshire for him.' Otherwise I kept everything local.

Billy Harding came up from Yeovil to be in charge of poster 'management' as he had been for all my previous campaigns. This time he brought Will Shead, one of thirteen children, who had left school at fifteen without any seeming knowledge of reading, writing or soap. He seemed fascinated by a collection of bits and bobs we have at home and kept picking them up, examining them and asking what they were worth, which aroused Sissy's sensitivities. He was particularly interested in a chess set in which the pieces represented political figures. Tom Oliver, who is the son of a former bishop of Exeter and therefore nicknamed 'Vicar', had come down from Oxford to help. He had never come across anyone like Will before and offered to teach him some basic moves. It took just twenty minutes for Tom to throw over his king, after which no one else dared challenge Will. I learned later that Will would only do the job if he was paid by piece work for every poster put up or pulled down. He was a young proponent of Theory X.

Not everything went smoothly. Four nights before the election Billy and Will decided to take the night off in pursuit of two girls they had come across. Andy, my second son, and two friends, Paddy Connor and Brizie Lochead, begged to be put in charge of poster 'protection'. Billy gave them precise instructions. If they could not resist the sight of an orange dayglo Lib Dem poster, they were to be very discreet and leave no evidence.

As they slowed at a well lit roundabout on the outskirts of Cricklade, Paddy jumped out and started wrestling with a well wired stake attached to a gate. On the other side of the roundabout was a police car with its lights off. Too late – panic. Paddy jumped into the back of the car and they raced past the police with their lights full on, turned right round the roundabout into a housing estate, parked the car and ducked down.

A few minutes later the police car, lights flashing, stopped alongside them. Andy, Paddy and Brizie were each pulled out separately, frisked and accused of preparing to rob the house opposite. The car was searched – inside were the remains of a Liberal poster, a balaclava and some nails, supposedly, according to Brizie, for a student party in Manchester. All three thought this was the end of their careers before they had begun. The police told them to follow them to the station where they would be charged with attempted burglary. Their names were taken. 'Are you related to our MP?' one of the officers asked Andy.

'I'm his son. He will kill me if he finds out.'

'Stay in the car.'

Five minutes went by, and then the other policeman walked over and shone his torch into Andy's face. 'Say good luck to your dad for Thursday,' and went back to his car. The three returned home, without a word to us about what had happened but doubtless very relieved, and poster responsibility reverted to Billy and Will.

Paddy Ashdown always came at least twice during a campaign to support the Liberal candidate. In 1992 he was leader of the Liberal party and a popular, attractive figure. I had a lot in common with him; he had been brought up in Northern Ireland; and he was complimentary about me in his memoirs. We had similar views over Europe and on social issues. But ever since I had found him practising his Malay language skills on Sissy on Ham Hill outside Yeovil, when we were walking the dachshunds, I had never really warmed to him. When talking to you he hooded his eyes like a mandarin. He lacked a sense of fun. He took himself very seriously, which led to him being occasionally pompous and self-important. Anyway, he was campaigning to get rid of me and Chris Patten!

My election team was run by Johnny McLaren, a bachelor and former Scots Guards officer turned PR consultant. It was decided that we would send a welcoming party to greet Paddy on his walkabout in Chippenham. So Johnny set off with half a dozen young university friends of my son's and my daughter's. They all met up on the bridge over the Avon in the centre of the town. The adoring, if elderly, Paddy fans looked on admiringly at the arrival of the smartly turned-out young helpers. But then their smiles turned to outrage as my team unfurled posters printed with 'Paddy Pantsdown', 'How can we trust you if your wife can't' and 'This way to Luckington' (where his former girlfriend had lived). A mini riot developed as the Liberals tried to snatch the posters from our team. Somehow, in the melee, the keys of Christine Napier's battle bus disappeared, causing further chaos.

My campaign was funded largely by gifts from Northern Ireland businesses, which was generous in the extreme as they must have known I was likely to move on. John Carson, the former unionist mayor of Belfast, came to canvas and taught us the Ulster way of getting votes. This was, in essence, to promise the voters what they wanted. Wherever he went he found former Belfast voters who knew someone he knew. The most elegant import from the Province was the Duke of Abercorn. He was immaculately turned out. At every door he announced himself with 'I'm sorry to trouble you, I am calling on behalf of Richard Needham, the Conservative candidate.' What effect these visits would have had on the council tenants in Corsham, had they known there was a real live duke standing on their doorstep, we shall never know.

At the hustings meeting in Malmesbury, which was Christine Napier's home patch and where she had tried to pack the audience, she was pincered by Christine Reid, who would have made an excellent MP, and me. She mouthed platitudes but had no grasp of detail and could not remember how much money the council had raised from the sale of its housing stock or how many council houses they had sold even though she was chairman of the finance committee. She wasn't seen again.

Towards the end of the last week in the campaign, I got a call to go down to Bath to see Chris Patten. We met in a lay-by opposite the entrance to the university. He told me he had lost. The Labour vote was haemorrhaging to the Liberals, despite Neil Kinnock's personal plea. It was a disaster. He was to be the next chancellor of the exchequer to replace the tricky, not-always-on-message Norman Lamont. If Chris were to lose, how would he ever get back into the Commons? He had only been an MP for thirteen years.

But much more importantly, the Party and the country would lose one of its brightest, most international statesmen. Chris was the Tories' strongest advocate and practitioner of Theory Y management in government. By becoming chairman of the party and having to defend Thatcher's indefensible poll tax, he lost his seat and sacrificed his own political future for that of his friend John Major. If I had a criticism of him, it was that he was too nice, too discursive, too unwilling to go for the throat. Although when he did bite, the injury was deep and fatal but he was too honourable to do that kind of damage in Bath. Liberals rejoiced when he lost, the right wing of the Conservatives drank champagne, and the rest of us cursed because we could see what a hole was left in John Major's cabinet. Chris had not, however, forgotten me.

CHAPTER 26

Minister of Trade

THE RESULT OF the election that took place on 9 April 1992 was that I had a majority of 16,388 – 56 per cent of the vote. The Liberal vote had declined by 5.8 per cent. As usual Labour was nowhere. I was safe – more than safe! On Friday afternoon I finally got hold of Chris Patten, primarily to commiserate over his losing Bath, but I was also keen to know what was going to happen to me. He said he expected me to go to the Department of Trade and Industry. Wasn't that what I wanted? I blew him a kiss down the telephone line. I phoned my private office in Belfast to tell them that I was off. They were pleased for me but genuinely sorry after I had been there for so long.

The next Tuesday I was told to report to Number 10 at 12.30 to see John Major. As I went up the stairs to his sitting room, I was passed by Jonathan Aitken coming down. He had been offered minister of state for defence. I was slightly miffed that he had got in before me. As charming, able and clever though he is, I felt that at the time there was something slightly whiffy about him. His weaknesses were yet to be exposed.

The prime minister was alone except for a private secretary. He congratulated me. We empathised over Chris Patten's result. He told me he wanted me to work for Michael Heseltine as a minister of state responsible, he believed, for energy, although it was up to Michael to decide how to task his junior ministers. This rather set me back as I was hoping for trade, which would have made me Michael's effective deputy and put me at the centre of Britain's global trading strategy. I didn't argue and went off to a celebratory lunch in Sloane Square with John McLaren, Christina and one of her friends. I was still over the moon.

After lunch I caught the tube to Victoria, walked down Victoria Street and went into the DTI reception at Richmond House. I told them who

I was. The receptionist searched down a sheet of paper, told me to wait and made a call. A few minutes later a tall, good-looking Lancastrian appeared and said, 'I am John Warren, the private secretary to the minister of trade. Welcome!' I had got it! Northern Ireland has 5 per cent of the UK population. Now I would be presiding over the overseas expansion of services and manufacturing across the entire public and private sectors of what was at that time the fourth-largest economy in the world.

We went to the top floor and then into a wide, modern, open-plan office, where John introduced me to his team: two assistant private secretaries, a diary secretary – who, to my delight, came from Enniskillen, so I wasn't completely cut off from my Ulster roots – two correspondence secretaries and a driver. After about ten minutes, as I sat admiring my desk and an enormous bank of telephones, the permanent secretary Sir Peter Gregson walked through the door. No knocking. No announcement. Permanent secretaries are senior to every minister except the secretary of state and call ministers by their Christian names. 'Richard, I am delighted to meet you. Mr Heseltine intends to be called "President", as in President of the Board of Trade. So please make sure you abide by that.' That was the sum total of his advice – apart from telling me that his door was always open, which would have been fine if I had known where it was!

My office had a connecting door to that of the 'President', which was an even more palatial suite. I stuck my head around the corner and he summoned me in. I hardly knew him. Our paths had never crossed. I had admired him as one of the few businessmen politicians who understood and supported industry. He was clearly a royalist rather than a roundhead, and wherever he went, he got stuff done. He was also an inspirational orator and led from the front. I also thought of him as being slightly aloof, even occasionally arrogant. I did not appreciate at the time that in private he is a shy man. He doesn't mind being ribbed and challenged. He has the ability to laugh at himself, which partly comes, I suspect, from being joshed by his powerful and forceful wife, Anne. He can be good fun. He has beautiful manners, and he is eclectic in both his tastes and his choice of friends.

Michael had radical plans for the department. He wanted to divide trade policy from delivery because he felt that they required different disciplines. He hired Andrew Fraser, a marketing wizard, to be in charge of inward investment and to concentrate on bringing foreign companies to Britain as their base for the European Single Market. As far as exports were concerned, he wanted to help smaller British companies into Europe and to encourage them to look further afield, especially to the fast-growing Asian countries. To do this, he suggested taking on a hundred export promoters from the private sector to spearhead a programme supported by government-backed financial incentives to push British business towards these new markets. I was to head this up.

He then asked me for my ideas. I told him I wanted to set up market plans for over a hundred countries. We would use each ambassador or high commissioner as the marketing director. We would do a SWOT (Strength, Weakness, Opportunities, Threats) analysis in each market. We would get each embassy to set tangible concrete objectives on which their performance would be judged. Michael approved. As I was leaving, he said, 'I've got another piece of news. The permanent secretary lives with his mother in Croydon and has never been to the US or China.'

'That's dreadful!' I said.

'No, it's not. It means he hasn't the background or knowledge to interfere and undermine our plans. One other thing. You have a reputation for pushing the boundaries. I will stand over your mistakes, but I expect to share the credit!'

A month after my appointment in June 1992, a profile of me appeared in *The Engineer* entitled 'Wet drops into trade job'. It continued, 'Richard Needham, once described as a raindrop because he was so wet, has in the past criticised government industrial policy. Now industry wants to see whether a trade minister will toe the party line.'

The party line had long been established by the monetarists and the free marketeers in the Treasury. Their mantra was open competition, free markets, minimum subsidies, let the market decide. Government assistance for featherbedded industry undermined productivity and reduced consumer choice.

My predecessors in trade had gained the reputation of being Treasury puppets. As minister of trade my role was to support and promote British business to gain orders against overseas competitors. If our rivals bent the rules, which most of them did, either we would have them stopped or we would bend the rules. Business had to know that we were their friend 'in need and deed'. We had to develop relationships with them across sectors and regions that would strengthen their confidence to invest overseas, and to attract outsiders to set up throughout the UK.

Michael Heseltine may have been a Theory Y manager and a friend of business but he was no featherbedder. He introduced radical reforms into civil service structures. He flattened the organisational pyramid. Each manager had to have at least four subordinates. He insisted on tough private sector controls on performance. Verifiable and measurable targets were introduced. Regular performance appraisals tested the competence and commitment of every grade. By dividing policy from delivery, he improved specialisms and reduced the number of generalist all-rounders. The DTI had long been the Cinderella of the major economic departments. The best fast-streamers were attracted to the Foreign Office and the Treasury, both of which looked at the DTI with some disdain and condescension. We were determined to get it back its mojo, and its reputation for innovation and support.

The strategy that Michael Heseltine and I had agreed on was to seek out those new and expanding markets that the limited resources available to British business could profitably concentrate on. The overwhelming majority of these were in the Far East, India, ASEAN, China and Japan. Russia was a basket case with no government-backed credit facilities for exporters. Eastern Europe was small and German dominated. South America was corrupt and risky. Companies by and large knew their way around the European Single Market, while too many others fell over their feet in the United States, wrongly thinking it was like the UK because it was English speaking.

A day or two after Sir Peter's brief introduction, Christopher Roberts arrived. He was the deputy secretary in the department and in charge of all trade-related matters. He was quite a grand panjandrum, and gave me a loud and thorough briefing regarding his responsibilities and my duties. He told me he had never heard of me before but, on investigation, had discovered that I had been seven years in the Irish bogs – a fate he could hardly imagine and a backwater he had hardly heard of. Now I was in the mainstream he was clearly unsure whether I would be up to it! I was back at the bottom of the ladder. I nicknamed him 'Sir' Christopher, a title that he clearly wanted but never attained.

Fortunately, he spent most of his time at international congresses and conferences as he didn't much rate the businessmen with whom I travelled the world. Selling and marketing were skills with which he was not acquainted. The only times he appeared were during prime ministerial overseas visits, when he was in permanent attendance, armed with helpful background notes and various alternative 'lines to take'.

The first weekend after my appointment I was catching up with my constituency backlog when John, my private secretary, came on to tell me that Philip Morrice, the director-general in Taiwan, wanted to come and see me. I told John I was having a few days off. Could he possibly see somebody else? 'Sir' Christopher maybe? Half an hour later Philip was on the phone from the train giving me a fearful wigging. DTI ministers didn't care, always looking after themselves unlike their other foreign opposite numbers. Mr Jeffrey Koo was coming over with £80 billion of gold in his back pocket to store at the Bank of England and there was no minister available to receive him. I calmed him down and gave him lunch.

The next day Mr Koo arrived and presented me with a teapot to give to Michael Heseltine, which I kept. I promised to lead a business delegation to Taiwan later in the year and everyone was happy. I soon realised that the schedule of a trade minister does not include time for sightseeing or reflection.

A fortnight or so later John burst in to tell me that the Prince and Princess of Wales were visiting the British pavilion at the Seville Expo '92 over 20 and 21 May. Sissy and I were to accompany them. There was a potential whipping hiccup in Parliament as the visit would be at the same time as the debate and vote on the Queen's speech. No problem. John hired a Learjet for the two dates and off we went. This was a step up from Northern Ireland, where hiring a taxi had required permission from the accounting officer. We met up with the royal couple at a service held in Seville cathedral, a huge, imposing, gloomy, Gothic tomb, filled with chanting and clouds of incense. We sat through an interminable service. The Prince spent the time drawing various columns on the back of the service sheet. Princess Diana fidgeted on the hard pews. When Widor's organ Toccata struck up, the Prince looked up and remarked brightly that they had had the piece at Diana's father's memorial service the previous week. After an hour Diana leant over to me and said, 'I'm dying for a gin and tonic. How about you?' I fell in love with her on the spot!

Over the two days we were with them I gained a small insight into his difficulties in being married to this beautiful, strong-willed and temperamental woman. His upbringing had not prepared him for such a role. It was like pairing a Suffolk Punch with an Epsom-trained filly.

The next day we toured the exhibition. The UK pavilion was beautifully designed and constructed by Nicholas Grimshaw but the contents were pitiable. The best offering of British innovation was an electric Sinclair C5 scooter, one of the biggest disasters in the history of technology. And the other eye-stopper was an empty, locked-up Range Rover lying at an angle. The remainder of the space was filled with bars, lounges and walkways. Clearly the private sector sponsorship money had run out. The marketing departments of large British companies had decided not to be involved. I rang up George Simpson, head of Rover, and gave him an earful but it was too late. We spent two hours touring the site. Not a word passed between the royal couple. There was a water fountain with a wishing well into which the Princess threw a borrowed coin and whispered to me cryptically, 'You can guess what I am wishing for?'

Later we went into a vibrating, circular, 3D cinema that 'flew' the shaking audience over a precipice. This was too much for Diana, who disappeared for an hour. Nobody knew where she had gone. When she returned, having found the gin and tonic, her mood had passed.

At the end of the visit they asked for a private word. They wanted to know how my phone had been hacked during the cow affair. They had been warned by their personal protection officers (not by the Met) of the dangers of being listened in to, but neither of them was aware that they could be voice taped with perfect clarity. They were shocked.

The British Expo Hall was a classic example of inter-departmental cock up. The Foreign Office wanted a substantial British presence to fly the flag and not upset the Spanish government, who were trying to boost one of their most deprived areas. The Treasury were not prepared to commit additional public funds on what they considered (rightly) to be a white elephant. So, the poor old DTI were sent off to persuade the private sector to pay for sponsorship. The private sector understandably was averse to supporting a temporary pavilion of no commercial benefit. Ministers dithered. Result: a dead Range Rover and a clapped-out motorcycle together with an international reputation for being past it. It is what had happened at previous expos (where the Sinclair C5 had also been a key exhibit) and would happen again at future ones.

I am sure the Prince would vote LibDem if he was a private citizen. He is a Theory Y man, as far as any future monarch can be. He cares deeply. He is dedicated to improving the lot of 'his people', particularly the most vulnerable. He is an understanding, sympathetic and thoughtful man who works immensely hard on all his causes and who cannot bear to see so many problems unaddressed. Although sometimes he appears to carry the burdens of the world on his shoulders, he has a quirky sense of humour that allows him to see the funny side of life. On occasion he can appear removed from the harsh climate of reality and the limitation of resources.

In the spring of 1993 I received a letter from the Prince's private office. The letter complained that British business was hardly visible in the Czechlands and the country was overrun with Germans looking to capture the market. Was this not another example of British short-termism and lack of ambition? The Prince was right, of course, but to persuade UK businessmen to travel to a small market already well served by its neighbours was like pushing water uphill. Nevertheless, in September 1993, I headed to Prague with a small trade mission of bankers and investors.

There I was to experience one of the most memorable evenings of my life. It so happened that we were there for Battle of Britain Day, on 15 September. David Blighty, the ambassador, was holding a reception at his residence for the surviving Czechoslovak fighter pilots and their families. He wanted Sissy and me to be the hosts. About twenty pilots and their families came, the pilots either in their RAF uniforms or in the dark blue uniforms of the 1939 Czech Air Force. Many of the wives were English – they had married during the war and gone back to Czechoslovakia with their men at the end of it. Some of the pilots were on sticks, some in wheelchairs, but mostly they stood straight as ramrods. As young men they had trained in the Czech Air Force. After the annexation of the Sudetenland they joined the Polish Air Force and, following the invasion of Poland, they had escaped to France and joined the French Air Force. Then when France fell, they escaped to Britain.

Of all the countries to send pilots to the Battle of Britain, Poland sent the most, followed by New Zealand, Canada and then Czechoslovakia. They formed two squadrons, 310 and 311, and their contribution was legendary. In all, over one thousand pilots served in the RAF. In 1945, nearly all those who had survived went home, many taking with them their newly acquired English brides. Slowly they were discredited, persecuted and imprisoned without trial by the Communists. Many were beaten, tortured and sent to concentration camps. Once they were released, they became labourers or miners. There were 180 who managed to escape back to Britain. The remainder were consigned to hell.

They stayed in contact with one another and they never wavered. At the reception all the English-born wives crowded together to share family stories and experiences. It could have been a gathering of the Women's Institute. Nothing was off the table: cake making, flower arranging, dressmaking, cooking and family gossip. I asked the tall, distinguished, white-haired wife of the general (the commanding officer had been promoted to a general after the overthrow of the Communists) what had happened to her. She told me her husband had gone back in 1945. When he saw the Russian threat, he begged her to stay behind in England but she was determined that the two of them and their children should remain together. I asked rather naïvely if she had any regrets. She tartly replied, 'Don't be ridiculous, young man. I've had the most wonderful life with the most wonderful man.'

I asked one man in his RAF uniform with a chest full of medals to tell me his past. In 1938, he had gone from the Czech air force to the Polish air force. He been captured by the Russians when they invaded eastern Poland in September 1939. He escaped, fled through Romania, Bulgaria, Turkey and Syria, and when he arrived in Egypt, he caught a ship back to England. He joined up. He fought throughout the War. He returned home, leaving his wife and baby son behind, was locked up for five years and spent the remaining thirty-five as a railway ticket clerk alone in Czechoslovakia. I asked him why he appeared so happy. 'Look over there,' he said, and he pointed to a handsome young man in a pinstripe suit who spoke with an American accent. 'That is my son, he is a banker and he has come back to help us. My life may have been wasted but his has not!'

The general made a speech. I thanked him, but whatever I said felt hopelessly inadequate in the presence of so much unrewarded sacrifice. They had come from a country we had abandoned as a 'quarrel in a faraway land between people of which we know nothing' (Neville Chamberlain, 1938). They had lost everything. They then sang the Czech national anthem followed by 'God Save the Queen'. There were no tears.

To me the whole point of the EU is that we could never have a war in Europe again. I am afraid the UK leaving is unlikely to do much to advance that objective. Nor can I see how it will lead to a growth in our ties politically and commercially in central Europe.

As a family we have one tenuous connection with Czechoslovakia. Sissy's father had served in the Luftwaffe's 39 Flak Abteilung Division, and he and her mother had spent their two-day honeymoon in the Carpathian Mountains, where Ernst was stationed and where she was conceived in the summer of 1943.

★

A month after the 1992 election the UK assumed the presidency of the Council of the European Union. As trade minister I became president of the Single Market Council. On my first visit to Brussels I was greeted at the door of the meeting room by Jaques Delors, the president of the commission. 'Minister, I hope you follow the instructions of your former prime minister and give the Union a lead in putting through your Parliament the rules governing the Single Market,' he said. The Single Market was the key to increase growth and she was right to compromise on other areas of sovereignty, disadvantageous for us, such as the rules of the CAP (Common Agricultural Policy).

The Single Market revolutionised trade across Europe. Nearly all the other members had designed crafty ways of protecting their products. For example, the Germans had rules that stated that beer on sale in Germany had to be brewed using German hops! As an open trading nation, we were the ones that suffered most from the mercantilist behaviour of our competitors. The biggest prize for us was the introduction and the enforcement of the rules of the Single Market. The arguments of the Brexiteers – that we abandon it in exiting the EU in order to agree trade deals independently with other countries, which will become more beneficial to us than those we already have – are baloney. Furthermore, the deals we will have to negotiate with Europe after the withdrawal agreement has taken place cannot possibly be an improvement on what currently exists.

The commissioner for the Single Market was a large, boisterous, Theory X, boring federalist German called Martin Bangemann. He was a former leader of the FDP. He viewed the Brits as the awkward squad who kept asking difficult questions and wouldn't go along with his compromises and cosy behind-door deals. He had once spent a holiday with his family in St Ives, where a mixture of Cornish weather and Cornish wit had not gone down well. After a few months I gave him dinner in the House of Commons, which reminded him of a mausoleum, he said, and he lectured me on his plans to regulate the noise of motorbikes. He didn't like hairy bikers. I immediately became an ardent defender and supporter of them.

However, in many ways we were our own worst enemy. As we didn't trust or like the Commission we did not do enough to gain influence among its permanent officials and we were often out-manoeuvred by the French and Germans, despite having a wonderfully capable 'divide and rule' permanent representative in Sir John Kerr. When 'push came to shove' they invariably formed an alliance that won the day.

At my first meeting of the Council in Strasbourg I soon discovered how cut off we were. All my colleagues were multilingual and appeared to know each other. They spent time chatting, laughing and patting each other on the back, ignoring me. The only one to come up to me was the Irish minister, who I knew anyway. I had to build alliances, and quickly. My predecessor was Portuguese so I sought advice from him. He suggested that I invite everyone over for a weekend so we decided to have a big jamboree at Brocket Hall and invite all the trade ministers of the EU. Michael Heseltine provided a Welsh voice choir and then disappeared, as his wife, Anne, was recovering from an operation. He claimed that too much time with his opposite numbers would drive him to becoming a Eurosceptic. Sissy came and I persuaded her to chat up Jürgen Möllemann, the German Federal Minister for economics. He asked if she could arrange to have a former RAF officer who had been stationed in Germany at the end of the War, contact his mother. But, unfortunately, after much effort tracking him down, the officer refused. We got on famously but it was all in vain as a short time later, when Möllemann found himself under investigation for a business scandal, and his parachute failed to open while he was skydiving and it was claimed he killed himself.

The Italian minister of foreign trade was Claudio Vitalone. He greeted me with a kiss and confided in me that his wife was chairman of Rome's largest hospital. She had only received two cases of Brunello as a Christmas box from the newly appointed representative of a big British drug company. Vitalone suggested that orders might start drying up if more was not forthcoming! He was a close ally of Giulio Andreotti, the Italian prime minister. He had been charged, along with Andreotti, with the killing of journalist Mino Pecorelli, which had taken place in 1979, but was acquitted twenty years later. Not all the others were such colourful characters. I was to discover later that corruption in the EU was as nothing in comparison to most developing countries.

Although the EU was full of flaws and scoundrels were well represented, it was on balance of huge benefit to British business and most of the time we could get our way on trade matters by securing 'opt-outs' and finding blocking alliances. Britain very quickly became the country of choice for companies outside the Single Market wishing to set up factories and offices to trade within it. Seventy per cent of British manufacturing is now owned by non-EU entities that are primarily using us as their European base. Leaving quite clearly puts that investment at long-term risk.

As minister of trade I decided there was a limit to what I could do to assist UK business in the Common Market. It was open and up to British companies to make their own way through Chambers of Commerce or trade associations. There was little role for government other than to ensure the rules were kept to and we stood up for those supporting open trade.

Neil Hamilton, who was a junior minister in the DTI, agreed to take over attending the Single Market Council from me. Although he was an ardent 'leaver', he was also very fond of things German. He could be good fun and he got along well and enjoyed the nights out with his colleagues.

I wanted to go to where I could add more value. That was in the fastest-growing emerging markets of ASEAN (the Association of South East Asian Nations), China, Japan, India, parts of the Middle East, Africa and South America. We started off with eighty different markets. It was too many. So we excluded those where it was impossible to get credit from the banks or from ECGD, the government's credit agency, like Russia and Iran. We also left the United States off our visitors' list because, like the EU, it was an open market with the same language and well catered for by independent consultants and advisers.

CHAPTER 27

Selling Britain Abroad

IT HAS LONG been the anchor role of the minister of trade to take missions of businessmen overseas, to gain access for companies at the highest level, and to act as a door opener and facilitator for closing deals and arranging partnerships. But in recent years, it seemed to me, there had been little structure to the visits and it was almost always representatives of the same companies who went on them. Missions were often promoted by local Chambers of Commerce and trade associations. Scotland, Wales and Northern Ireland ploughed their own furrows. Running missions was a major source of income for the private sector bodies as, unlike Germany, we have no statutory framework of chambers. In the eyes of the chambers and trade associations, the five-star missions and the best ones to get on to were prime ministerial visits, followed by those led by the president of the board of trade, and next in line were mine.

We decided to up the numbers of ministerial missions, up their profile and up their significance. Too often trade ministers were happier seeing their opposite numbers in Victoria Street rather than in Singapore, Hong Kong or Jakarta. We broadened the scope of the missions by involving the British Council, the universities, the banks and the denationalised utilities. We were keen to attract a greater diversity of companies and sectors.

The ambassadors and the trade attachés had to put forward annual plans with targets and objectives and provide a SWOT (Strengths, Weaknesses, Opportunities, Threats) analysis of their markets. One of the core requirements was to make more use of existing bilateral groups that fostered improved business, social and cultural ties. The Indo-British Partnership, China-Britain Trade Group, Malaysian Society, Anglo-Japanese 2000 Group and Anglo-Korean Forum for the Future all became involved, and were closely linked to the embassies and the local British

Council offices. Too often the Council's officers went their own way and didn't see the connections between trade and the arts.

Unlike so many of our major competitors – who treated aid as a route to trade – the Department of Overseas Development had a huge budget but was so even-handed in its dispersal of funds that many in business thought it was an offshoot of the United Nations.

Our plan was to show off Britain's dynamic, multicultural, international business elite, representing an old country undergoing a modern, twentieth-century regeneration. It didn't always work out that way.

The overseas missions were usually comprised of twenty or so different companies whose representatives came in all shapes and sizes. Unfortunately, at that time most English businessmen – there were very few women – were a fairly conventional tribe: mid-forties to fifties, often overweight, and predominantly interested in football, golf, the weather and their products. They tended to be woefully short of understanding the politics, the language and the culture of the countries they were visiting. If they had done history at school they had long since forgotten it. They often thought of themselves as captains of industry but they were more of the army than the navy variety.

They were cautious about expressing views on anything other than their own narrow field of expertise or giving away 'confidential information'. They were scared to put their heads above the parapet. In meetings with prime ministers, presidents or ministers most of them stayed frustratingly silent, putting more pressure on the head of the mission, the minister and the ambassador to keep the dialogue going. There were of course notable exceptions, and these were the people on whom I relied to carry me through the banquets, the press conferences, the meetings, and the seminars and who helped me with the content of my speeches.

Generally speaking, our competitors were more sophisticated. The Germans, for example, have English as their second language. In learning it they have broadened their cultural and social awareness and as a result they tend to be more open and informed than their English counterparts. The Americans were about as awkward as we were, bellowing at people on the assumption that whoever was listening wouldn't be able to understand them.

The missions were exhausting. Travelling to Asia, they generally involved a long overnight flight, arriving at our destination in the evening. After a fitful, wide-eyed night, the next day would start with a 7 a.m. breakfast briefing from the ambassador. By mid-afternoon most of the participants were nodding off. They then came round for the evening's entertainment and, because of the time difference, they were wide awake by night time, and stayed at the bar until 2 a.m.

One of the main hurdles was the food. In China, twelve-course banquets always formed part of the schedule, not least because it was an opportunity for many of the Chinese hosts to enjoy a feast they certainly wouldn't get at home. The DTI section head, Alan Murray, was usually with us and would help translate the menu, and advise us on what could be skipped and what delicacies it would be rude to refuse. Sea slugs and bamboo water rats in aspic were memorable specials that it was hard to persuade our international travellers to sample with expressions of enthusiasm.

Korea was one of the countries to which we supported missions on a regular rota, and these trips were perhaps the most difficult. Known as 'the Hermit Kingdom', it has been trampled over, annexed and pillaged by Japanese and Chinese invasions in rotation for more than fifteen-hundred years. Koreans trust no one, believing every visitor has a raft of ulterior motives and a desire to shaft them. Their national dish is kimchi, cabbage and Korean radish fermented with scallions, garlic and ginger. It is sour and spicy and extremely smelly. The Korean idea of bliss is a banquet featuring eight different varieties of kimchi. The only mitigating factor was that each guest had a beautiful Korean girl beside him who would feed him the kimchi with chopsticks. Every mouthful was accompanied by a shot of soju. There was usually a Korean band in the corner playing rather sad folk music on a wailing string instrument. After an hour or so the participants were reeking of garlic and legless.

On one such mission we were invited to attend the anniversary of the Battle of Kapyong, which was fought between 22 and 25 April 1951 when a Chinese army attacked the Commonwealth brigade. It was an epic struggle in which some of the American supporting troops ran away, together with a whole division of South Koreans. The US Air Force managed in error to napalm the Australians. It ended in victory for the Commonwealth with thousands of Chinese soldiers killed. Every year there was a service of remembrance and I was asked to take the salute at the march past by the veterans who had returned to visit the scene of the fighting.

We decided to take the mission members and their Korean opposite numbers, together with some of the veterans, to the site of the battle to remind the Koreans that we had had to save them from the communists.

With us on the bus was General Sir Anthony Farrar-Hockley, the official historian of the Korean War who was known as 'Farrar the Para'. He had been captured at the Battle of Imjin and had spent two years in a prisoner of war camp where he had been tortured. He was a legend.

He was giving us a lecture on the battle on the way up to the site in the bus from Seoul. Most of the businessmen on either side had very hazy memories, if any, of the Korean War or what the Koreans had done since 1951. The landscape changed from that of a desert to a carpet of cherry blossom. 'Oh,' blurted out one of the participants, interrupting the general in full flow, 'look at those glorious flowers on the hillside. Aren't they charming?' 'Not if you have to fucking fight through them,' was Sir Anthony's brusque retort.

Over the years not everything went to plan. In Tokyo I went shopping one day and couldn't understand why the platforms on the underground were so empty. It was 20 March 1995, the day of the Tokyo subway sarin attack. When I returned, I found the embassy in turmoil. Had I been gassed? Had they 'lost' a minister? I was given a real dressing down by one of the embassy officials who said I had no right to go shopping when time had been put aside for a ministerial briefing on the upcoming meetings. Unusually for me I lost my temper!

In Hong Kong I was invited on to Peter Woo's yacht on Grand National day in 1993. Peter is the son-in-law of Sir Yue-Kong Pao, founder of the largest shipping company in the world. Also on board to watch were Cap Weinberger, former US secretary of defence, and Steve Forbes, editor of *Forbes* magazine and a former Republican presidential candidate. We settled down to watch the world's most famous race. Captain Keith Brown, a former guardsman, was officiating as starter on his last race before his retirement. On Brown's first attempt to start the race the tape shot up but became entangled with several jockeys. He frantically waved his flag, signalling a false start, as did his assistant further down the track. After ten minutes of untangling and resetting the tape, the captain tried again. The tape shot up, this time wrapping itself around the neck of jockey Richard Dunwoody. The captain signalled another recall. But unfortunately, on this occasion, his flag failed to unfurl, so thirty horses thundered down the course and completed the race, leaving seven at the start. The result was cancelled. It was the greatest farce in the history of British racing. It did nothing for our reputation.

CHAPTER 28

Confronting the Dragon, Humouring the Elephant

R ELATIONS WITH CHINA in the run-up to the 1997 handover of Hong Kong were by far my biggest challenge. Chris Patten, the governor, was my closest friend. He was determined that Britain should leave a functioning and semi-independent world-class city with as much democracy for its people as he could squeeze. The fact that previous governors had done little to introduce democratic institutions prior to his arrival had not impressed him. His was the Theory Y stance. He was supported by the prime minister, Douglas Hurd (who was foreign secretary at the time Chris was appointed) the Americans and most MPs.

The Theory X supporters wished to avoid upsetting the Chinese at any price. They believed that what had been agreed under the Joint Declaration of 1984 was as far as it was possible to go before the Chinese moved in their tanks. Britain had huge investments in Hong Kong which would be put at risk in any fallout with Beijing. Hong Kong was the gateway to the Chinese market. Business was the be all and end all in their eyes, way more important than the democratic rights and freedoms of the inhabitants. After all, in their eyes, Hong Kongers were only interested in making money and improving their standards of living. The campaign was led by the big international trading companies, such as Jardines, and the banks, such as HSBC and Standard Chartered. They were backed up by the UK infrastructure manufacturers, such as GEC and Rolls-Royce, and were also supported by the Hong Kong Chinese conglomerates of Li Ka Shing, Peter Woo and Lord Kadoorie's China Light & Power. To keep them all sweet previous governors had showered them with honours. They all kept British passports in their back pockets and most of them had invested in UK estates just in case another Mao showed up! There were a few brave souls such as Simon Murray and David Tang who remained steadfast.

The pro-Beijing lobby could count on the help of willing lackeys in the Foreign Office – 'old China hands' who had spent their careers in the Far East and could look forward to lucrative non-executive directorships when they stepped down. The most egregious of these was Sir Percy Cradock, a mournful mandarin, who spent his retirement trying to undermine Chris Patten's measures to extend democratic rights. On one occasion I ran into him in a queue at a reception waiting to be introduced to a visiting Chinese minister. I told him that his disgraceful interventions were deeply damaging to government policy; that if this had been 1939 and he done the same he would have been locked up for treason. Unsurprisingly we never spoke again.

He was not the only shameful example. Norman Tebbit and others did all they could to oppose any immigration from Hong Kong after the handover. Much of Hong Kong's population had fled the Communist terror of 1949 and had made new and happy lives for themselves and their families. It was despicable to suggest that money and greed was their main motivation. The hundreds of thousands that turn out to demonstrate against the Chinese government at anniversaries of the Tiananmen Square massacre are proof of that.

Chris Patten was right to push for reform. China was also changing. Behind the walls of the Forbidden City there were debates about how China should introduce reforms encouraging innovation, creativity and entrepreneurialism. Men like Zhu Rongji, former mayor of Shanghai and a vice premier, later to be premier, had visited MIT and Harvard. I had met him on several occasions and he told me that his biggest task was to reform authoritarian Theory X management. More participation, less Confucianism was his mantra. He came to London in 1993 with a business delegation including Madam Wu Yi, the Chinese Thatcher. But inevitably, wherever he went, he came up against what was happening in Hong Kong, even though the vice premier kept repeating that it was not part of his portfolio.

The visit concluded with a dinner in the Foreign Office. There were two tables of eight. One was hosted by John Major and one by Douglas Hurd. I was on Douglas Hurd's table. Douglas was never one for much small talk. John Major made a welcoming speech which brought up Hong Kong. Zhu Rongji looked frosty. It was not a happy affair. The food remained on the plate and the white wine was warm. I decided we had to lighten it up. So, I asked Madam Wu Yi, who was sitting opposite me, to teach me some useful phrases in Mandarin. After some banalities she came up with '*lao wai da bi zi*'. That, she explained loudly, is what we call foreigners.

'What does it mean?'

'Big-nose, old, foreign chaps,' she translated and burst into a fit of giggles.

'I'm not going to give you any aid money if that's what you call me,' I told her. The mood lightened.

Somehow, I had to balance supporting British companies trading or wanting to trade with China with my support for the governor's policy reforms. I spent a lot of time talking to Ambassador Ma, inviting him and his wife privately to events where he could vent his fury with the governor. Michael Heseltine would express sympathy with his position and somehow we kept up cordial personal ties. Life was made difficult for our businesses but not impossible and I continued organising trade missions across different cities through the China-Britain Trade Group. In 1997, Britain left Hong Kong after five years of Patten's governorship with our heads reasonably high and with an agreement far more favourable to Hong Kong than if it had been left to the kowtowing, cock-hatted Sir Percy Cradock and his acolytes. We closed the final outpost of the Empire with our international reputation intact and with a great deal more success than the present government's disastrous handling of our exit from the European Union.

Over the years there was an increasing number of Chinese delegations. I always found time to take them round the House of Commons and give them a full tour of both chambers, letting them watch a debate from the visitors' gallery and then go to the bar. Two years ago, out of the blue, I got a call from the Chinese chargé d'affaires. He told me that President Xi Jinping was coming on a state visit and would like to see me. Apparently, he had been part of a delegation as party secretary for Fuzhou twenty-five years previously and I had taken him out. This meant I had been classified as an 'old friend'. He would like the opportunity of seeing me again, with a small number of his other acquaintances, in his hotel room at the Mandarin in Knightsbridge.

I asked the embassy official what I should say and for how long I should speak. 'You have ten minutes,' he told me, 'so talk about how you see Anglo-Chinese relations developing.' As the president only had one hour and there were ten of us, with Gordon Brown kicking off, I realised that some were unlikely to get in. I prepared my contribution, checked it out with the embassy, and was third in line, to be followed by Michael

Heseltine, John Prescott, Peter Mandelson, Charles Powell and the others. Michael told me that he didn't wish to say anything and was happy for me to go on for as long as I liked. I did. As a result, Prescott, Mandelson and Powell were cut down to two minutes each. I heard afterwards that they were far from pleased about the length of my comments as they had very important matters to raise. I had done exactly what was asked of me by the Chinese embassy. None of them had ever involved me while they were in government. I didn't feel too sorry. The overriding impression I got from the president was his concern about how the United States would react to the rise of a new global power. The disappointing part was that I had absolutely no recollection of setting eyes on him before!

Unfortunately, President Xi has turned out to be the worst kind of Theory X communist autocrat. In his interview with us at the Mandarin Hotel he proclaimed the importance of handling the US sensitively and carefully. He said he had studied Thucydides's Trap, which had led to the war between Sparta and Athens. But his threatening behaviour is comparable to that of Kaiser Wilhelm II before the outbreak of the First World War. His treatment of the Uighurs; his sabre-rattling over Taiwan; his disregard for the 1997 Agreement with Britain that guaranteed freedoms for Hong Kong over fifty years; and his expansion of Chinese naval power in international waters belonging to Vietnam, Thailand, Malaysia and Indonesia are antagonising not only his neighbours but moving the world in a very dangerous direction.

If China was my biggest challenge, India was my biggest opportunity. Ever since independence, India had been a closed, incompetent, poor, ramshackle, underdeveloped socialist economy. Tories liked to remember the Raj, pig sticking, durbars, maharajahs and viceroys. They whitewashed over the legacy of Britain's imperial past, the massacre at Amritsar, the so-called Indian mutiny and the sack of Delhi in 1857. The Labour Party, many of whose leaders had gone to the London School of Economics, had close but rather patronising ties with the leaders of the Congress party who had also studied at the LSE. They celebrated the independence of India as one of the great successes of the Attlee government, although millions had died during partition, partly due to the vanity of the viceroy, Mountbatten.

The Indian aphorism – 'Why is it that the sun never set on the British Empire? Because God doesn't trust her in the dark' – needs to be remembered by British companies wishing to do business in India. India must be treated with respect and humility. We are now the bird sitting on the shoulder of the elephant, feasting on the ticks.

India entered my life early. My Grenadier godfather, Colonel David Beaumont-Nesbitt, had spent several years in the 1930s attached to the Indian Army and had fallen in love with everything Indian. Curries became and remain the dishes I die for. He read me *The Jungle Book*, *Kim* and the *Just So Stories*. I adored them. After Uncle David died, India disappeared from my life for twenty-five years except for a very great friend I made at law school, Bhaichand Patel.

I determined on a major government initiative to promote closer commercial relations with the UK throughout India by strengthening and financing the Indo-British Partnership. It was obvious to me that India was on the move and we needed to find ways of exploiting and building on the long and sometimes bitter path which had left our relationship uneasy and often fraught. The government, particularly a Tory one, had to show it took India and its opportunities seriously. We needed to welcome and encourage the increasingly powerful, non-resident Indians in Britain and their families, to use them as a Trojan horse, to promote investment and trade in both directions.

To kick off this new initiative, we arranged a major trade mission to Bombay. Our star attraction was HMY *Britannia*, with her resident Royal Marine Band that beat the retreat at sunset. No other country boasted anything like her. But by 1994, the navy said they could no longer afford her and the DTI could not find sufficient private money to retain, man and repair her. Her decommissioning was another example of Britain's declining influence in the world.

The high commissioner, Sir Nicholas Fenn, was in charge. He was a nervous man. We were invited to attend a reception run by the British Council for graduates and their parents at the University of Bombay outside the Rajabai Clock Tower – a wonderful piece of late Victorian architecture, designed by Sir George Gilbert Scott and modelled on Big Ben. I asked Sir Nicholas whether I was expected to make a speech. Absolutely not, he forcefully assured me.

The vice-chancellor's oration reminded the visiting delegation of all the wickedness of British rule, not least because the tower and the adjoining library were falling to bits. Sir Gilbert had shipped all the drawings and materials out from England with a Meccano instruction booklet on how to put it all together. Unfortunately, this did not include ways in which to make and repair stained-glass windows. Most of these had now collapsed and the pigeons were inside the library rather than outside. The vice-chancellor then invited me to address the four-hundred-strong audience and tell them how we could redress this failure! I rose and responded. Never before had I been given the chance to deliver a speech which had not been drafted by civil servants, especially when it came to the spending of money. As I had no draft, I was free to say what I liked. I agreed with the vice-chancellor's every word. We had behaved disgracefully. I would pledge the government to train up young Indians at York Minster cathedral in the replacing and repairing of stained-glass windows.

There were cheers. The high commissioner sat pale and trembling. 'I have no budget! You can't do this – this is monstrous. You will have to pay for it yourself,' he fumed. 'Well, I have just done it and I won't pay for it myself.' It took four years for the British Council to find some funds, supported by my own endeavours. Now the not-so-young Indians are at York Minster repairing our windows as we have run out of stained-glass craftsmen.

Encouraged by our success in Bombay, the next mission was more ambitious and involved renting a Concorde for a week in November 1993. A hundred businessmen were selected to cover four cities: Delhi, Calcutta, Madras and Bombay. Many of the hundred businessmen were large and Concorde's seats were narrow. Because we were flying overland for most of the way we had to travel subsonic. It took around six hours to reach Jeddah, by which time tempers were getting frayed and we had consumed a combined total of 166 bottles of champagne and white wine. However, we did have the thrill of crossing the Bay of Bengal at Mach 1.2.

The organiser in India was the Confederation of Indian Industry (CII). The CII was chaired by Jamjed Irani, one of the most senior directors of Tata and the most wonderfully relaxed and amusing man. He took me aside after the first day and asked me to solve a dilemma he was wrestling with. He found it very difficult to get on with the Japanese. What was the problem? Was it that he could not get their names right? They all sounded the same to him. No, I told him. Having worked with the Japanese for over ten years I suspected I knew what the problem was. When the Japanese first arrive, the plane door opens and in rushes a blast of heat, followed by dust and some smells that are new to Japanese nostrils. At the bottom of the gangway the Japanese visitors are greeted by large gentlemen with beards wearing what to them look like nightdresses and carrying garlands, who proceed to embrace them. By and large, Japanese people do not like facial hair and are not partial to being kissed by bearded men smelling of garlic. After a lot of shouting and yelling they are bundled into waiting, sometimes un-air-conditioned cars and whisked off through chaotic traffic for lunch or dinner. The Japanese are not on balance overly keen on hot curries and find Indian-English hard to follow. They finally lose interest in doing deals when they have to spend the next two days on the khazi. 'Ah, I see,' he said. Two years later he was presented with an honorary KBE by the Queen and I happened to be at his inauguration. He said to the Queen, 'Richard Needham has done more for Anglo-Indian relations than any former minister.' 'Really' said the Queen and moved on to my neighbour.

We went to Calcutta, the capital before Delhi, and met with the communist chief minister, Joyti Basu, a shrewd politician, who did not make life easier for himself or his people by wanting to nationalise everything. The next stop was Madras to call on Madam Jayalalithaa, a famous former south Indian film star. She was covered in solid gold bangles and bracelets that tinkled whenever she moved. She told us of all the opportunities we could profit from on the back of her new low tax development zones, although of course, 'we look at everything on a case by case basis'. Swraj Paul, later Lord Paul, who it was alleged had been Mrs Indira Ghandi's bag carrier, blurted out, 'Surely a suitcase by suitcase basis.' This brought matters to a premature close.

The missions did succeed in improving our relationships across the board. India remained a difficult market but the old stereotypes were dispelled on both sides and a much deeper understanding, helped enormously by the large Indian community in Britain, emerged.

Post-Brexit, our relationship with India is perhaps our most important, second only to that with the USA. The Indian community in the UK is one of the most – if not the most – dynamic, successful and entrepreneurial. We must welcome and support them, particularly the students. One of the most encouraging trends in the Tory party is the increasing number of Indian-descended MPs. It cannot now be beyond the realm of possibility that in the not too distant future we might have a prime minister of Indian descent.

One of the elephants in the room for the trade minister was how to handle corruption. Those who now claim that, free from the European Union, we will have wide new opportunities to increase our trade with the developing world ignore two points. First, they cannot define these prospects even if we manage successfully to negotiate trade agreements that match those we already have inside the European Union. Secondly, how do we avoid the huge, endemic levels of corruption that pervade the markets in Asia, Africa and Latin America? Our prospects are not improved through the passing by a Conservative government of draconian anticorruption legislation which, whether we like it or not, puts us at a massive disadvantage compared to our competitors, whose noses are not as sensitive as ours.

When news of my plan to promote closer commercial relations with India became known, my first cousin, Robin Needham, got in touch. Every generation of Needhams contains a saint and Robin was the one in mine – he had dedicated his life to the charitable sector. He tragically drowned in the great Thailand tsunami of 2004. He lived for three decades on the subcontinent, ending up as director of Care UK in Nepal. He had spent several years in Calcutta and Bangladesh, where he adopted two little girls.

Robin told me that while in Calcutta, he had found several Needham graves in the huge ex-patriot local cemetery. There were rumours of a tribe of Indian Needhams somewhere to the north but the trail had gone cold. Perhaps in my new exalted position I could pick it up. I asked my private secretary, Rozmin Llada, whose family originally came from Gujarat, to help. She contacted the high commissioner in Delhi. After several months, an Indian businessman phoned Rozmin and said that there was a tribe of Needhams in Shillong in Assam. They were the descendants of one Francis Jack Needham. Jack Needham turned out to be a very remarkable man. Born in 1842, he had gone off to Calcutta in the mid-1870s where he had joined the Bengal police force. In 1888 he was made assistant political officer and sent off to control the wild tribes of the north east. He was to spend the rest of his days disappearing for weeks at a time with a handful of men, pacifying the local population and exploring the jungle.

After several years of learning the ethnic languages and looking in vain for the source of the Bramaputra, he became a distinguished botanist and settled down with a local Assamese woman called Mary, by whom he had eight children. He stayed there for the rest of his days and died in 1924, a Fellow of the Royal Society and a Companion of the Indian Empire. His descendants, meanwhile, had fanned out across the globe.

On the trade mission to India when we travelled on Concorde, I arranged to bring my three distant cousins from Assam down to Calcutta. Two of them were teachers in a primary school and the other was the caretaker. There was no obvious evidence of my distant Needham relative, except for their sense of humour and their love of playing whist. They were Khasis, which meant they followed a matrilineal tradition. So, the Needham connection had become a little hazy. They had never flown anywhere before but a trip round the bay in Concorde singularly failed to faze them and I have been trying ever since to get them over to visit their original Irish roots – but Concorde seems to have put paid to any further desire to travel.

When I first became trade minister in 1992, I was determined to make Indonesia a priority market. Sissy spoke Bahasa as did Ilse, her mother. My stepfather-in-law was one of the top businessmen in Jakarta. He represented Racal electronics among other mainly German companies. Sissy and I had helped to bring up Melvin Korompis, whose father, Gino, owned the largest sugar refinery in Java. Ilse had adopted an Indonesian boy, our children had Indonesian au pairs and we had remained friends with Dewi Sukarno, the first president's wife.

The Indonesian leaders had strong connections with Germany, the United States, Japan and increasingly China, but their dealings with Britain were limited. The country was the fourth most populous in the world, approaching two-hundred million people. It had a successful, long-established and extremely powerful Chinese community that had integrated into the local population, and a growing middle class.

The ambassador, Roger Carrick, was a get-up-and-go character and was delighted to have a minister of trade interested in his country. At the end of 1992 we had travelled to Hong Kong to see Chris Patten and his family, and Roger invited us to call in and stay with him on the way back. He arranged a dinner for many of the great and the good and a number of government ministers, at which Sissy was a huge success because she spoke the language.

Over the next three years I took as many trade missions to Jakarta as I took to China. I became friends with Rahardi Ramelan, the trade minister, and his boss, the Japanese-speaking Johnny Ginandjar. I courted my opposite number BJ Habibie (who later became president) and his brother Fanny, who was ambassador to London. I persuaded the Treasury to authorise tens of millions of pounds of ATP (Aid Trade Provision), which was taken up by companies such as Balfour Beatty and Trafalgar House and used to build roads and bridges across Java. I struck up a friendship with Murdaya Poo, the third richest man in the country – but his partnership with Balfour Beatty never reached the heights he achieved with Nike or Hitachi. Nor was he able to persuade me that he should manufacture for Dyson, despite being the world's largest supplier of trainers.

Indonesia did not have the sub-contractors that existed in Malaysia. Malaysian manufacturers used imported Indonesian labour so there were no savings to be made. We supported the British Council's efforts to broaden cultural relations and attract students to UK universities. I established the Indonesian Business Council to produce a strategy for improving our trade. Unfortunately, after ten years, it closed down. Despite all our efforts nothing much changed, except for a joint venture between Jardines and Honda that produced five million motorcycles a year. Indonesia, like Brazil, was always about to happen. But our relationships with both these countries have never taken off. Indonesia is our forty-fourth largest market in terms of exports and imports, below Egypt and Pakistan, and half the size of Malaysia's, even though Indonesia has ten times as many people.

CHAPTER 29

The Trip from Hell

O NE OF THE conventions of modern democratic governments is that
when a prime minister or president goes overseas, they take the press
with them. When I accompanied John Major on a visit to the Far East in
September 1993, we travelled in an elderly TriStar. The PM sat in seat A1
at the front with Norma in A4, on the other side of the aisle. Behind him
was his private secretary, Rod Lynne, then me, then the ambassador and
finally John's doctor.

The prime minister and Norma both had curtains and bunk beds, which
gave them total privacy when they wanted it. The middle of the plane
was taken up with the Downing Street garden girls who had to decant
from Number 10 and carried on working as if they were overlooking
Horse Guards Parade. No one seem to worry about sitting down or
wearing seatbelts when we took off or landed. Business continued as usual.
Behind the 'office' was a business class section for the senior directors who
accompanied the prime minister, hoping to sign deals in his presence.

There were some special seats for a variety of unconventional passengers.
I had arranged for two sixth formers from a grammar school in Northern
Ireland that had twinned with a school in Japan to come along and meet
up with their penfriends. At the back, squeezed into the economy section,
well supplied with booze and with nothing much to do, steamed the
lobby. They had no interest in the commercial opportunities and many
of them not much knowledge of the places and people we were going to
visit. Many of them spent the journey getting tight and working out how
they could trip up the prime minister at any press conference he might
hold. Far from home politicians can lower their guards and sometimes
forget that the golden rule is to try to avoid the press whenever possible.

On the Japan leg of the flight John felt sorry for the huddled masses packed in the back of the plane begging for interviews. So, he went to talk to them and soon found himself in a lively argument about the problems he was facing with rebels in the party. While on the plane, he was quite measured but by the time we were at a press conference in Tokyo he became increasingly tetchy. To the bemusement of the Japanese press corps, every question was a barrage of hostility on petty party-political infighting. He unwisely called some of his more prominent right-wingers 'barmy' – which of course they were – but from then on he was hounded by requests for 'clarification', 'responses to his critics', and questions about whether there was going to be an election and who he was going to fire.

I got fed up with this. I told John Sergeant, the BBC's political correspondent, to stop damaging the image of the country with his petty point-scoring, which wasn't of the slightest interest to anybody other than him and his mates in the Westminster bubble. Sergeant is somewhat opinionated. Not used to taking criticism from middle-ranking ministers who are meant to hold him in proper respect, he gave me an earful about his Oxbridge background and his loyalty to the country, and said it was his duty to get to the truth. I said he should stop being pompous.

The trip, which had been heralded as an assembly of the most powerful delegation of businessmen ever to fly out of the UK together and had the purpose of gaining orders in the Far East, had turned into a public relations disaster. Gus O'Donnell, who later became head of the civil service and was at that time the prime minister's press secretary, must accept part of the blame as he did not do enough to shield John from the bored pack of ravenous hacks. They seemed determined to outdo each other in their resolution to embarrass and humiliate the prime minister in front of his overseas counterparts. It became known as 'the trip from hell' and it got no better when we arrived in Malaysia.

On the first evening of the visit Dr Mahathir – the feisty, competitive, acid prime minister – launched into a vituperative attack on Britain's policy in Bosnia and how we were doing too little to protect the Muslims there from the genocidal attacks of the Serbs under Milosevic. This led to a row. Major was furious and threatened to get on the plane and fly home. Mahathir had a point. He knew the position on the ground because Malaysia had sent a contingent of troops.

The next day the toxic atmosphere continued. Finally, at about 6 o'clock, before a private dinner in Mahathir's residence, I confronted John in the gents and told him to calm down. Our discussion ended with me throwing a towel at him, and him telling me that I could have 'the bloody job if I wanted it'. We went outside and I asked the steward to bring two large gin and tonics. The gin and tonics arrived but before we had time to sip them, the door burst open and in came the lugubrious high commissioner Duncan Slater accompanied by Najib Razaleigh, the defence minister, who later turned out to be one of the biggest rogues in Asia. The gin and tonics were deposited into a nearby flowerpot – alcohol was supposed to be forbidden – and we trooped off to dinner fearing another bust-up. I decided to put on a cabaret and performed my full repertoire of jokes, accents, stories and impersonations. It appeared to work because I heard later that Mahathir said Malaysia needed a Needham in its cabinet.

During the flight back, John asked me to give him my thoughts for his Party conference speech. Afterwards he wrote me a very nice personal letter thanking me 'for the part you played in making it such a success'. I read the speech several times to see where my contributions had been included but I was unable to find any! Although the political side of the trip was a disaster, the businessmen were delighted with the high-level contacts they made on the back of the prime minister's sponsorship.

Four months later I nearly did end up in the Malaysian cabinet as a furious row broke out between the two countries. There had been rumours and accusations that in order to win billions of pounds worth of defence contracts the British government had used the Aid Trade Provisions to support building a dubious dam at Pergau in northern Malaysia. The grant amounted to £234 million and rumour had it that chunks had disappeared down local throats. All major economies supported similar deals in Asia and we would probably have sailed through (at least the dam worked!) except that Andrew Neil decided to publish a lengthy article in *The Sunday Times* in February 1994 accusing Wimpey of trying to bribe Dr Mahathir. Bizarrely the story had been leaked by the Merseyside police who were searching the Wimpey offices looking for evidence that the company had been involved in some fraud with the militants then running Liverpool Council.

Unsurprisingly Dr Mahathir reacted with fury and retaliated. On 25 February, Anwar Ibrahim, the finance minister, and his deputy announced a boycott on British companies tendering for public projects. It was the reintroduction of the 'buy British last' policy from a decade earlier. Andrew

Neil added a firelighter by refusing to retract, and comparing Mahathir to Hitler.

The prime minister and Michael Heseltine summoned me, and told me to get on the next plane to Kuala Lumpur and sort it out. I decided to take a small team of trusted businessmen with me and seek an interview with the prime minister. Luckily for me, Andrew Neil had not cleared his lines with his boss Rupert Murdoch, who was trying to gain access across all South East Asia for his Star Television channel. That too was now under threat.

I was told that Dr Mahathir would see us but that he was still outraged. When we arrived at his offices in Carcosa I told my team that they had to stand up and clap as soon as he entered the room. This did not go down well, particularly with Mervyn McCall from Northern Ireland who, before Mahathir arrived, remarked to me that Mahathir was a racist bigot. He claimed that had he treated Catholics in Belfast in the same way that the Malaysians treated the Chinese, he would have been locked up. I told him to shut up and follow my briefing.

When I got into the prime minister's office there was a press photo call that records Mahathir looking relaxed. He asked me what I wanted him to say. I said, 'Give them an indication of how long the boycott might last.'

'I can't do that,' he replied. 'You know what our policy is. Draft me a few speaking notes.'

I said, 'I'm a British minister preparing notes for you criticising my government?'

'Yes,' he said, 'unless you don't want me to say anything.'

We went downstairs to a conference room. The team dragged themselves to their feet and clapped in a half-hearted sort of way. Mahathir growled at them, 'Richard told you to do that, didn't he?' He then took my notes out of his pocket, unfolded them and started off. 'I'm now going to read out what Richard has prepared for me.' He then lambasted me, the government, the Press and former colonialists. I was humiliated. But so what, if he felt better?

I was then sent off to see Anwar Ibrahim to get the details of the boycott. He sat me down and told me that he had heard I liked scones. He proceeded to butter me one while telling me how many hundreds of millions of pounds of business we were likely to lose. I realised then that their hearts weren't in it but we had to get them off the hook. The hook turned out to be Rupert Murdoch. Murdoch had flown over for a secret discussion with Mahathir and a deal must have been struck.

A few weeks went by and two things happened. Narasimha Rao, prime minister of India, came to London on an official visit. A fortnight before his arrival there appeared a hagiographic interview with him by Andrew Neil, who had been sent out to Delhi, by *The Sunday Times*. Rao was small, round and reportedly open to offers. Neil's interview painted him as being somewhere between Mahatma Gandhi and Pandit Nehru. The Star Television Contract was also up for licensing in India! John Major, who had been kept informed on what was happening, asked me to sit on Rao's right at the Downing Street lunch and we gave him a blow-by-blow account of how 'poor' Dr Mahathir had been hung out to dry by *The Sunday Times* and the not-so-nice Mr Neil. He kept spitting out his specially prepared bowl of rice as we deluged him with the deviousness and danger he might expect from allowing the Murdoch press into India.

Two months later Andrew Neil left the editorship of *The Sunday Times* and departed for New York. Years later he rang me up and asked if I had been involved in any way in his move. I reminded him of his assassination of my privacy over the cow affair and told him that one good deed deserved another.

About a year later the boycott was quietly dropped and business returned to normal. I had formed close links with Malaysia that were to become an important part of my life over the following twenty years.

Anwar and I had hit it off. Between 1995 and 1998, after I had left government and joined GEC, I went to Kuala Lumpur several times, and Anwar always saw me. He introduced me to his wife, Wan Azizah, a Dublin-trained ophthalmologist and Nurul Izzah, his eldest daughter.

In late 1997, Anwar and Prime Minister Mahathir fell out over the Asia contagion financial crisis. Mahathir was determined to impose capital controls and Anwar, as finance minister, wanted to stay in the open trading system. Instead of sacking Anwar and replacing him with somebody else, Anwar was arrested on bogus sodomy charges (a crime in Malaysia), thrown into prison and beaten up by the chief of police. Since then, Anwar has spent almost ten years in prison, much of it in appalling conditions. Every attempt by the government to break his will has failed. He has never flinched. He has never faltered. He has never backed off.

Although Malaysia is a relatively small economy compared to Indonesia, Thailand and the Philippines, it should be a key player in establishing a plural, multi-racial, liberal Muslim country based on the democratic rule of law. Whether it succeeds still depends on whether Anwar becomes Prime Minister. Unfortunately, other ASEAN countries have usually been run by dictatorial, corrupt, military juntas, headed up by former generals.

Anwar, before his arrest, had long been campaigning for a reformed society under the banner of 'Reformasi'. For much of that period while he had been in jail, he and Wan Azizah led the main opposition party against the corrupt Umno government. He had powerful and influential enemies who were determined to bring him down. For the last twenty-two years I have done all I can to support Anwar, his wife and family. I have raised money, shouted through a loudhailer outside the House of Commons, lobbied ministers and members of parliament, written letters and made a thorough nuisance of myself. Throughout I have been backed up by my friend Chris Patten. What has the British government done to support this 'prisoner of conscience', this beacon of hope for millions of oppressed peoples and minorities? What have they done to tackle the appalling levels of corruption resulting in laundered billions sitting in London bank accounts? For the most part, they have done nothing more than lift the occasional finger while doing all in their power to support the British arms industry to sell jets and tanks that arguably the Malaysians don't need.

Extraordinarily and unexpectedly, after winning the last election from his prison cell, this wholly remarkable man, who has been supported by his equally remarkable family, appeared to be right on the edge of achieving his dream. Prime Minister Mahathir was 93, and had agreed to stand down and hand over to Anwar in the following two years. Then the wheel turned. The prime minister resigned in early 2020 and, instead of Anwar gaining power, the old corrupt Malay-dominated parties, supported by the king, scraped together a coalition to install Muhyiddin Yassin. By jiggery-pokery and patronage, he has so far survived and once again Anwar has been thwarted. His hopes for an inclusive democratic multicultural Malaysia seem to have slipped from his grasp. But the dream lives on.

'The night has ended. Put out the light of the lamp of thine own narrow corner smudged with smoke. The great morning which is for all appears in the East. Let its light reveal us to each other who walk on the same path of pilgrimage.'

Rabindranath Tagore

CHAPTER 30

Trying to Please Everyone

IN LATE APRIL 1993, Tristan Garel-Jones asked me to come to his room in the Foreign Office. I had just come back from four days in Korea and Hong Kong and the next day I was leaving for a Single Market trade ministers' meeting in Denmark. Tristan, the supposed model for Frank Underwood in Michael Dobbs's *House of Cards*, sat in an armchair. He had no desk. 'I have decided to move on in the near future. The worms are in the apple. We have got Maastricht done. We have had a good innings and there are other things to do.' He went on to tell me that he had recently come back from a trip to Colombia with John Major and that they both agreed that, once it got a grip on drugs and related violence issues, it was a country with huge potential. He told me that Colombians love us because of how we helped Simón Bolivar at the Battle of Boyacá in their war of independence in the 1820s. The rich families send their children to schools in England, have homes here and escape here in times of trouble. They are a democracy and always have been. Tristan had spent a lot of time on building our relationships and believed Colombia should be a focus in Latin America. John Major agreed and he wanted me to take over from Tristan.

Colombia! I had trouble trying to fit in Brazil and Argentina let alone Bogotá. All I knew was that we had special forces committed there, we bought a huge quantity of cut flowers from them and that Northern Ireland's power stations relied on Colombian coal. I also knew that the IRA had sent top bomb makers to teach the FARC (Fuerzas Armadas Revolucionarias de Colombia; the Revolutionary Armed Forces of Colombia) how to kill and maim.

Orders are orders. The office put together a rather thin trade mission, which would take in Brazil as well as Colombia. One difficulty was the journey: there were very few flights between São Paulo and Bogotá, the journey takes six hours, longer than crossing the Atlantic, and all the flights seemed to land at three in the morning.

Before I left, I discovered that my opposite number in Colombia, Juan Manuel Santos, had been in London for several years, when he was an international delegate to the International Coffee Organisation, and he had studied at the London School of Economics. He had stayed with Yolanda and Douglas Connor, parents of one of my son's best friends. Yolanda gave me a letter of introduction. When Juan Manuel and I met, we hit it off immediately. He has charm, humour, determination and courage. He is also a real friend to Britain.

The ambassador to Colombia, Sir Keith Morris, was outstanding. There was nothing he did not know and no one he hadn't met. He had an accomplice, Malcolm Deas from St Antony's College, Oxford, and together they acted as consiglieres, advisors and Machiavellis in the complex world of Colombian political parties.

Everyone on our mission was treated like royalty and we met everyone from President Samper down. Colombia is supposed to be to Venezuela what Ireland is to England. However, Bogotá has magnificent squares and palaces to rival those of Madrid. The country is one of, if not the most beautiful biodiverse nation in the world (for example, it has twenty-one species of cuckoo). Over the space of two hundred miles, from the east to the west, it covers three different climates trapped between huge mountain ranges. It has everything except peace.

Juan Manuel had me to stay at his stunning estate, high up in the Andes. He told me his priorities were protecting the EU trade agreement that allowed cut flowers tariff free into the UK and was designed to reduce the growing of coca. Some 70 per cent of cut flowers sold in Britain came from Colombia. Secondly, he was keen to increase inward investment. BP was developing a huge oil field at Cusiana, which he insisted I visit despite the occasional terrorist attack. After all I came from Northern Ireland! Thirdly, the government needed support from our special services. Colombia is twenty-five times the size of Ulster and had twenty-five times the number of terrorists.

I took the trade mission to Medellín, where I agreed to address an investment conference. We drove through the Andes from Bogotá, accompanied by Noemí Sanín and Álvaro Uribe. Noemí was the elegant former foreign minister, presidential candidate and ambassador to the UK. Unfortunately, she did not speak any English nor I any Spanish. Álvaro Uribe had studied at St Antony's College, Oxford. He was the mayor of Medellín and would go on to become governor of Antioquia and president of Colombia.

We had open-backed, pennant-flying lorryloads of troops in front of and behind our armoured BMW. I kept my fingers crossed that the IRA with their FARC friends had not placed a roadside bomb in our path. Every twenty miles we stopped at a roadside watering hole to allow Noemí and Álvaro to meet and greet the locals. We were bombarded with tapas and aguardiente, the local equivalent of poteen. Noemí seemed quite unaffected by the fire water and kissed everyone who came up to her. By the time we reached the conference hall I was exhausted, suffering from violent indigestion and blotto.

As I struggled through my presentation, I looked down and saw Pat Dougan, CEO of Mackie's Engineering in Belfast, standing below me, waving his arms and pointing to the back of the hall. I told him to be quiet and sit down. As soon as I had finished, he dragged me off in a taxi and, to the horror of the security guards, we rode off into the countryside. After twenty minutes we came to a giant, sack-producing, jute factory, puffing out steam and dust. It turned out that all the machines had been manufactured by Mackie's of Belfast in 1953.

Mackie's on the Springfield Road in West Belfast was well known for its Protestant connections. It was one of the world's most famous designers of linen and jute machines. It was regularly blown up by the IRA as part of their strategy to bring jobs to West Belfast. All the company's customer records had been destroyed. They had no knowledge of the machines they had built forty years before and were still working. The owner gave Pat an order for three-hundred-thousand-pounds-worth of spares. It was a reminder of what a great industrial centre Belfast had once been.

Pat was a remarkable man, a nationalist rugby-playing back row forward from North Antrim. As a child, he spent some time during the Second World War stealing hand grenades from the back of army officers' jeeps, blowing up salmon in the river Bann, and then selling them to the officers' mess. For a time, he became a runner for the IRA, before founding the immensely successful screening and crushing company Powerscreen. When he left, I persuaded him to come to Mackie's as its first Catholic managing director. It could have been very dangerous for him, but everyone was soon captivated by this bear of a man. He worked unceasingly to try to save the company by developing new products and reinvigorating the foundry. But the downturn in investment in the linen industry was too severe and soon after he had welcomed President Clinton to the factory on his first visit to Belfast, the company – like so much of manufacturing in Northern Ireland – was forced to close.

In total I visited Colombia three times and as words spread about the opportunities, so the numbers of participants on my missions increased.

Foreign leaders liked to come to London during June and July when they could watch Wimbledon and Ascot and their spouses could shop in Harrods. The DTI, together with the London Chamber of Commerce, the CBI or the Institute of Directors, would arrange a conference for the leader and his accompanying delegation. I would give the welcoming introductory address and the president or prime minister would respond, outlining the wonderful investment opportunities that existed in his country for British business.

I quickly developed a format: out and out flattery. What a wonderful country. What a wonderful leader. I would have got the in-country post to give me particular nuggets of information in advance so I could sound much more knowledgeable about their culture, art, constitution and history than I really was.

I came unstuck at a lunch in Downing Street for the president of Turkey, Süleyman Demirel. I had given a gushing introduction at an investment conference prior to the lunch, and lavished praise on Turkey as being one of the great civilising empires in world history with an empire the size of Britain's and a colonial history to match. He was delighted. At the lunch he leant over to the prime minister and the foreign secretary and said it was high time for Britain to upgrade its relations with Turkey and put someone in control of turbocharging a new mutual commitment. Pointing at me he continued, 'Someone who is clearly a great expert on and fan of my country.' Two pairs of glasses swivelled in my direction and, in unison, John Major and Douglas Hurd blurted out that I knew nothing about Turkey. 'That's not what the president thinks,' I answered.

So off I went to Turkey with a team of expectant companies who were hoping to be involved in the country's new programme of privatisation and infrastructure development. Amongst them was Pat Dougan again.

We were given an unprecedented hour-long slot with the president. John Goulden, the ambassador, advised us to give Demirel space to expand on his *Weltanschauung*.

Before the meeting the president invited me in for a one-on-one. What did I want him to say? 'We would love to hear your views on current disputes and your ideas for solving them,' I replied. That was enough: once the delegation was shown in, Demirel embarked on a history tour of Turkey and its glorious past, tactfully omitting the 1915 Dardanelles campaign. Then we had the present and the future. Turkey sat at the anvil between Europe and the Middle East and was the crucial power on which the future of Europe, Russia, Iran and Egypt depended.

It was a hot day and the air conditioning was intermittent. My team of bankers, salesmen, engineers and consultants nodded off.

When he had finished, the president asked for questions. Eyes popped open but then there was silence. I glared expectantly at Dougan. 'Mr President. In the papers today I read about the terrible deaths of your brave young soldiers at the hands of Kurdish terrorists. I come from Northern Ireland. I have lived through what you are now going through. You have to stand up to these people and bring them to justice.'

I blinked. Was this not the man who in his youth had been a member of the IRA?

'What is your name?' Demirel asked.

'Dougan, Sir.'

'What do you want?'

'The Izmir water project, Sir.'

'You shall have it, Mr Dougan, you are a true friend and supporter of Turkey!' Unfortunately, it was not enough to save Mackie's in Belfast, but Pat had shown the others how to win an order.

Meanwhile the veteran British ambassador to Morocco, Sir Allan Ramsay was persistent in demanding I take a mission to Rabat. After a year I agreed. When I landed in Casablanca, I was met by a Berber guard of honour. When they presented arms, I noticed the magazines had been removed, which was a relief. The finance minister, Mohammed Saghou, came straight to the point. Why were we buying cut flowers from Colombia not Morocco? Why were Moroccan tomatoes subject to prohibitive tariffs, protecting Spanish producers and causing higher prices for UK consumers? 'You have a choice,' he told me. 'Either you buy our flowers and our tomatoes or we will send you our cannabis! And if you won't take our cannabis, we will send you our Moroccans!' He had a point. British consumers would be better off buying from Morocco than Colombia but how could I let my friend, Manuel Santos, down? The same principle applied to Colombian bananas, which were bigger and cheaper than those from the West Indies. But I was confronted by the prime minister of Dominica, the formidable Eugenia Charles, who stormed into my office with the same arguments as the Moroccan minister.

Had I been less 'wet', I might have done something. But politics is the art of the possible and I decided to leave things as they were. There were more important battles to fight.

At the end of April 1994, I led a mission to Oman and Bahrain. Bahrain was ruled by a Sunni family under the emir, Isa bin Salman. It has a large, deprived, discriminated-against Shia working-class majority. It relies heavily on the support and patronage of its neighbour Saudi Arabia. It is poor compared to the other Gulf States but still generous to visiting British businessmen.

On the last afternoon of my visit the ambassador, Hugh Tunnell, insisted on accompanying me back to my hotel room. Sitting on the bed was a smart, black leather despatch box. I opened it. Inside was a small treasure trove: a Chopard gold watch, a red jewellery box containing a string of pearls and a pair of gold cufflinks. 'Oh dear,' said Hugh. 'I think this comes to rather more than the £75 for gifts allowed by the Treasury. Unless you want to behave like Alan Clark, who stuffed the watch into his pocket, you will have to hand it in.'

When we went down to the lobby the businessmen were all looking very smug, sporting their new gold watches. 'I'll take care of yours,' insisted my private secretary Andrew Dobbie when we got back to London. 'Hang on,' I said. 'I want you to find out what happens now.'

A few days later he came into my office with a glum face. 'You can keep the despatch box and the pearls are fake. The rest goes into a private auction.'

'Why private?'

'Well, if it went into a public auction the emir might discover and he would not be pleased to see his expensive personal gifts sold off to pay down the budget deficit. But I'm afraid it's worse than that. The private auction is a ring with allegedly Jewish connections. So, the price obtained is a fraction of what the items are worth.'

'Oh, that would delight the Emir even further,' I replied. 'I suggest we sell the watch at a public auction and give the proceeds to an Arab charity. Meanwhile I am locking them up in my desk while you investigate further.'

A couple of weeks later, after a visit to Colombia, I sat down and opened the drawer. It was empty. The gifts were gone!

'Come here, Dobbie,' I bellowed. 'I don't know how any of this electronic paraphernalia on my desk works but there is an outside line and if that watch is not back in here in five minutes, I am phoning the police and reporting a theft!'

Four minutes later, the permanent secretary, Sir Peter Gregson, arrived. 'Richard, rules are rules, I'm afraid, and the Treasury is adamant that they must be sold.'

'Okay,' I said, 'then why don't we call in the Bahraini ambassador, explain the situation and get him to sell them and give the proceeds to a charity?'

'I wouldn't recommend that. I'm sure the ambassador would be only too happy to take care of them but I doubt whether the proceeds would end up in an Arab charity. I'll have one more walk around the park and see if anything can be done,' said the retreating Sir Peter.

The following afternoon I picked up the phone and a silky-smooth voice announced, 'I am the head of the middle eastern department in the Foreign Office, Minister. I hear there is a small problem with a gold watch. I'm sure we can find a way of solving it. As you will appreciate, ambassadors are presented with gifts for themselves and their wives on numerous occasions. It would be unthinkable for them to be sold. The rule is that the recipient wears the gift on behalf of the government and when he or she leaves, it is handed on to his or her successor. There is also the option of buying it. In your case, Minister, I'm sure the government would be delighted for you to wear the watch while you remain minister of trade and when the unfortunate time comes for you to move on, you will have a chance of purchasing it or handing it on to your successor. By then, if you have worn it regularly, it may be somewhat tarnished and lost some value. By the way, do you have a small wrist?'

'Quite narrow,' I replied.

'Well then, that also limits its value if the links you removed have disappeared.'

So, for the next year I enjoyed wearing the watch. The day of reckoning arrived when I resigned. I phoned Andrew Dobbie. I said I'd go and get a valuation; he was quick to point out that there was a government-approved list of valuers.

I chose Bonhams. The wristwatch expert peered through his eyeglass. 'A thousand at auction,' he opined. Then came the sting. He looked at me. 'Who are you? Were you a government official?' I nodded. 'Special rules for you, mate: willing buyer, willing seller. Two thousand.'

I bought it with my redundancy money. It has been an appalling investment as it regularly breaks down and has to go back to Switzerland for a two-hundred-pound service. Meanwhile the government's policy on gifts remains watertight.

On 7 September 1994 I did an interview about the Malaysian boycott with Nick Clarke on BBC Radio 4's *World at One*. At the end of it, I said, talking of *The Sunday Times*'s article accusing prime minister Mahathir of taking bribes, 'Words are lethal when dealing with people you had a close colonial relationship with, and it as true of Malaysia as it is of Ireland or anywhere else'.

Nearly three weeks later Norman Tebbit wrote to the prime minister, attaching a 'transcript' that alleged that I had said 'and it is as true of Malaysia as it is of Ulster' – he had underlined this part. He went on to demand that I should keep my views about the relationship between England and Ireland to myself. This infuriated me. Firstly, he must have known what he had done and secondly, he inferred that I was comparing Ulster to Malaysia as examples of former colonies. He was understandably bitter about what had happened in the Brighton bombing and had adopted a hard, uncompromising, unforgiving stance as far as Irish nationalism was concerned. But he knew little of Northern Ireland; hardly ever went there. Ulster people of either community knew little about him. He had a strong dislike for me because of the cow affair and I was sure that he would go out of his way to stop me being promoted. He was a Theory X politician who, with his vicious tongue, had the ability to frighten and bully. Michael Foot had described him as giving a 'famous imitation of a semi-housetrained polecat'. In public he often lacked empathy and sensitivity. He had no time for those he thought were 'shirkers' or 'wasters'.

I drafted a short, balanced and polite response for the prime minister to send and received back a proof on Number 10 notepaper. John Major had drafted, in my opinion, a rather pusillanimous, feeble reply that ended with his hopes of meeting up with Tebbit at the party conference. Major clearly believed he already had enough problems dealing with his right wing without further antagonising Tebbit by defending me. I happened to be in Hong Kong at a private dinner when I received the reply. I thought I was out of earshot of Number 10 when I unwisely remarked that where we had been landed with Major, Hong Kong had Chris Patten, and that I knew which one I would have preferred! A few days later this was reported back to Number 10. Panic. A reshuffle was coming. I rang John Parker, who had been on the mission, to ask him what he thought I should do. John was the former chief executive of Harland and Wolff and was now chair of Babcock International. Later he would go on to become chairman of Anglo-American Plc and senior non-executive director of the Bank of England.

Unbeknown to me John immediately wrote to the prime minister, saving my bacon. A few days later he received a personal reply thanking him for his comments. Disaster was averted thanks to my Northern Irish friend. The lesson is that you are never safe from being found out wherever you are, and reacting to criticism only makes matters worse!

Babcock International Group PLC

Chairman **Dr. T. John Parker** FEng	Badminton Court, Church Street, Amersham Bucks. HP7 0DD Telephone: 01494 727296 Fax: 01494 721909

19 October, 1994

The Rt Hon John Major, MP
Prime Minister
10 Downing Street
LONDON SW1

Dear Prime Minister,

Often we industrial leaders are critical of Government and of particular Ministers.

I thought I should write to you, and the President of the Board of Trade, to say that I have just participated in a Trade Mission to Hong Kong led by Richard Needham.

I have been doing business in Hong Kong for more than 20 years but I have never experienced a Marketing Mission led with such vigour, drive and personal charisma, all of which went down particularly well with the major business leaders we met.

Clearly, Richard Needham's sterling efforts, since becoming Minister for Trade, have made a deep impression on our potential customers around the world. I thought I should record that we, as a group, particularly appreciated this form of support from Government.

Yours sincerely

T. John Parker

Copy: President of the Board of Trade

Babcock
International

Registered in England No. 234 2138. Registered office as above

CHAPTER 31

Plugging the Gaps

IN SPITE OF a few hiccups, after two and a half years as UK plc's sales and marketing director in the new expanding markets of Asia and Latin America, Africa and the Middle East, I had a pretty good idea of our strengths and weaknesses. The companies that made use of ministerial support were nearly all large and international with access to export credit finance. They needed me to open the doors at the very top. The middle-sized and smaller companies relied on help from DTI regional offices, the country desks of DTI and, most importantly, the commercial offices of the embassies, which had been strengthened by the arrival of one hundred private sector-sponsored export promoters. The quality of service provided by the department had improved enormously.

But it remained the case that, compared to the Germans, our manufacturing exporting base was narrow and losing market share. Most service companies had a dearth of product offerings that attracted overseas interest. Our designs lacked style and taste. Spending on research and development was often minuscule. The quality of our management was variable and our language skills generally non-existent.

I decided to concentrate on the strategy to tackle design failings. Firstly, I persuaded the British Council offices to integrate more with the embassies' commercial departments to promote British design and British culture. The Design Council concentrated too much on how things looked rather than how things worked. Reinforcing the need to do something, a government survey had found that only 8 per cent of senior managers in either the civil service or the City thought that design was of significant importance to running a business.

Terence Conran, who had spent millions investing in the Design Museum to showcase British innovation, was rightly outraged by the lack of government support and interest. One of the obstacles was that no single government department owned design as a responsibility. Nominally it fell under the industry side of DTI, which was run by an oil man. The Royal College of Art was a university. The British Council was an outpost of the Foreign and Commonwealth Office. There was a limit to what I could do, but I could highlight the need for supporting new and existing initiatives.

One such case was London Fashion Week. Fashion was dominated by the Italians and the French, but we had some wonderful young designers coming through and they wanted help promoting UK creations. I went to see Rick Greenbury of Marks & Spencer and he nominated his deputy Clinton Silver, former chief clothes buyer at M&S, to become chairman of London Fashion Week. Clinton reluctantly agreed. He was a hard man but a very shrewd and determined one. We had to give life back to a dying national treasure.

After two years in the role, Clinton remarked that dealing with the ruthless Italians and French was the hardest time of his business life. However, Bruce Oldfield said it was impossible to overestimate Clinton's importance – he had a wonderful knack of getting the best out of and winning over the often moody, temperamental, selfish, politically iconoclastic Vivian Westwoods of this world. He got Vidal Sassoon and Marks & Spencer to sponsor Fashion Week. The Princess of Wales became an unpaid mannequin for British ideas. London Fashion Week is proof that government intervention at the right time with the right people can change industries without the need for handouts or subsidies.

One of my strongest allies and supporters of my trade promotion strategy was Bob Ayling, CEO of British Airways. Bob has always been a design enthusiast, and he got himself involved in exciting if contentious, eye-catching developments. He had reorganised British Airways into 'the World's Favourite Airline' by a series of measures which included investing in the London Eye, and building a world leading open plan office complex near Heathrow called 'the Waterside', nicknamed 'Ayling's Island' and costing £200 million. He had internationalised the company by introducing language training for all the cabin staff. His most controversial move was an amazing series of designs for the tails of his planes. Some of them were perhaps a step too far, especially for Mrs Thatcher, who once draped her scarf over a display model.

Sometimes his enthusiasm got the better of him and he became a divisive figure. This led to his demise at British Airways, which then returned to money making Theory X mediocrity, and his loss of the chairmanship of the company building the Millennium Dome, which is now a world-famous entertainment venue. In both cases he was disgracefully let down by people who supported him at the start but abandoned him once they heard the sound of gunfire.

My next action was to build on the efforts being made by Sir Peter Parker to improve the language skills of Britain's younger businessmen. Sir Peter Parker was a great man, one of my idols. He learnt Japanese before the war and became an interrogator of captured Japanese officers during it. He joined the Intelligence Corps in 1943, serving in India, Burma and later the United States. He was a linguist. He studied history at Oxford. He was the best undergraduate actor of his day. He was a passionate Theory Y manager and for a time he was head of the overseas department of the Industrial Society.

We concentrated on Japanese. I went on a course at SOAS for a day to find out how the language worked and it was one of the most useful days of my life. Language determines the culture of a country and the social relationships between old and young, men and women. It can either make it easier to relax and relate or it introduces barriers and makes it harder to establish trust and intimacy. To understand the structure of a language is a crucial building block in understanding how individuals will react and behave in any negotiations or discussions. Thirty years later the Sir Peter Parker Awards are still running.

Following the annual awards ceremony, Peter and I shared a car back to the DTI office. It suddenly occurred to me that I would like to find out what would happen if someone phoned up the DTI switchboard and asked in Italian to be put through to the minister. Exactly what a mischievous journalist might do to make us look ridiculous. So, I rang through.

'*Buon giorno. Per favore, posso parlare con il Ministro Commerciale?*'

'Could you say that again?'

I repeated my request.

'Ethel, I've got some Spanish guy on the line.'

'Give him to me.'

'Hello, Ethel here. Can I help'?

I tried again. There was a pause.

'Stop taking the mick, Minister!'

So ended my efforts to introduce multi-language skills to the DTI switchboard.

For a country that is an island and that once controlled half of the world, it is surprising how insular and ill-informed we have become. Most British governments have left businesses to their own devices when going overseas. Most medium and small companies dip their toes into the water, find it too cold or too hot, and stick to their home markets or to making components for their larger customers.

For many years most British companies have been deeply reticent about attempting to penetrate overseas markets. Exporting is expensive. Most companies have tight gross margins, at best 20 to 25 per cent. Selling abroad requires extra marketing funds and high distribution margins, sometimes tariffs, product adaptations to suit local needs and higher transportation charges. Many companies are run by accountants who focus on margins, bottom lines and shareholder value. Twenty-five years ago, very few companies knew about government-supported export advice and accompanying services. Those that did didn't like being charged for them and didn't think they were particularly good value for money. The marketplace was often confused by accountancy firms offering their own professional advice. Trade associations and Chambers of Commerce, unlike their statutory counterparts in Germany, only served a relatively small number of enterprises.

Michael Heseltine and I determined on a nationwide campaign to support new exporters. I crisscrossed the country from Salford to Newcastle and from Plymouth to Norwich holding seminars and manning exhibitions. At the Salford conference, the North West regional office had decided that such an important visitor as me should be properly looked after. Rather than putting me up in the local Holiday Inn, I was booked into the bridal suite at the Midland Hotel in Manchester at £600 per night. I left without unpacking my bags, a vision before me of what might have appeared in the *Manchester Guardian* had the story got out!

The numbers of local companies wishing to export were depressingly small. Our manufacturing base had hollowed out through years of low productivity, low investment, Theory X-based bad industrial relations and poor design. Mrs Thatcher's disastrous high interest rate, high pound, demand-reducing policies of the early 80s had been the added nails in the coffins of many industries. The future growth of the economy would have to rely on inward investment and the expansion of soft services.

Amongst the murk there were occasional lighter moments. From time to time I used to visit Rick Greenbury, chairman of Marks & Spencer, in Baker Street for a chat and an update. He told me in October 1994 that he had just seen samples of wool clothing from Korea. They were superb in quality, design, range of garments and price. He could not see how the Yorkshire cashmere woollen industry could survive. He asked me to pass this on when I had the chance.

It so happened that I had been asked to be guest speaker at the annual dinner of the Worshipful Company of Woolmen at the Saddlers' Hall, which would be attended by the Princess Royal, the Master and all the luminaries of the wool industry. There I intended, in a tactful way, to pass on the news that the chairman of Marks & Spencer had given me.

On the day of the dinner Andrew Dobbie, one of my assistant private secretaries, asked whether I had white tie and tails. I had not looked at the invitation, so I had no idea that this was the dress code. It so happened that I had been married in white tie and tails thirty years earlier and, as far as I was aware, they were in a cupboard somewhere at home in Gloucestershire – they had not had an outing since the wedding. However, the starched shirt and waistcoat would be yellow with age and my waist was not what it once was. I told Andrew to ring Moss Bros and hire what I needed. There wasn't a suit to be had anywhere in London. They were all out on hire. A new one would cost eight hundred pounds and it would be weeks before it would be ready.

I rang Sissy and explained to her what was required: cufflinks, buttons, studs, stick-up collar, white tie, waistcoat, watch chain, black patent leather shoes. Sissy put everything in a suitcase and raced to Swindon to catch a special express service that was due in Paddington at 6 o'clock. By the time it arrived at the office it was 6.45 and the reception began at 7.30. It was unpardonable to be late for royalty.

The private office was assembled to dress the minister. The trousers had to be cut open at the back but no one would see it. Everything was assembled. Then disaster struck – Sissy had sent up a morning suit starched collar not a stick-up! Panic. Andrew rang round the other ministerial private offices. This really would prove whether the civil service was the Rolls-Royce it always claimed to be in a crisis.

Hallelujah! Earl Ferrers, DTI minister of state in the House of Lords, kept one in a box in his desk in case of emergencies. He was a 6'3" former Coldstream Guards officer. He had a rugby player's 18-inch neck. His

Election night, 3 May 1979.

Tea ceremony, Tokyo, September 1985.

My two Permanent Secretaries – Gerry Loughran (left) and John
Murray – making a presentation to me in 1991 to mark my tenure
as the UK's longest-serving minister in Northern Ireland.

CastleCourt, Belfast, 1992.

Visiting Cusiana oil field, Colombia, 1994.

Me, Dr Mahathir, Sir Charles Powell and John Major,
September 1993.

Celebrating becoming the UK's longest-serving and
most-travelled Trade Minister since World War Two, 1995.

John Major, Ivan McCabrey of Mivan, Yasser Arafat
and me, 14 March 1995.

The Blue Chips dining club, 1983.

Blue Chips, thirty years on.

Friends at Last! Left to right: Mitchell McLaughlin (Sinn Féin),
me, senior civil servant Declan O'Hare and
Glenn Barr (formerly UDA), 2 June 2016.

With Yukio Hatoyama in our wood in Wiltshire, 17 May 2004.
Julia Boyd, wife of our former ambassador Sir John Boyd,
is in the background with Sissy behind her.

Holidaying on the Helford River, Cornwall, August 1997.

collar wrapped twice around my throat. I got hold of a knife to make a hole for the stud further around the collar. Unfortunately, the knife went through the collar into my finger and splattered the shirt and collar with blood.

There was nothing more to be done – I raced off. I got to the Saddlers' Hall just as Princess Anne was going up the stairs. 'What kept you?' she asked, and then seeing the state of my collar, 'What on earth have you done?' Once we had sat down and I'd explained what had happened, she asked, 'Do you want to tell them or shall I?'

'They'll think I've tried to kill you! You do it, Ma'am,' I said – and she did!

By the time I stood up to respond the starch on the collar had melted, the stud shot out, and the collar flew open. Any chance of me passing on Rick's message disappeared in gales of laughter. I'm afraid the future didn't contain too many laughs for the Yorkshire woolmen.

CHAPTER 32

Time to Go

JOHN MAJOR'S EQUIVOCAL reply to Norman Tebbit's complaint about me in the autumn of 1994 had started me thinking about my future. I had been minister of trade for nearly two and a half years. The Department had been reorganised and become more integrated with the Foreign Office. Ambassadors now had to produce annual business plans and forecasts of the levels of exports and inward investment. One hundred outside export promoters were embedded in overseas markets. The rules governing export finance had been relaxed. Both the British Council and the Department for International Development worked more closely in promoting Britain's commercial and service businesses. Although the rules and disciplines of the civil service favoured a top-down 'do as I say' Theory X style of management, the atmosphere tended to be more relaxed and easy-going than in much of the private sector.

I had achieved a lot. I had been made a privy counsellor in June 1994. I was a regular visitor to Number 10 and to Chequers. In March 1995 I was invited to open the debate at the Chequers seminar on future foreign and trade policy, which was attended by the most senior members of the Cabinet. I pointed out that the UK's share of world trade had almost halved over the last twenty-five years from 9 per cent to 5 per cent, while Germany's had remained at 9 per cent. Economic might drove political and military influence. What were the policies we should avoid and adapt to halt that decline? Twenty-five years later our share has reduced to 2.5 per cent. Germany's is at 7.5 per cent. However, the debate soon deteriorated into arguments about what we should do to win the next election and which department could squeeze the most out of the Treasury. No one suggested that one way out might be to leave the EU!

Michael Heseltine had in 1992, tongue in cheek, promised to take credit for all my successes – but at a conference in Birmingham which was celebrating the centenary of the first car built in the city in 1895, he announced that it had been my idea and I was the best minister of trade since the War.

Minister of trade was a top, even *the* top, position below the cabinet. So, I had to be in the frame for promotion. Nicholas Soames had told my uncle John Sheffield that I was definitely going into the cabinet. But where? Gerry Loughran thought as secretary of state for Wales after a pretty average performance from John Redwood, who had made a fool of himself for not having learned the Welsh national anthem at Cardiff Arms Park. But I was not so sure. The government was deeply unpopular, riven by dissent and scandals. I had gained a reputation, unfairly for the most part, as a bit of a loose cannon. I had the support of my blue-chip friends, but Chris Patten had disappeared to Hong Kong. My postings were in Ireland and in trade so I was hardly ever in the House of Commons to push my case in the bars or the Chamber.

Tristan Garel-Jones told me that he thought it was time to get out. We could not win the next election and we could be out for years. The right wing of the Tory party would oppose my appointment to any position in the cabinet and the prime minister might well think it wasn't worth moving me when I was doing a good job.

I had a wonderful parliamentary private secretary, Andrew Rowe, MP for mid Kent, who had worked in Central Office before heading up the Conservative trade unionists in the 1970s. He was founder of the UK Youth Parliament. He was decent, kind, loyal and honest man; too good in some ways for the cut and thrust of politics. He died bravely and early from prostate cancer in 2008. He was a living example of Theory Y in everything he did. He was not sure that Major would promote me unless he was pushed hard to do so. John was the key but I am not sure what the recommendation of Richard Ryder, the chief whip, would have been.

John Major has become a better prime minister the longer he has not been prime minister! He now has gravity and statesmanship. He is measured and authoritative. He has behaved impeccably since he stood down, unlike his two predecessors. I had got to know him quite well, had seen him in action when he travelled abroad and had watched his performances in the House. Under the smile, the wit and the apparent single-mindedness there was a caution, a lack of certainty. He was averse to taking risks which sometimes made him appear weak.

Perhaps it was his difficult upbringing. His failure to go to university ate at his confidence and made him doubt his own judgement. I watched on several occasions, as he sparred with officials over advice that they had given him, and he was reluctant to accept. Like only really clever men, he was capable of looking down the telescope backwards and coming up with startlingly creative suggestions and solutions, which nonplussed the civil servants briefing him.

There were a number of times when I witnessed him tearing the official 'line to take' to shreds, but then he would back off and move on to something else. He had been dealt a terrible hand when he became leader and, after the European Exchange Rate Mechanism fiasco, he had a dreadful time. He also had to live with kamikaze rebels, who he sometimes tried to bribe and conciliate when he should have kicked them in the balls. When he finally did it was often too late. His determination to wade into the Ulster bog and bring peace was probably his greatest legacy – for which he is not properly recognised. In Blair, he had one of the most decisive and attractive politicians of the last century as his opponent. John Major was not a great prime minister but he was a good one, and – as importantly – he was and is a good man.

As for me, I had lost my feeling of excitement and enjoyment when I entered the House. The thrill had gone. Then I was stopped by a policeman at Palace Gate who greeted me with 'Nice to see you're back, Mr Benyon.' Tom Benyon was an MP who looked a bit like me but who had stood down in 1983!

After ten years as a minister, constantly travelling, I was quite worn out and the money had run out. It turned out I was not the only one in the family thinking it was time for a change. One weekend in early 1995 I came home to find the family waiting for me. Robert told me that we were to have a conference about my future. I asked whether my future had anything to do with them. They replied firmly that it didn't – but that it had a lot to do with their mother and she had had enough of being the surrogate MP for North Wiltshire while I had been away for ten years. 'We think it's time that either you take the role back or you give up. We have decided that the family should have a vote. Each of us children and our mother has one vote, as do you, but in the event of a tie you can have the casting vote.' It never came to that as I was out-voted four to one!

There then arose a bigger question. Who was going to give me a job?

In the middle of January 1995 Jim Prior, chairman of General Electric Company (GEC), asked if I would go to see him for a private chat at the tatty company offices in Stanhope Gate, next to the Dorchester, off Park Lane. When I arrived, I was surprised to see that Sir Arnold Weinstock, the founder and CEO, was also in attendance. Jim came straight to the point. The Tories were not going to win the upcoming election and I wasn't going to make the Cabinet. 'I suspect you're out of funds. Would you like to come and work with us as a full-time executive in charge of international business on £200,000 a year?' Of course, this would mean my standing down from the Commons and the end of my parliamentary career.

This was money I had never dreamt of. I did not tell him that the die had already been cast by the family vote a few weeks earlier. I asked for a few days to reflect. There followed a few horrendous months. At the end of January, I flew to Malta for two days. I was the first trade minister ever to visit. From the 18–26 February, I went to Sri Lanka. From 11–14 March I was in Jordan and Tel Aviv with the prime minister. I came back for two days and then departed for Japan, arriving on 17 March and departing on the 22nd. From 26–31 March I led a trade mission to South Africa. I was in Paris for the weekend of 7–11 April at an international conference on export credit guarantee schemes. I headed up another trade mission to Korea, returning via Malaysia, from 17–25 April. When I finally got home, I finished the week canvassing in support of the local election candidates. On the Monday I phoned Jim and said I would accept. I had fallen into the Theory X trap: money was a motivator!

First, I had to tell Michael Heseltine. He said he quite understood but would be sad to see me go, and told me to inform the prime minister. John was able to see me straight away. He said how lucky I was, that he quite understood, didn't blame me at all and would do exactly the same himself if he had the chance. I asked him for a reference. A small part of me still hoped that he might offer me something. But he didn't. He asked me to stay for a few weeks so my resignation would be part of the reshuffle he was planning.

As it turned out, by early summer 1995, John Major had become so exasperated with the 'bastards' on the right of his party that he decided that he had to take drastic action. He decided to resign as Party leader and put himself up for re-election while remaining prime minister. One evening I was waiting to see him with Tristan Garel-Jones in his room behind the Speaker's Chair to discuss some South American issue. He stormed in, having had a blazing row with about fifty of the Eurosceptic rebels. 'I've had enough. I don't need any more of this. As you know, Tristan, I never cared that much for the job anyway. There's plenty of other things I can do with my life!' We calmed him down but it was clear he had to face down his critics by regaining control of his party, or he and his government were finished.

He did this by resigning as leader of the party on 22 June but staying on as prime minister and putting himself up for re-election. Robert Cranborne, later the Marquis of Salisbury, backed by Alastair Goodlad, the deputy chief whip, were put in control of his campaign. I offered to help but I think Robert probably had me down as a Heseltine spy! Michael Heseltine told everyone he would do all he could to support John Major and he did. His only chance was if John did not get enough votes. He did, by three! That was the end of Heseltine's hopes of ever becoming prime minister and any lingering chance of me making the Cabinet.

A week into the leadership campaign I had jetted off to Chicago to study the courses offered at the Institute of Design, part of the Illinois Institute of Technology. It had originally been called 'the New Bauhaus' and was the greatest centre of industrial design in the world. It was also a centre of Theory Y management practice. I wanted to know how we could persuade them to set up a campus in the UK. It was one of the initiatives that died with me.

I went back to London for a day and then took off for my final trade mission, which was to Malaysia. I had finally succeeded in attracting entirely new types of company on such missions, and my last one included a business that was the world-leading provider of lighting in nightclubs, and a Blackpool company that made 'The Big One', which turned out to mean that they fabricated huge funfair wheels.

On the way back to the airport, Duncan Slater, the high commissioner, told me the outcome of the vote and that there was to be a reshuffle announcement the following morning. I would find a brown envelope waiting for me when I touched down. It contained my resignation letter. Ministers do not get fired, they resign. This avoids any need for redundancy payments. Theory Y management methods do not apply. I drove straight into Ashdown House on Victoria Street to say goodbye.

The reshuffle had been announced and Michael Heseltine had become deputy prime minister. As soon as I arrived, I went into his office. He was very matter of fact; I was quite emotional. I really had loved working for him. He had got the best out of me. He was inspirational, fun, loyal to his subordinates, someone you wanted to follow and emulate. I would miss him. I went through the connecting door to my office. Who was there but 'Sir' Christopher Roberts waiting to wave me goodbye and welcome my successor. Ulrich Mathaler, my principal private secretary, had already transferred his loyalty and was keenly preparing for the newcomer. I agreed with all the others that we would stay in touch and we have. Even now, twenty-five years later, we still meet up from time to time.

I went back to my flat around the corner. For the first time in ten years, that night I caught a tube to a reception at the Victoria and Albert Museum. Meanwhile I was still an MP with a constituency to nurse and I had to make plans as to when to announce I was standing down and moving to GEC. I wasn't the only one leaving the ship.

In fact, I was joining a long and distinguished line of ministers, who had either been asked to resign, decided to retire or been offered jobs outside Parliament. John Nott had gone to Lazards, the first ex-minister reportedly to earn £1 million a year; John McGregor to merchant bank Hill Samuel; Norman Lamont to Rothschilds; Tristan Garel-Jones, along with Leon Brittan, to UBS (Tristan rather bizarrely claiming that now he was convinced that John Major would win the next election he was no longer required!); Peter Walker to British Gas and Francis Maude to Salomon Brothers.

In 1994, the government established a Committee on Standards in Public Life under Lord Nolan. This was a result of a drip of revelations about MPs – mainly Tories, but not always – abusing their positions. Neil Hamilton, amongst others, had apparently asked questions for Mr Al-Fayed of Harrods in return for cash. Jonathan Aitken had lied about his hotel bills in Paris. After sixteen years in power, the Tories were stale and divided. Tony Blair presented a bright, exciting, clean new Britain in comparison the one offered by the sleazy Tories. The country was ready for a change and the media of all descriptions was with the country.

No one in the media had picked up that I had left the government following the reshuffle. I decided to lie low over the summer and try to work out a plan to play down the inevitable row that my joining GEC was bound to cause. At the end of July, I wrote to Robin Butler, Head of the

Civil Service, to ask his views about my applications after a three month gap to join GEC and Mivan as a non-executive director. He replied saying if I had been a civil servant, I would have been given approval. He passed my letter on to Lord Carlyle, chair of the advisory committee on business appointments. He came back at the end of August saying that, although the government's proposals were yet to be formally adopted, my application would appear to meet fully the criteria recommended by Lord Nolan, and that his Committee would have endorsed the appointments. I had met all the criteria of a Cabinet Minister even though I wasn't one.

I decided to hold a press conference on 3 September 1995 to reveal that I would be standing down at the next election, to announce my new appointment and to head off some of the criticism that was sure to follow. But I was too easy a target for the opposition to ignore. I was front-page news. *The Sunday Times* lead splashed 'Minister lands Tories in new sleaze scandal'. Malcolm Bruce, the Liberal Democrat Treasury spokesman, was quoted in the article as saying, 'It is really using the privilege of recent office to line your own pocket! It smells of something getting close to corruption.' 'Needham is crawling under the fence before it is nailed to the ground,' squawked Brian Wilson, the Labour trade spokesman. 'Mr Needham, like so many ex-Tory ministers, regards it as his right to collect directorships like confetti'. Brian Wilson went on to a highly successful business career, collecting directorships with organisations including Celtic Football Club, AMEC, Foster Wheeler, Harris Tweed and Airtricity plc.

Trevor Kavanagh, political editor of the *Sun* – of whom it was said that when he bit you, you turned septic very quickly – could not resist weighing in. We had had a row in Jerusalem on a trade mission with John Major after he and his mates had daubed the businessmen's bus with 'fat cat' slogans. He claimed I had helped GEC get cash before taking a job there and got a quote out of Brian Wilson: 'You can't have a minister who in July was approving funds for GEC and then in September is sitting on its board.' These were downright lies.

Fortunately for me, my critics had gone too far. I had studiously ensured that I had kept to every instruction and abided by every rule. This time I could call in the law without having to seek the authority of the attorney general. The *Sun* had to contribute five-thousand pounds to charity and Messrs Bruce and Wilson had to apologise and undertake not to repeat their libels.

I did, however, have as many friends as enemies. Peter Riddell wrote a very supportive piece in *The Times* that began, 'Richard Needham has done nothing wrong. Far from being an example of sleaze or scandal, it is a sensible move which more politicians should seek to copy.' The supportive letters far outweighed the vituperative.

September 1995 was a traumatic time. I was giving up everything that had dominated my life for over thirty years, and any ambition I'd held of getting further in politics was over. My life as a public servant was at an end, although I still had two years until the next election so I would remain a member of parliament. I determined to do all I could to ease the way for my successor, even though he came from the other side of the Conservative party and I disagreed with him on most issues.

Giving up politics also meant giving up the partnership that Sissy and I had developed to run the constituency together. It had been a foundation stone of our relationship for over twenty years. After thirty years of marriage, how would we cope with our lives being more separate than they had been since our engagement?

Interaction with constituents is the lifeblood of any MP. It keeps you sane, your feet on the ground and in touch with the hopes, fears and the day-to-day lives of those around you. My decision meant that I would lose many loyal friends who had helped me get elected and re-elected.

I felt guilty that I was giving up a theory Y existence and going off to earn money on the back of what I had learnt in politics. On the other hand, I was exhausted, and many of my friends in politics were also standing down. It was time to move on and do something different – to start again, and to return to a life of business at a level way above that which I had left when I entered the House of Commons.

CHAPTER 33

The Family

A WHOLE HOST of reasons drive men and women towards political careers – ambition, a sense of duty, and a desire to wield power, to improve things and to be famous. Very few who start down the road realise just how long, twisting and potholed it is. Nor do they realise the demands it will place on any family that they might plan to have along the way.

I had decided in my teens that politics was the career for me. But I also wanted to have a beautiful wife, beautiful children, a beautiful house and lots of money. Unfortunately for me, there was no money in the kitty so I knew that I would need to achieve my dreams by hard work and a dose of luck.

Sissy and I married very young, and our two boys arrived soon after our wedding – Robert in 1966 and Andy in 1969. Christina was born a decade later in 1977. I started my first business when I was twenty-five. From then on, for the next twenty-seven years, I worked flat out. When I was not travelling the country selling, I spent six days each week at the factories in Yeovil and Crewkerne. When I was elected a county councillor and had to go to meetings in Taunton – twenty-five miles away – several times a month.

Once the companies I had set up were up and running, I bought a one-bedroom flat near Victoria station and spent several days a month in London, pursuing my political career. In 1975 I became Jim Prior's political assistant and the workload doubled. Once I had become an MP, I spent my first few years in parliament building up my majority. This involved spending four days a week at Westminster and the rest of my time – including Saturdays and most Sunday evenings – working in the constituency while remaining involved with the companies. The situation did not improve when I was in Northern Ireland, and had to stay in Belfast for four or five days per week and needed the weekends to concentrate on the constituency. As minister of trade I travelled extensively. How could I be a Theory Y husband or father if I was only there for the family at Sunday lunch?

Sissy had to take on most of the parenting as well as being, at the start, the book-keeper and financial controller. She later became my main constituency secretary. Without her total commitment, both to the family and to my career, the ship would have foundered.

We also had the responsibility of looking after two Indonesian boys – Johnny, the adopted son of my mother-in-law, lived with us from the age of five until he was twelve, and Melvin, whose parents had decided to send their son to school in England, lived with us in the exeats and holidays.

When we had first married and were living in Somerset, the plan was that the children would go to a local day school and then move to Sherborne public school at twelve or so, attending as day boys. The plans for our children to remain day pupils were blown apart when I was chosen as candidate for Chippenham and we had to move house. We had to decide whether to use the state system or go private. After much soul searching, particularly as Sissy was deeply uncertain about sending children away at a young age, we approached Eton. Raef Payne, the teacher who I had had real affection and respect for while I was at the school, was by this time a senior housemaster and he agreed to take on Robert and Andy if they passed the common entrance.

Once we'd moved, Robert went to a local crammer, Washbourne's Place, to prepare for the common entrance. Andy was still at Sherborne and became a weekly boarder. He was deeply miserable. Sissy collected him every Friday, by which point he was already crying at the prospect of having to go back on Sunday. We moved him to a more local preparatory school, Beaudesert, which he could attend as a day boy. He had to attend a pre-common entrance interview at Eton. Andy had no idea what to expect and Beaudesert had done nothing to prepare him, so I told him that he should take charge of the interview and ask questions of the interviewer, rather than allowing his own academic shortcomings to be revealed. A few months later, I went to rather a grand dinner at Eton, where I was sitting opposite a French teacher. When he discovered who I was he burst out laughing. 'Your son spent the whole interview asking me about my football team. I am gay and I hate football, but after about twenty minutes I had become quite an expert. I never got round to asking him anything, but he was so different to all the others that I had to pass him.' There are advantages to having a politician as a father!

In due course Andy went to Washbourne's Place too for his last year before Eton. This draconian local crammer was run by a martinet couple. The boys worked for twelve hours a day without any recreation. Fear of a variety of ingenious punishments together with brigade squad discipline got them through. Robert's pass mark was one above the minimum. Theory X can work on occasion, when there is no alternative.

We would have preferred to save the money and send them to the nearest state school. However, the results were the wrong side of mediocre and my parents-in-law agreed to help with some of the costs. Years later, when I was an MP, I arranged a comparison between a comprehensive school in Chippenham and a similar school in Hong Kong. It turned out the main difference between the schools was in the amount of time the teachers spent with the pupils. In Hong Kong the children had much more invigilation and much more homework. They were also much more disciplined. Although the results were similar, in terms of the number of pupils who were passing exams, the grades within the overall results were far higher in Hong Kong. The same is true of the differences between the state and private systems in the UK.

So off Robert and then Andy went to Eton, the school to which I had vowed not to send my children. Were they happy? Not particularly. They were both unlucky in having some contemporaries who were bullies. But the out-turn was a lot better than that of the local comprehensive in Cirencester. Robert became captain of his house and got a place at Lady Margaret Hall, Oxford – the first Needham to have gained a university place by merit rather than by birth. Andy went to Edinburgh where he was meant to be studying history. There followed four years, most of them spent chasing girls and starting a successful directory for students, which he sold to the Daily Mail Group. He still managed to come out with a 2:1.

Our daughter Christina had had an idyllic early childhood, going to the local primary school in South Cerney and being looked after by Lillis, our doting Indonesian au pair. But, aged eleven, she went to St Mary's Calne, a smart girls' public school about twenty miles from home. She was as unhappy as Andy had been at Sherborne. Like him, she came home at weekends, but was always in floods of tears as Sunday evening approached. She complained then – and still does – that she was without a father for almost all her teens.

In 1983, when Robert was sixteen and Andy thirteen, Tim Young, an inspirational Eton teacher who went on to become headmaster of the Royal School Guildford and who had spent time helping Robert to prepare for his common entrance, unexpectedly arrived at our home. He told me I was making a mess of my relationship with my children. I was not giving them time. I wasn't listening to them. They were scared of me and, much as they might have admired me, they felt I was showing them insufficient love, encouragement and understanding. This was shattering for me. I had become obsessed with my career. I was publicly promoting Theory Y while behaving like the worst sort of Theory X sergeant major toward my sons. Sissy and I had fallen out badly with both our sets of parents and vowed that the same would never happen with our own children. Being an MP in a marginal seat was tough and tiring, and there had been too little room for being a dad. I had to change, and fast.

There was a limit as to what I could do after Tim Young's visit as I had no career to go to after politics. At that time there was no realistic likelihood of anyone hiring a former junior Northern Ireland minister and I wanted to go on as I knew I was capable of doing more in the government. I did, however, listen more to the children and do everything I could to be with them when they wanted me. One day I got a frantic message from Andy that he had to see me that night in his room at Eton. I rushed down from London and got there, only to find his room empty. I waited an hour. At last he arrived and told me that he had sorted it out, whatever 'it' was. The positive outcome was the discovery that Andy had my number and wasn't scared to use it, and that I had reacted straight away when he called me.

I realised that politics is a potent driver that seduces you into believing that you are in the middle of what matters; that you are significant and making a difference. But ten years as a minister and twenty years as an MP – unless you are Winston Churchill or Kenneth Clarke – is long enough. You have to know when to go. My only plea for mitigation to my family is that I did make it up to them in the end – I had much more time once I'd left politics.

CHAPTER 34

GEC – A Giant with Clay Feet

Y EMPLOYMENT WITH GEC was to start with a six-month stint as a non-executive director on £35,000 a year. After the first six months I was to be appointed director of exports with a salary of £200,000 per year together with a pension plan, expenses, and the use of a car and driver. I was required to buy £30,000 worth of GEC shares – I had to borrow the money from Jim Prior as all my savings had long since gone. There was an understanding that I would be made vice-chair when Jim Prior stood down as chair (despite there already being a vice chair in Michael Lester, the company solicitor).

GEC was the creation of one man, Arnold Weinstock, a poor Jewish boy from Stoke Newington in North London who married the boss's daughter. He set about building one of the greatest industrial empires in Europe. His vision was to create market monopolies through which he could dominate his customers. As a consequence, he did not need very many. He became the main supplier of generating and transmission equipment to the Central Electricity Board, who supplied power to all the area boards throughout the country. The second customer was the Ministry of Defence. GEC provided everything from submarines and wireless sets to rockets and avionics. His third customer was the Post Office. The telecommunications side was spun out by the government and privatised to become British Telecom. He manufactured all the switchgear, the handsets and the telephone lines. GEC also had very substantial stakes in the transportation industry. Weinstock was a clever mercantilist who built his empire through takeovers.

He allowed all his subsidiaries to retain their identities so as to disguise their true ownership. But he controlled them through ruthless financial oversight from the centre. He was not interested in branding or marketing or innovation or design. He was interested in profit. He was the purest example of a Theory X tycoon. Whenever there was a chance to expand on the cheap, he would take it. He went into medical imaging, lifts, scales, cookers and washing machines. He never visited a factory or asked for a marketing report, and was more interested in his horses than in the managers who ran his businesses. Until the early 80s he prospered mightily. But then he came under huge competitive pressure. Two of his biggest customers were privatised and opened their supply base to foreign competition. The arrival of North Sea oil hiked up the exchange rate; that led to a recession and a reduction in government expenditure, which dried up his orders. He decided to save his empire by embarking on joint ventures. He went into a fifty-fifty joint venture with the French giant Alstom, which he hoped would give him access to the European market. But because the French were undertaking a massive expansion of nuclear power and the British were not, he soon found himself to be the little brother in the relationship. He tied up his Plessey Telecom and cable entity in a joint venture with Siemens. He tried working with Hitachi in mobile phones but, unsurprisingly, they fell out and, unwisely, he abandoned the wireless and mobile phone market. A few years later, this decision was to prove the company's undoing.

He had a board of sixteen, whose non-executive directors he largely ignored. His management team comprised competent and professional administrators, but entrepreneurs did not last long in the company. Only one of the board appointments was a woman, Sara Morrison. I had come across her first in Gravesend in 1974, and subsequently because she was the wife of Charlie Morrison, the MP in the neighbouring constituency of Devizes. She kept her dog under her desk and her considerable influence on Arnold was often damaging and divisive.

The board met four times a year at 3 o'clock in the afternoon. The timing of Arnold's arrival at the meeting would depend on whether one of his horses was running and whether he could listen to the commentary on his ancient battery run Toshiba radio. Every meeting consisted of a series of reports on the trading and financial position. The minutes of 6 December 1995 state: 'in consumer goods, results continue to be disappointing, new management is being sought.' Debate was not encouraged. There were few critical interventions from the non-executive directors or detailed discussions about policy and strategy. Once when I tried to raise an issue of general concern, I was told afterwards that such contributions were not welcome. The board meeting was usually over in an hour or so.

Arnold ran GEC as if he owned it. All decisions were taken by a small coterie of his senior managers including John Lippitt, the procurer of overseas contracts. Jim Prior was the front man and the public face to the media and Parliament. He tried always to tread a conciliatory path. There were those who thought he was too weak in exercising governance and, on occasion, more craven than required. His ambassadorial role and reputation covered up a range of far-from-savoury activities. Jim's advice to me was to lie low for the first six months as a non-executive director and get to know the general managers of the various divisions, and prepare to take on an executive role thereafter. I had an office and shared John Lippitt's secretary, Liz Robertson, so he would know everything I was up to, which he made certain wasn't much. I did make one trip to Hong Kong, where the representative of the joint venture, GEC Alstom, made it clear he took his orders from Paris not London. I also made one trip to Rio de Janeiro to promote a possible contract with the Brazilian navy. However, the financial controllers in GEC Marconi decided that Brazil was too big a commercial risk so nothing came of it. It became obvious very early on that neither Jim or Arnold had worked out what my role would be or how I would fit in the existing structure.

GEC was run by divisions, all of whom had their own sales and export specialists. The company was stuffed with outside consultants who worked either on commission or directly for a subsidiary. Many of them were retired, high-ranking service officers and ambassadors supplementing their pensions. At the centre of the head office web was a very large spider, John Lippitt CB. He had been deputy secretary in the Department of Trade and Industry for many years. His obituary in the *Telegraph* described him as an 'unorthodox, swashbuckling civil servant'. The *Observer* was kinder. He was 'shambling, belligerent, with immense energy'. He described himself as 'a real bomb-thrower'.

It is generally true in human affairs that cock-up is more prevalent than conspiracy but in Lippitt's case it was the reverse. Over the years he had established a network of agents across continents and industries. He was Arnold's bag man. He knew where the skeletons were hidden and there were coffins full of them.

It was proposed that I take over from Lippitt but the idea was preposterous. Firstly, I was never going to be involved in anything that smelled of corruption and many of GEC's businesses, particularly in the

Far East, India, Africa and South America depended on huge commissions for their orders. Jim Prior told me some years later that he was appalled to discover that after Lippitt had left the board of GEC as a consultant he had earned £20 million in fees. When confronted Lippitt retorted, 'I paid tax on all of it!'

I, therefore, had no troops, no Treasury and no authority. Lippitt tried to find far-flung places where he could send me to keep me out of the way. I did have a small success in setting up a factory in Pudong, Shanghai, making fibre-optic cable for the Chinese Ministry of Transport, which wrapped it around railway tracks and used it for high-speed telecommunications links.

John Lippitt had made himself indispensable to GEC. Weinstock and Jim Prior should have reined him in. It became clear to me quite quickly that my predecessor was to become my successor. Which he did. Lippitt was a Theory X icon.

In the spring of 1997, George Simpson, GEC's new chairman, called me in and told me I was not going to be made export director and that he was keeping on John Lippitt in his existing role. George wanted me to stay on as a non-executive and additionally become chairman of GPT, the telecoms division that was owned 40 per cent by Siemens. I had seen this coming and knew it was time to end an unhappy relationship. I had built up a lengthy list of potential alternatives – although in some ways it was still a wrench to leave as I had always wanted to end my career as chairman or vice-chairman of a FTSE 100 company.

CHAPTER 35

Gleneagles and the Heart Hospital

A s I was a non-executive director for the first six months at GEC, I had time to take up other directorships.

Gleneagles Singapore is the largest private healthcare provider in South East Asia. In 1995, Gleneagles had decided to take over and refurbish the Heart Hospital in Westmoreland Street in London (the NHS had declared it surplus to their needs in 1994). It was the world's first specialist cardiac centre, where Donald Ross had performed the UK's first heart transplant operation.

Many of Singaporean consultants had been trained in London under the direction of the top Harley Street cardiologists and surgeons. Six of the Harley Street doctors got together and asked Gleneagles if, in return for them sending the Heart Hospital all their private patients, Gleneagles would refurbish and re-equip the facility. The cost would be in the region of £30 million; Gleneagles would have 50 per cent and the doctors 50 per cent.

Albert Hong, who was an old friend from my days at the DTI, was asked to be the project manager and architect. He was the richest and most successful architect in South East Asia. Out of the blue, in the middle of August 1995, two months after I had resigned from the government, I took a call from Singapore from Albert, who said that he wanted to see me urgently. I was on holiday in Cornwall. 'I will take the next plane and come and see you there tomorrow,' he said. I picked him up from Truro station and took him to the Pandora Inn at Restronguet. As Albert slurped oysters and drank black velvet (half champagne, half Guinness), he told me that the CEO of Gleneagles, the cardiologist Dr Lim Cheok Peng, was looking for a chairman for the Heart Hospital. The role would require no more than a day a month. I agreed on the spot, took him back to the station and he caught the night flight back to Singapore.

Things started to go wrong quite quickly. The structure of the company was deeply flawed. The six consultants who were directors and shareholders had invested no money. Their only commitment was to provide as many of their private patients as they could. The Heart Hospital relied on loans from Gleneagles, who were allotted two board members, Dr Lim Cheok Peng, and me as chairman. The CEO was Richard Dodds – a capable, kind, hard-working Theory Y manager – who was liked by the staff but who found it difficult to control some of the consultant directors.

Consultants are renowned for being awkward. Outside their clinical disciplines, many of them are opinionated and set in their ways. The doctor directors of the Heart Hospital were the top heart specialists in London, if not Europe. They earned hundreds of thousands of pounds a year and had international reputations. Getting their time and attention and finding common positions was like herding cats. Their spokesman was Dr John Parker, from St George's Hospital in Tooting, who was a wise man and respected by all. Sadly, after six months, he contracted a tumour of the brain, which necessitated him standing down from the board, and he died in early 1998. This placed an extra burden on me in managing the demands of the doctors and supporting Richard Dodds. The building and fitting-out of the hospital were constantly delayed by disputes with Westminster Council over amendments required to existing planning regulations. There was one particular councillor who appeared to have an unhealthy interest in delaying the hospital opening.

The London private healthcare market was dominated by a massive American private care multinational, HCA. It owned the Wellington Hospital and the Harley Street Clinic, the two largest private cardiac units in London. They were determined to do everything they could, by hook or by crook, to keep Gleneagles out. Patients tend to go for treatment where the consultant suggests but the health insurance companies have to approve and license the facilities and the fee structures of the treatment centres. The largest insurer in the UK is Bupa but, in London, PPP is the dominant provider and PPP owned 49 per cent of HCA's London hospitals. Disgracefully and without any medical justification, they refused to recognise or approve their patients for the new Heart Hospital.

It was a blatant attempt to maintain a monopoly and to stifle competition. As soon as the delayed hospital opened for business in 1997, it started losing money; £1 million a month. It was always half empty. Richard

Dodds did what he could to drum up business overseas and attract patients from other insurers but it was not enough. Our directors were bringing a high proportion of their non-PPP patients but they were not prepared to lose their PPP patients to their colleagues who were working at the Wellington and at the Harley Street clinic when PPP refused to let them use the Heart Hospital.

I was now deeply involved several days a week in trying to save the hospital from bankruptcy. Something had to be done – and quick! I contacted Keith McDowall who ran a political relations agency. He was a lot more than a run-of-the-mill PR man. For many years he had been a journalist with the *Daily Mail*, and then went on to become one of the feared industrial correspondents who were the hyenas to the lions of the TUC. They fed on the titbits thrown to them by the union barons. Ministers trembled before their leaks and forecasts. From being industrial editor at the *Daily Mail*, he went into the civil service and became Willie Whitelaw's press secretary in Belfast. In total he served fifteen ministers of both political persuasions. He was a journalist to his fingertips. Tell him anything and he'd be looking for an angle, a story, a twist that could inform and embarrass. He knew government and industry inside out. He was married to Brenda Dean, the determined General Secretary of the print union SOGAT. She was the first woman to head a major industrial trade union. In her private life, Brenda was the kindest, nicest, most understanding person, but put her on a platform and she became a female Michael Heseltine. By 1997, her trade union days were over but she was vice chairman of the University College Hospital Trust Group and was to play a vital part in the future survival of the Heart Hospital. We also needed a good competition lawyer to challenge the market-rigging, competition-denying, unacceptable face of capitalism represented by HCA and PPP. We took on Cyrus Mehta from Nabarro Nathanson, who is a quiet, immensely knowledgeable and determined lawyer.

As it turned out, it was a war we could not win despite our detailed and well researched presentations submitted by Cyrus Mehta to the Office of Fair Trading. The OFT had already opened an inquiry into whether the private medical insurance industry was competitive, and in November 1999 they issued their report. It was an astonishing document. They found the structure of the private medical insurance market to be competitive, and open to new entrants and product innovation; that there was nothing untoward in the insurers directing patients towards hospitals in which they had an interest; that no one was being disadvantaged significantly; that the introduction of new players would increase costs because there was a surfeit of beds; that new entrants would therefore reduce occupancy. The report rejected any notion that new facilities would bring improved equipment, patient management, more competition and greater efficiency, as well as attracting new clients. In the confectionary market it would be like a report saying, that no new products should be allowed on retailers' shelves because Cadbury could provide all the chocolates required. There was no discussion about how fair trade could be promoted when the insurer had control of both the patient and their treatment. It was a government-supported monopolies charter.

Dr Adrian Bull, the chief medical officer of PPP, who should've known better, tried to bat off suggestions of any impropriety while denying the Heart Hospital a licence on entirely spurious grounds. Keith McDowall managed to have him badly mauled by Anne Robinson on BBC *Watchdog*. During the programme PPP had got over 60 per cent of the London private medical insurance market and the OFT report had been based on the whole country. He faced further difficulties when it was later discovered that HCA was at the centre of a major fraud trial in the United States.

We then asked the Monopolies and Mergers Commission to intervene. They responded by saying that they could only take on investigations above a certain threshold as their budget was ring-fenced by the Treasury and they did not have sufficient funds. It was also clear, as one of their board members came from the Department of Health, that they had little interest in getting involved in a spat between private healthcare providers that the New Labour government ideologically did not approve of.

Meanwhile Schroders had bought a large stake in Gleneagles and installed a tough Indian banker, Anil Thadani, as chairman. He soon decided they wanted out before losing any more money. I asked the Singaporean high commissioner to make representations to the British government. Surprisingly he seemed unwilling to support the interests of a Singaporean company. He claimed it was a private sector issue and he could not intervene.

In 2000 Gleneagles put the hospital on the market. Who would be the buyers? HCA reappeared and had the nerve to suggest that they would convert it into consulting rooms to reduce the number of private cardiac beds in London and thereby improve their monopoly position. The

Howard de Walden Estate proposed changing the planning regulations and turning the building into flats. The ideal purchaser would have been the London Clinic, which had no cardiac operating facilities, so I saw the chairman, John Biffen, a former cabinet minister. They were interested but didn't have the cash. Behind the scenes I had been working on Brenda Dean. She in turn had persuaded Sir Ron Mason, chairman of University College London Hospitals, to see Keith McDowall. Sir Ron and Robert Naylor, UCLH general manager, then visited the Heart Hospital and immediately saw the opportunity to reduce their cardiac waiting list.

Here was a golden chance to snaffle up an asset which government agencies, the OFT and the Monopoly and Mergers Commission had left stranded, and back came the NHS. Robert Naylor bought a spanking new, beautifully equipped, state-of-the-art cardiac unit for less than half of what it would have cost to build. The London cardiac waiting list was removed at a stroke!

There were casualties. The Singaporeans were so angry at the way they had been stitched up that they allowed the hospital to go into administration. All the small creditors lost their money, even though they had been told that Gleneagles would see them right. Tadhani's argument was that as he had lost a fortune – Gleneagles had lost upwards of £30 million – others alongside him should suffer too. The six consultants, who had lost nothing, took their private patients back to the Wellington and the Harley Street clinic and my role became redundant.

Unsurprisingly, the Singaporeans vowed never to invest in Britain's healthcare industry again. British governments like to trumpet how the UK welcomes inward investment, how there is a level playing field, how the rule of law protects all and how we welcome competition!

CHAPTER 36

Dyson

MY RELATIONSHIP WITH Dyson began when I was still at Westminster. In early 1994 I got a call from Malcolm Frith, one of the local BBC radio reporters. 'You're always going on about attracting and supporting new business but I've just been to a factory on Bumpers Farm in Chippenham making revolutionary vacuum cleaners. They've never seen hide nor hair of you. The man who owns it is called Dyson and he comes from Bath.' I rang James and went to visit him. I realised after five minutes that I was in front of a very remarkable man.

A few weeks later Geoffrey Howe, former chancellor, was booked to come to Chippenham to support Caroline Jackson, our MEP in the 1994 European elections. Geoffrey, although a lawyer, had always had an engineering bent and when I suggested he spent the afternoon in Dyson rather than meandering up and down Chippenham High Street, he flew at the idea – much to Caroline's displeasure.

James always insisted that any new 'hire' had to go on the production line and build a model, which Geoffrey enthusiastically proceeded to do. He left with his hand-assembled vacuum cleaner and showed it off when he got home to his wife, Elspeth, who happened to be on the board of Comet, at that time one of the UK's largest electrical retailers. She took it into the office, and a few weeks later James got an order. Several months later, I asked James if he would give us a demonstration of his bagless cleaner at my office in the DTI to see if the Department could help him overseas. Everyone was enthusiastic. Here was something invented in Britain, manufactured in Britain and uniquely different – and it worked!

Vacuum cleaners were, for most of the large domestic appliance manufacturers, a Cinderella product. They were an ancillary to the full range of domestic appliances. The money was made mainly through large ticket items: cookers, freezers, fridges, washing machines and dryers. A thirty-pound vacuum cleaner was a small but necessary item that helped make up the model range.

Very little new research and development had been done to improve their performance over several decades. Clunky, big, heavy motors produced initial high suction that forced the dust into a paper bag, but the pores quickly clogged up, reducing the suction. The money to be made was from the user having to buy new bags on a regular basis rather than from the sales of the machines themselves. There were two types of cleaner. The first was a cylinder version that sold mainly throughout Europe; this market was dominated by continental manufacturers led by Electrolux and Miele. The other model was the upright version, first introduced by Hoover in America, which dominated the US and UK markets. Into this dozy, complacent, backwater world strode James Dyson. Many, if not most great inventors, are constrained by their backgrounds, their experiences and the confines of their own expertise. Discovering a disruptive technology is one thing, but commercialising it requires a quite different mix of skills. He has them.

The man himself is complex and often contradictory. He can be obstinate, vain and sometimes aggressive, but at the same time, he has tremendous charm. He has beautiful manners, immaculate taste and is capable of gaining the loyalty and affection of his most trusted lieutenants, many of whom have been with him from the start of his extraordinary journey.

He has had two revolutionary ideas: the bagless cyclonic vacuum cleaner and the development of applications using small digital motors. His laser-like concentration on these two brilliant and original technologies have led to a huge business, turning over billions of pounds and making his family the richest in Britain. He has now largely debunked to Singapore. He is not a Theory Y people person. As one of his executive director colleagues said, 'When he visits a factory, he spends more time talking to the machines than the people running them.' He is feared rather than loved by many of his staff. He can be intolerant and critical, but he is often right and he gets stuff done. He is intensely focused and fit. Even though many of those who work for him don't like him, they enjoy striving for Dyson, and he attracts gifted men and women. He had a hard and difficult upbringing and to survive in his early years in business he had to risk everything. He was threatened with lawsuits and often deserted by those who he thought he could most rely on. This has left him cautious, suspicious and litigious in his dealings with others. He is the cat that walks by itself. I worked with him for over sixteen years and I made many, many friends in the Company with whom I remain in touch. I have enormous admiration for what James Dyson has achieved. I just wish he could have done it by giving more generous recognition to the extraordinarily talented people who have spent their careers making him into what he has become.

I had joined the board of Dyson in 1995 when I had left the government. James and I got on immediately. He was looking for a 'mate' he could confide in as an equal – that person would need to bring a breadth of experience that would add a new dimension to his company's management. I was looking for a role, and I realised immediately that my experiences and my international contacts could be invaluable to him. The company was growing at a phenomenal pace. Its turnover was six million pounds per annum when I joined and it was doubling every year. James offered me the role of international director but I did not want to be tied into a single executive salaried role. I could also sense that, as two powerful characters, it would not be long before we fell out. I agreed to three days a week with a roving remit that covered every aspect of the company's operations save design. In time I became deputy chairman; chairman of the audit, treasury and remuneration committees; chairman of Ireland and Germany; responsible for central government and local government support in Malaysia; and support for manufacturing and product development in China, Japan and the US. Working at Dyson was exhilarating, demanding and fun.

In 1997, we decided to hire a new senior management team. I suggested Korn Ferry, the head hunters we used at GEC, as the best of a poor lot. I have an aversion to head hunters, probably because only once in my career have I found a position as a result of their recommendation. Head hunting firms operate as revolving doors. They have a list of client companies, and a list of client managers and directors. Every few years they approach their clients and suggest it is time to either 'refresh' the board or 'refresh' their careers. So, a game of musical chairs develops. Each side relies on the other to find new opportunities. Handsome fees are earned in the process. Directors of public companies get posts commensurate with their status. A finance director of a 250 plc company will be found a role as head of the audit committee of a similar-sized public company. A senior partner of

PWC, KPMG or Deloitte will be put up for a slot when he or she reaches sixty, often to the board of one of their former clients.

One of the groups of professionals that are usually excluded from this merry-go-round are former politicians. Although senior ministers become non-executives, they are seen as mainly lobbyists and in-house PR consultants. Very few ever make it to chair or CEO.

Most senior ministers have a wide variety of talents. They speak well, they listen, they are confident, well connected. They make excellent chairs of meetings because their workload makes it vital that they manage their time effectively. They are good with people and getting the best out of them. As they do not employ their civil servants, they rely on their goodwill. Therefore, most successful ministers are Theory Y managers.

Head hunters seem to pigeonhole politicians into boxes labelled 'wind bags' or 'out of touch' or 'know nothing about the real world of business'. Perhaps I have an unreasonable prejudice. While I know they are necessary, I am not convinced that swapping people around is a proper job. It's not unlike being the lollipop person at the school zebra crossing.

In spite of my doubts about head hunters, Korn Ferry did find us three exceptional new people in 1998. Martin McCourt arrived as the commercial director. A funny, clever, canny Scot, whose grandfather had come from Derry. He had a background in marketing and selling with Duracell and Mars. He was the perfect foil for James. Practical, analytical and with his feet firmly embedded in reality, he was capable of picking out the wheat from the chaff. James had ideas for everything: fridges, washing machines, hairdryers, toasters, taps, hand dryers, there was no end to his ingenuity. Martin was the steady hand that dominated the process and the planning, and kept asking the difficult questions about how to prioritise and make best use of our resources. He and James spent a lot of time scrapping but in the end they would always find common ground and a common purpose. He was to stay for a further sixteen years and was hugely important in the success of Dyson around the world.

Neil Edwards became manufacturing director. He had spent time with ABB, Jaguar, Siemens Plessey and Phillips. He is a restless, fidgety man who is highly creative and technically savvy. He loves travel and new challenges. He wasn't afraid to take on James to his face. Even on one occasion offering to buy him out for £200million.

The third recruit was Peter Richardson, who once Martin McCourt was appointed chief executive, took on the position of chief operating officer. He had a bad back, so he never sat down. He was a top manager – of logistics, personnel, distribution, purchasing and IT. He was the engine room of the company and under his relentless eye the organisation hummed.

James also had a number of ultra-loyal followers who have been with him from the start. Head of engineering Pete Gammack is one. Quiet and modest, he was brought up on a farm in Devon. Farmers know how to put things right when there is a breakdown; they are good with their hands, resourceful, determined to find ways around problems. It was surprising how many sons of farmers came into the company as the number of dairy farms around Malmesbury declined.

James disliked, even despised, the typical suited, golf-playing, tie-wearing, overweight British businessman. He wanted to be different and do things differently. He took on a team of brilliant young female graduates straight out of top universities and put them in charge of marketing and public relations. They charmed everyone and they were tough.

At meetings, everything was up for discussion. Everyone was free to voice their opinions and given every opportunity to be unconventional and think radically. The marketing and public relations staff and some of the young engineers were invited into board meetings, which was only partially successful as they only felt comfortable discussing their own areas. There were no ties or suits. We sat in open offices, although James was paranoid about security in the development laboratories. Problems were there to be debated, analysed, tackled and solved. And they were.

For much of the time it was a Theory Y environment. James wanted his beloved engineers to be rewarded but he was less charitable in his approach to everyone else. The mixture of experience and youth within the Dyson team meant that we had an ideal balance of pragmatism and daring.

The company had more than its fair share of brilliant young men and women, often from surprising backgrounds. This was not least because James wanted to look beyond the head hunters' conventional candidates. For example, when it came to choosing a manager to run Japan, we were handed a list of American-trained consumer goods managers who were either married to someone Japanese or who were Japanese with American partners. Instead we decided to take on a senior diplomat at the British Embassy.

Diplomats may know nothing about domestic appliances but nor did anyone else when they were first recruited. Diplomats can, however, speak the language. They are clever and personable, charming and gregarious, self-confident and could quickly learn about vacuum cleaners. They are also self-assured and prepared to speak truth to power.

In Japan we had to design a small cleaner to fit into the smaller homes that are typical in Japan. To prepare for this, the ex-diplomat, Dr Gordon Thom, in a male-dominated society, hired an office full of women. When I queried this, he rounded on me: 'Women buy the machines, women use the machines – why would I not employ them to market and sell them?'

I did spot a single white male sitting alone among all the women. He had been sent over from Malmesbury to design the Dyson for Japan. He wore a scruffy T-shirt and sported an unkempt beard. I advised him to smarten up and shave off his beard. When I visited a year later, he was surrounded by adoring fans and Dyson had become a top seller in the Japanese market.

As the company grew, it became ever harder to match demand with supply. We needed to expand quickly. The ebullient Neil Edwards spent £10 million expanding production in Malmesbury. But this did not solve the problem that the only relevant plastic-moulding-machine manufacturer in Europe was Italian. They were technically excellent, but their machines were complicated and expensive to maintain.

We still relied on a large number of components suppliers for everything from motors to cables. The manufacturing base in Britain had long since been hollowed out and the European suppliers we had to use were often closely tied to Dyson's competitors. They were expensive, the quality variable and the delivery intermittent. We had to do something radical. We prepared plans for a large expansion on our existing site but we faced local opposition from the grandees, including Andrew Parker Bowles, who lived in a nearby village. Some didn't fancy looking at a factory from their bedroom windows or the wage increases that would be demanded by their cleaners. They were supported by my successor, the local MP James Gray. I told him bluntly that if we were not given permission to build on the existing site, it would not be a question of moving to Chippenham or Wootton Bassett but to Malaysia or China. He ignored us.

Neil Edwards was sent off to explore the overseas alternatives. I suggested we started with Malaysia. I had maintained my contacts there since my time as minister of trade and I arranged for Neil to visit some of the plastic moulders in Johor. Malaysia is small and its rulers have long had close links to Britain: most of its politicians, lawyers and business people have been educated in the UK, and many have homes in London. Its establishment is endemically and disgracefully corrupt. Its politics are dangerous, sectarian and homophobic, and often sexist and racist too. Against that unpromising background it has several advantages. English is the main language of business. All the big British financial and accountancy companies are long established. It is business friendly – at a price.

For Dyson, its most compelling attraction was its huge plastic subcontracting sector. The Japanese had descended on Malaysia in the 1970s and 80s when their labour costs had become uncompetitive. Most of the consumer goods giants established integrated supply chains in southern Malaysia, including Panasonic, Canon, Toshiba and Sony. They brought with them their technologies, their quality circles, the Kanban system and their just-in-time, lean manufacturing processes. Southern Malaysia had become one of the most productive and competitive industrial hubs in the world. Within twenty years, Johor had grown to be the Birmingham of South East Asia.

The local companies were Chinese-Malay owned; the workforces were local people or Indonesian immigrants, often supervised by Indian engineers. The factories are modern and the hygiene facilities excellent. It was not exactly Theory Y but the conditions were luxurious compared to life in the local *kampongs*. The hours were long and the work repetitive. The workers lived in hostels attached to the plants. Holidays were short. Many sent their wages back to their villages, aiming to work for five to ten years and save enough to go back to their families and work in the countryside.

The moulding machines were made in Japan or China, and were highly efficient, simple to operate and easy to service. The quality and reliability of their output could not be matched by Western competitors. There were no trade unions. The margins were tight but the volumes were huge. The closeness to Singapore gave them a direct outlet to world markets. In 1997 there was a global downturn and therefore considerable spare capacity. Neil Edwards's arrival could not have taken place at a better time.

We began by setting up two small production units to make a single machine so that we could compare results, one in the East Midlands and one in Johor with VSI, a publicly owned Chinese-Malaysian moulder. VSI were able to provide us with a spare bay, and all the equipment and labour we required. We shipped out a small team to work on the project, who lived on one floor of the Sofitel hotel in Senai. It was three months before the first cleaners rolled off the assembly lines. The Malaysian version won hands down in terms of quality and reliability. It was also 60 per cent of the cost of the British alternative.

The case for moving the production to Malaysia had become unanswerable. James decided that we would not reduce the price of the product; instead, we would use the increased margins for marketing and product development. However much sense it made to close our production in the UK, it was bound to have a major impact on the company's image which was synonymous with James'. It also dented James' image as he had become an icon for the British innovative manufacturing entrepreneur. A 1999 *Guardian* interview stated, 'The colourful entrepreneur said, "Britain should be making itself into a powerful manufacturing nation producing wonderful products!"' He had also become a vocal supporter of the British manufacturing initiative.

As James was always the public spokesperson and mouthpiece for the company, the public could be forgiven for believing he made all the decisions. In their eyes, he and he alone was to blame. The abuse was poisonous, especially from those claiming to represent New Labour. They had seen James as a 'cool Britannia' example of the new government's caring, Theory Y, exciting, modern alternative to the owners of the old, dirty, smokestack factories of yesteryear. One caller claiming to be Alistair Campbell, the prime minister's press secretary, got hold of James's private number and screamed abuse at Judith Hughes, James's PA, down the phone while I was listening. Luckily Judith had never heard of Alastair Campbell.

In fact, all James's senior managers and directors supported the decision to move, and the space created by the move was soon filled with design engineers working on new products. I was as complicit as anyone even though I had previously, foolishly, told the factory floor that I would oppose Dyson moving elsewhere. I had been the MP for Malmesbury, so it was my former constituents who were being made redundant. However, the move had no effect on Dyson's sales in the UK.

At that time James was totally unprepared to borrow capital. He had suffered enough previously from the effects of dilution and losing control. The downside was that there was no money to meet the requirements to open new markets with bespoke technology in Japan, the marketing costs of launching in the USA and to increase the rate of R&D (Research and Development) investment. Martin McCourt came up with a solution. Once we had tied up our subcontractors, he proposed a change in the business model to DDP (Delivered Duty Paid), whereby the responsibility for the product remained with the manufacturer until it was delivered to the port nominated by Dyson. It was Martin's single most important contribution to the growth and success of Dyson. In a single stroke, the DDP model saved millions. We no longer had responsibility for the supply chain materials and could outsource work in progress. We paid only once the goods had landed. As we moved models out of the UK, the cash poured in. Our subcontractors had the facilities and the equipment to match our expansion plans. We could now quadruple our research and development projects and increase our TV advertising across all our markets. We had cash to attack the Japanese market, supposedly the most difficult in the world, and get back our licence in the US from Phantom. They had made a complete mess of trying to sell Dyson's bagless technology in North America. I said to James that the biggest market in the world for upright vacuum cleaners was the US and we were the biggest manufacturer outside the US. It was an opportunity we had to go for. The price that the administrators were prepared to accept was a few million Canadian dollars and none of the local competitors had the wit to buy the licence. It was an open goal. James was against spending anything but was finally persuaded by the rest of the board. Within five years, using similar marketing techniques to those we'd used in the UK, Dyson became brand leader in both the US and Japan.

James and the board used me to undertake special assignments that they did not have the expertise or time to do themselves. When Dyson introduced its revolutionary hand dryer we were concerned that if it had a plastic moulded front it could be easily damaged or vandalised. We decided to look for a subcontractor who could make aluminium casings. Malaysia only had a very small metal-bashing sector so we had to go elsewhere. I contacted Mark Wong, my old acquaintance from GEC days, and asked him if he could find a company we could sub-contract to in China. I was particularly interested in Nanjing as I felt strongly about the rape of the city in 1937 by the Japanese and felt that it would be a nice gesture to establish a production unit there. Mark found a small, state-owned factory making automotive components that was ideal. It was run by a formidable female engineer, Sun Mei, who was extremely keen to expand her business into new areas. We sent one of our engineers over to assist her and within six months the plant was up and running. To celebrate the opening, I flew to Nanjing, visited the museum, which graphically portrays the massacre, and there attended a banquet hosted by Party Secretary Qi. During the course of the event, he asked me what my hobbies were, and I told him I enjoyed shooting. He suggested that the next time I came over he would like to invite me to a Chinese shoot. I asked him what would happen if we could not find any wild pheasants and he replied, only half-jokingly, that we should look for some Japanese! He was formerly the commander of a Chinese nuclear submarine. Unfortunately, the aluminium-fronted machines never took off as they were heavier and more expensive, and the vandalism we had worried about never materialised, so the joint venture was closed down.

One of my other tasks for Dyson in China was to investigate the possibility of selling hand dryers to the Chinese national railways. This required me to use a large number of Chinese railway toilets. It became clear that hand dryers would not be a priority for those using them. I had been against setting up an office in China before we had established successful sales in Singapore and Hong Kong, but the decision was taken without consulting me. Joc Stuart Grunbar, the Spanish-speaking head of our call centre in Malmesbury, was persuaded to up sticks with his family and set up in Beijing. Joc discovered that department stores in China are warehouses that rent space to manufacturers, and that it is up to the producers to provide the marketing, selling and servicing of their products. It was very clear that this would take a huge amount of time and money. At the same time, the global financial meltdown of 2008 took hold so we decided to close the office and bring Joc and his family home. Joc's wife blamed me for the fiasco but that was a case of shooting the messenger rather than the principal.

Over the years the board also asked me to research opportunities for the company in Brazil, South Africa, Korea, Russia, Greece, Germany, Italy, Benelux and the US, amongst others, and to make follow-up visits when local subsidiaries had been established.

Moving production to Asia paved the way for Dyson's future meteoric rise and also introduced a potential dilemma into the heart of the company's business model. It is always preferable, wherever possible, to have research, development and engineering as near to manufacturing as possible. Prototyping and testing is so much easier when it takes place next to the factory floor rather than at the other end of the world. Even making allowances for modern advances in video-conferencing techniques, practical glitches and unforeseen wrinkles can be ironed out by physical interchanges between the laboratory and production. Potentially costly reliability issues can be isolated, tools rejigged, and production run speeds altered and improved when both sides are working hand in glove.

As long as research and development are dominated by engineers working with James Dyson in Malmesbury, the core of the company's intellectual property and product development will remain in the UK. But now that the company headquarters have moved to Singapore, and the factories are a stone's throw away in southern Malaysia, how long will that remain? James is 73. The largest market is the Far East. Dyson's CEO recently stated that their headquarters should be near their major markets, and their centres of sales and production. How long will it be before most new product development follows and the UK becomes a satellite? Dyson has been complaining for years about the shortage of good new engineering graduates for his design laboratories in the UK. His advocacy of Brexit, many hoped, would mean him bringing some manufacturing back to the UK, not moving his Head Office to Singapore with its corresponding loss of tax revenue to the UK Treasury.

While escaping the clutches of the Corbynistas is understandable, leaving the rest of us to face the consequences while advocating we leave the European Union is either bizarre or verging on the hypocritical. There will be many who will find it hard to forgive him. It means a chequered end to what could have been a respected and admired lifetime of achievement.

I stood down when I reached seventy, in 2012. I had grown weary of arguing with James over what I felt was his Theory X treatment of his senior employees, and he had, no doubt, been irked by my criticisms. To have been an important part of such an extraordinary success story over some sixteen years and to have played a key role in the company's success was more than sufficient reward.

CHAPTER 37

Jack of All Trades

B Y 2000, I had built up a lifetime's experience in politics and business. I had travelled the world and knew many of the top leaders in Asia, Latin America and Africa. I had bags of self-belief and wanted to share my knowledge, skills and wisdom with others. I had a lexicon of Harvard Business School-type case histories to fall back on.

If Dyson was to take up two-and-a-half to three days a week, I had plenty of time spare for other opportunities. I had two red lines. I would not work for a Theory X style management and I would only accept a non-executive director role if there was an area in which my experience would be of particular help.

NEC Europe offered me the post of vice-chairman, and becoming their link to the government and the civil service. They were one of Japan's largest investors in the UK and I had known the chairman, Sekimoto, for many years. They wanted someone they could trust and who could help their Japanese managers understand and adapt to European practices and behaviours. I have now been in that role for twenty-two years although the company has had limited success. NEC now employs hundreds when they used to employ thousands. Japanese insularity and their slowness to adapt to changing circumstances and technologies have put them under the cosh of Korean and Chinese competition. With the banning of Huawei from the 5G roll-out NEC now has a real chance of recapturing a significant proportion of its former market share in Europe and the UK.

The late Mike Stacey, CEO of Meggitt plc, used to opine that non-executive directors resembled supermarket trolleys — you filled them both up with food and drink; the only difference was that the contents of trolleys were cheaper! Meggitt employed me to help establish a stronger foothold in South East Asia. Once that was done and my role was completed,

I left. I wanted to be different and to challenge existing management complacency; to internationalise the companies I had signed up with; to stand up for the risktakers and the ambitious; to be confrontational when necessary.

I have been involved with a whole variety of industries, covering different sectors and sizes. Sir Peter Mason, CEO of AMEC, the billion-pound upstream and downstream oil and gas company, and its international director, Ian Thomas, approached me to be one of their political advisors. Ian was a consummate operator who could handle most solutions without any input from me. As a consequence I ended up being responsible for the company's operations in Libya, which Ian did not particularly fancy. Tony Brown, the local AMEC manager, and I used to travel to Tripoli every six months to visit their subsidiary MAPEL, run by Adrian Ward, which provided the nationalised oil companies with European engineers to repair and maintain their pipelines.

On our visits we often paid a courtesy visit to the British ambassador at his residence on the Tripoli shore front. In January 2001, al-Megrahi had been convicted of the Lockerbie bombings. Colonel Gaddafi whipped up anti-British feeling in Tripoli and there were large demonstrations targeting British assets. We arrived the day after the announcement of the verdict and asked the ambassador, Richard Dalton, if it was safe to come and see him. 'No problem,' he responded, so Adrian, Tony and I set off. When we got to the embassy we could see a crowd had gathered outside the front gates. So we decided to enter by the side entrance. Once inside we sat down to discuss the existing political situation; we could hear Richard's wife with friends playing tennis outside. Meanwhile, in the background the noise of the crowd was growing to a crescendo. Having seen us go in through the side door the protestors had followed us, perhaps in anticipation of our leaving. As the ambassador continued his analysis, the uproar intensified. A few minutes later, the first secretary appeared to say he had told the staff to keep away from the windows. As the ambassador continued, we became ever more nervous. We could still just make out the tennis match. After a further ten minutes we had to lip-read what the ambassador was saying. The tennis game had stopped. His wife appeared, completely unruffled, to say that the mob was trying to climb over the back gates and she had given instructions for all the cyphers to be locked in the embassy safe. Looking at us, she suggested it was time we left. The ambassador reluctantly agreed and made his way up the ramp to peer over the front gate. On his instruction the gate was opened and we made a sharp exit.

To our horror, we could see a second mob approaching us. There was no other option than to continue. I was sitting in the front, Adrian was driving and Tony was in the back. When we got closer, we could see that the crowd was being orchestrated by a number of extremely smart women wearing Gucci headscarves. We were forced to a halt and I lowered my window, smiled, waved to them and wished them good morning. They did not seem to know quite how to react but then the lady nearest to me waved back and beckoned us on. This one was clearly a Gaddafi-sponsored rent-a-crowd, designed for show rather than substance. We decided we'd had enough of Tripoli for that day and drove out to Leptis Magna, the famous Roman ruins and the city of Septimius Severus, the African emperor, who died in York in 211.

Another business appointment was to become chairman of an AIM listed bus company in south Wales, 2 Travel plc. I discovered too late that the business was more about the value of housing on the bus depot sites than the Gurkha-driven buses that were parked there. I was director of a public relations company that morphed into an AIM listed African goldmine. I was engaged in Indonesia by a Northern Ireland building firm, Mivan, which moulded concrete for apartment blocks. They left without paying some of their bills and without telling me. The next time I went to Jakarta airport I found myself under interrogation for the non-payment of taxes!

There was one instance when I ignored one of my two red lines. In 1999, I went to work in the City at the request of my friend Paul Zuckerman, the son of Lord Solly Zuckerman, the former government chief scientific advisor. Paul asked me to become a consultant to Caspian Securities in Asia, an emerging markets investment bank chaired by Rupert Pennant Rae, former deputy governor of the Bank of England, whose time came to an end when he committed an indiscretion in the governor's dressing room.

I was curious how the City worked. It turned out that one of the biggest investors in Caspian Securities was Tan Sri Arumugam, the agent for GEC/Marconi in Malaysia, and one of the Malaysian prime minister's bag men. His investment was tens of millions of pounds. Where had the money come from? Commissions from GEC-Marconi arms contracts was one probable source.

Their offices were in Broadgate. The atmosphere was toxic. It was a cut-throat jungle – there was no job security and investment teams came and went, poached from one bank to another. HR departments were not considered relevant or necessary. Rewards were based on commission on deals done, together with bonuses. But as the deals dried up it became even more of a dog-eat-dog, ruthless world. Steve Clayton, the general manager for Malaysia, described the overall behaviour as resembling rats shinning up drainpipes. Compliance was where ever possible token and to be avoided. The people who worked for Caspian were, by and large, clever, fun and committed (if only to their own self-interest) but the system moulded their behaviour and forced them to react like carnivores. Everything I read about greed and trickery in the City turned out to be true. It was Theory X gone mad.

The bank had opened offices in America, Europe, India, Hong Kong, China and ASEAN. The prime mover was Christopher Heath, who had made a fortune while at Barings in the early 1990s out of Japanese government bonds. He could not have chosen a worse moment to launch. Just as he set up, emerging markets blew up and it took two years before Caspian went under.

During my time there I made several trips to Asia. At the end of May 1998 I was asked by Sean Hughes, Caspian's manager in Jakarta, to visit him and help him gain a mandate from the Indonesian government. They wanted to raise a fund to invest in expanding palm oil production. I knew the trade minister, Rahardi Ramelan, well. When I arrived at Jakarta airport, I was surprised to find the airport terminal packed with passengers trying to leave and noticed that very few people appeared to be arriving. On our journey into the city centre we passed miles of traffic going the other way. We had arrived at the start of a revolution to replace President Suharto. Somehow, we managed to get to the minister's office. He was sitting behind a large desk in front of a large panoramic window and we were placed opposite him. As we discussed the potential loan, we could see smoke and fires raging across the city. The police had lost control and the rioters were looting and pillaging, mainly in Glodok, where the Chinese community lived. They were also attacking the smart new shopping malls which had recently opened.

After about twenty minutes of us staring out of the window, Rahardi turned round, saw the chaos outside and brought the meeting to a swift close. I rang my godson Melvin Korompis and asked if he could come and fetch us. We made our way to the Mandarin Hotel and went to the bar on the top floor, from where we watched the destruction of a great modern city. It was a frightening and horrible sight. It became clear that the police had abandoned any attempts to restore order. After a further hour or so the army started to deploy, arriving in Saracen tanks. I had been responsible for licensing their sale several years previously when minister of trade. To gain approval for the transaction, I had to attend a cabinet committee, comprising the prime minister, the chancellor, the foreign secretary and the president of the board of trade as there had been concerns that the tanks could be used by the President Suharto to suppress his own people. Now they were being used to protect the Chinese minority from the Muslim majority who were attacking them, just as I had predicted at the meeting. The manager of the hotel sent his staff home. Many were in tears, terrified for the safety of their families.

When evening came, we could see that the roads were deserted. I told Melvin that, from my experience in Belfast, the looters would return home to enjoy the goods they had stolen. Perhaps we could go out in one of his battered old cars and get a better idea of what had happened. We set off through the debris-strewn streets, past burnt-out and smouldering buildings. The smell was indescribable. We ended up at the front of the president's palace, the impressive Istana Merdeka. The gates were closed but the palace was ablaze with lights, awaiting the president's return from a visit to Egypt. Two soldiers rushed at us, one of them pointing his rifle at my head, and shouted at us 'pergi tjepat sekali' (move on quickly). We made our way back to the hotel. The following day Suharto returned and, having driven around the city and seen for himself the wreckage that his corrupt rule had brought about, resigned. Every flight out was booked by Chinese-Indonesians trying to escape the turmoil but fortunately, we had return tickets with Singapore Airlines.

Over the last twenty years I have either been chairman or non-executive director of a further four listed companies and numerous start-ups. Biocompatibles plc was the only one for which I was headhunted. I joined in 2000 to replace the existing chairman, Jeremy Curnock Cook.

My time at the Heart Hospital counted in my favour. Biocompatibles was an innovative medical device company started in 1984 by Professor Dennis Chapman who stood down when the company became public. He had patented and developed a water-based coating that could be used to reduce irritation on contact lenses. Later the company developed a polymer system that could act as a reservoir for drug-delivering medical devices, for example cardiovascular stents and anti-cancer drug-eluting beads. The beads were saturated with Doxorubicin, a standard anti-cancer drug, and delivered a high dose of drug into the tumour, with few of the side effects associated with systemic intravenous delivery. The company was 100% British and required considerable amounts of cash to develop its products. Its CEO, Crispin Simon, was a motivating Theory Y manager of the highest calibre. I found it a joy to work with him.

The City had problems in understanding the value of complex medical devices and therefore tends to stay clear of them. The shares of these companies are therefore often at a discount to their assets. Into this space climbs the 'vulture capitalists'. They thrive on market failure.

Out of the blue, early in 2002, JO Hambro Capital Management Limited (JOHCM) bought 27 per cent of Biocompatibles shares on the open market. The shares of these companies are often at a discount to their assets. Into this space climbs the vulture capitalist. They thrive on market failure. JO Hambro was run by Christopher Mills. His modus operandi was to buy just below the limit of 30 per cent, which would have required him to make a bid for the entirety of the company, but enough to give him effective control. He had researched Biocompatibles and knew that its assets were worth considerably more than its share price. His next step would be to appoint his own nominee as chairman and instruct the company to sell off its various components so that he could make off with the cash. If his raid was successful, Biocompatibles would be left as a hollowed out shell.

My job as chairman was to stop this happening. Our first step was to talk to those companies who had already been pillaged and work out our defence. We made it plain to Mills that we would resist his attempt to destroy a small but valuable British-based medical device company and would use every avenue both public and private to discredit him.

As a part compromise, he agreed to put James Hambro, one of his colleagues, on the board. James very quickly realised that what Mills was proposing would be devastating. I played on Hambro's desire to be seen as a responsible city investor and to support the company's development strategy. After a few months, it was clear that Mills did not want a full-scale fight. The price of the shares had risen by 20 per cent so he sold out, took Hambro with him and went off to prey on some other unfortunate. The destructive nature of these raids on well run, successful businesses is the unacceptable face of capitalism. Thereafter, because of what Crispin and I had achieved with the support of the remainder of the board, the company went from strength to strength.

After six years as chairman, I stood down in 2006 and a few years later British Technology Group (BTG) bought the company at a substantial premium to the price at which JOHMC had sold. It was the right place for the company, its technology and its staff.

Crispin Simon left and joined the Department of Trade and Industry, where his private sector experiences were of huge value, and thereafter he continued his public service by becoming deputy high commissioner in Mumbai. He remains a true friend.

During the early nineties and as the Dyson story became more widely known, I started handling requests for speaking engagements. There are a large number of speaking agencies that offer their customers a range of options based on the fame and topicality of their clients. Speakers come in bands. At the top of the range are the Bill Clintons at over a hundred thousand dollars an appearance. Lower down come the two- to three-thousand pounds a gig.

The market is segmented. I was put forward for after dinner slots ranging from the Annual Australian Burns Night Ball at the Dorchester Hotel in Park Lane to PwC's West of England Chief Executives post-conference dinner. The daytime engagements included an afternoon session for a Barclays Bank workshop entitled 'Manage your cash in small businesses' and a local government seminar on 'How to be an entrepreneur in today's financial climate'.

I developed a series of differing contributions depending on the occasion. The after-dinner speeches had more jokes, which needed to be classy, original and, if possible, personal. The core of the address needed a theme based upon the audience's make up and background. I concentrated on case histories of Theory X and Y successes and failures in politics and businesses. The ending needed to be uplifting and if possible inspiring, leaving the audience with a particular message to take home.

Over the years I built up quite a successful if small 'Needham' brand, earning me between £30,000 and £50,000 a year. As soon as I reached 75 it fell off a cliff. I went from hero to zero. A lot of my bookings were because of the Dyson connection so when Martin McCourt left the company he stole some of my slots. An ex-CEO has more insights to divulge than a former deputy chairman or so bookers used to believe. My attraction as a former trade minister was eclipsed by Lord Digby Jones, even though he had only been in the job for a year and had never been an MP.

I enjoyed fifteen years of travelling around the country and sometimes abroad, although a one-day trip to Karachi stretched my stamina. There were bear traps to be avoided. One evening I had to address the annual dinner of the World Wheat Convention at the Grosvenor House. Half the delegates didn't speak English, and a lady from the UN food agency harangued them for three quarters of an hour on how they were destroying the planet with pesticides. The acoustics were appalling and by the time I rose half of the audience were drunk. The only people who listened were on the top table as everyone else was either talking amongst themselves or wandering around between the tables.

It is best to avoid appearing on the same platform as Rory Bremner, particularly if he is on first. He will always steal the show and nothing that you can say will be funnier or more arresting. It takes time for confidence to recover after being drowned out for half an hour, despite the chairman's vain pleadings for quiet.

It was prior to one of the after-dinner events that a most rewarding and interesting opportunity came about. In 2006, Stephen Harrison, the head of PwC in the West Country and an old friend, had asked me to perform the after-dinner speech at his annual party for directors of AIM-listed companies. He told me he didn't want to hear about my successes – they were few enough and he could cover them in the introduction. It was my failures he was more interested in.

I worked out that of all of the companies I had been involved with since leaving the government eleven years earlier, eleven had failed and six had either been sold or were still trading. 'At least you were no longer a director at the time when most of those went under! I'm sure my clients would like to know how you abandoned so many sinking ships and scrambled onto the quayside,' Stephen said. I began my speech by alluding to my record as Stephen had asked me to, but pointed out that in most of the cases, PwC had been the accountants.

At the end of the evening he introduced me to Terry Stead, CEO of Avon Rubber plc, an accountant. Stephen told me that Terry was looking for a new chairman and that I could fit the bill if I followed the Dyson rather than the GEC path.

After going through an expensive head hunter-led process, the board appointed me, although not without opposition from the chairman of the interviewing panel. He was a not very distinguished accountant from a water company who had been told by the head hunters that they had found more relevant candidates than a former politician. I gave him lunch and stood him down.

Avon Rubber had a worldwide reputation going back over a hundred years. When the pneumatic tyre was invented, Fullers, the Brewing Company, branched out and founded the Avon India Rubber Company. Over the next century Avon Rubber became a worldwide conglomerate, either developing or buying rubber-related businesses. It became the Army's supplier of gas masks in both world wars. It made every variety of rubber component for trains and then cars. It built up an inflatable boat operation. In the thirties, forties and fifties Avon employed thousands of people, mainly in Melksham and Bradford on Avon in Wiltshire. It was the major employer in the area and its bright red circle in the middle of each logo was an internationally recognised brand, even though unkind locals had nicknamed it 'the dropped bollock'. My little company in Yeovil had had the contract for signwriting all their delivery vans.

The Fuller family had joined forces with the Moultons to make the company the Dyson of rubber. But the following generations, with the exception of Alex Moulton, were not cut from the same cloth as the founders, and – like so many old respected British industrial companies – it started to fall apart. When the company became public, 'the Avon' became subject to the curse of accountants.

I do not favour head hunters but I have even less enthusiasm for accountants. I am not opposed to any young man or woman gaining an accountancy qualification. It is a passport into any career, public, private, services, industrial or charitable. On its own it is woefully insufficient. Most accountants spend their time introducing processes to control costs and monitor output. Not many of them have experience of Theory Y management and they place insufficient importance on putting their customers first or on being innovative and creative. Terry Twigger, the admittedly highly successful accountant trained CEO of Meggitt plc had a range of 'Twiggerisms', including, 'Every silver lining has a cloud' and 'Why spend time with customers? All they do is whinge and ask for discounts.'

Accountants demand budgets are adhered to, often disregarding the information they have been given by the marketing and sales staff. Because they are remote from the battlefront they are often slow to pick up changing market trends and alter direction accordingly. The results are often disillusioned staff who cannot meet objectives set by outsiders who undermine their ability to be fairly rewarded for outstanding effort. This increases staff turnover, reduces risk-taking and hampers a business's capacity to compete and develop new solutions.

Avon Rubber was run by cautious and unimaginative men who were unable to find ways of competing with the new, low-cost, Far Eastern subcontractors, except through redundancies, cost cutting and disposals. This was the position in much of engineering in the seventies, eighties and early nineties, not helped, it is true, by high inflation and a high pound. As the UK OEMs (original equipment manufacturers) declined, their subcontractors had nowhere to go and no capacity to develop other lines in other markets.

In 2007, when I arrived, Avon was in its death throes. Its profits and sales had declined relentlessly. So, it needed to make a go of what was left, but the management lacked the skills to do so. I was determined to turn Avon into the mini Dyson it had once been a century earlier. There were two diamonds left. The first was the military gas mask division, which had just lost the new design order for the British Army, but – perversely – had won the contract from the United States. There was also a dairy company making rubber liners for milking machines, which had a patent on a potential design for a much more efficient and productive liner. I decided to 'let the CEO go' and reluctantly took on his CFO, an Afrikaaner accountant called Peter Slabbert. I feared originally that a dour South African who lived sixty miles from the head office would not be ideal. But I was wrong. He understood that we needed to make use of our brand, create products, sell direct, cut out the OEMs, spend more on R&D, and shift our production overseas if necessary, to improve our gross margins while investing in sales and marketing.

I began by asking my old design partner from thirty years ago, Richard Hazelton, to modernise the logo. With Peter's agreement, I hired Matt Evans, a left-wing ex-British Aerospace Theory Y advocate, to lead our marketing transformation. Over the next five years, under Peter's management and my chairmanship the company changed out of all recognition. I was able to bring to bear the knowledge that I had acquired over 50 years in politics and business. The shares were priced at £1.65 on my arrival and after six months they were down to 25p, but by the time I stood down in 2013, they had risen to over £4. Now, with brilliant direction from Paul McDonald, who has risen through the ranks, and the outstanding former Dyson design engineer, Jamie Wilcox, they are over £30. The company is the best-performing stock in FTSE All Share Index. Over the last ten years its shares have risen 3146 per cent. It is considering bringing some of its manufacturing home. It is growing organically and through acquisition. Stock market rules state that chairmen should step down after six years unless there are specific reasons for not doing so. I was seventy, coming up to seventy-one, and I had a vice chairman, David Evans, who was keen to take over. The groundwork had been done.

CHAPTER 38

The Final Call

B Y 2010 MY political life was fading into the past – but occasionally it returned with a bang. I was sitting in an Indian restaurant in Sloane Street in June 2010, having had too much prawn madras and too many Tiger beers, when the phone rang. A voice said, 'This is Juan Manuel Santos, president elect of the Republic of Colombia. Is that Richard Needham?' For a second I thought it was a trick. Although Santos and I had become firm friends when I was his opposite number as minister of trade, we had not been in touch for ten years. He continued, 'Where are you? I need your help. Can you come to see me?' He was in London for a few days, staying with the Ambassador, his brother-in-law, Mauricio Rodríguez, at the official residence in Sussex Gardens. I told Santos I would be there in ten minutes. I waved to the waiter, and asked for mouthwash and the bill.

A couple of years before this call I had received another, this time from Sean O'Callaghan, 'the Informer', the most important British and Irish government spy inside the IRA during the Troubles. He wanted to have lunch with me and Henry Robinson, his friend and partner, to discuss a project – to provide anti-terrorist consultancy to governments – that they were planning. We met in a small, inconspicuous Albanian restaurant, Café Koba, in Soho. Henry had been in the Official IRA but now both he and Sean were atoning for their sins and doing all they could to help the victims of terror, particularly those who had lost loved ones in the Omagh bombing.

They sat with their backs to the wall, peering out of the window, checking for possible assassins. Sean smoked incessantly, drank relentlessly, ate nothing and never drew breath. He wasn't so good at listening or delivering. But we all became friends, particularly Henry and me. Because Henry had been in the 'Stickies' he wasn't considered as much of a traitor as Sean, who had been with the IRA – but Henry had spent time in the Maze for kneecapping a member of the Provisionals, and they would certainly have killed him if they'd had the chance.

Both Sean and Henry had not forgotten how to think like terrorists. They were steeped in Republican history, Marxist economics, nationalist hatred of the English, disbelief in the motives of others and distrust in the solutions of 'do-gooding' interlocutors.

Now, two years on, I sat on Mauricio's sofa in the Colombian residence, concealing my eructations, while the president elect outlined his strategy to bring the FARC in from the cold, demilitarise them and involve them in the democratic process. Juan Manuel was using Jonathan Powell, one of the architects of the Good Friday Agreement and Tony Blair's private secretary, to mentor the negotiators. He wanted Mauricio to get over to Northern Ireland and meet with all sides, particularly Sinn Féin, who had a notoriously close relationship with the FARC. He needed to get a 'take' on how to proceed, and learn from all sides about their experiences of the peace process.

Colombia has an image problem in the United Kingdom. The Labour Party and the trade union movement have long supported a campaign against supposed human rights violations in Colombia, outwardly fronted by outside NGOs, but in reality, infiltrated by the terrorists. There has been a never-ending stream of allegations about the excesses of the security forces and their failure. There is something arrogant, condescending and patronising about the failure of the far left in Britain to maintain a balanced view – much like Jeremy Corbyn's and John McDonnell's support for the likes of Gerry Adams in Northern Ireland. The vast majority of those who supported these claims had, of course, never been to Colombia, had no idea of the difficulties in dealing with an armed Marxist terrorist insurrection, and a right-wing fascist military faction of ex-soldiers and police, as well as the richest most ruthless drug cartels that supply the US with cocaine.

This country of forty-five million people is 70 per cent larger than France. Much of the land is covered with impenetrable jungle. Its neighbours such as Venezuela, are often anything but helpful – they harbour the terrorists that are trying to destroy a democratically elected government. Amazingly, the Colombian government, unlike pretty much any other in Latin America, has in its history never defaulted on its debts. Over the last fifty years, five million people have been displaced and 220,000 killed. Due to the war it is poor.

There had been violations of the rule of law. Amnesty was right to focus on 'prisoners of conscience', but there was no even-handedness in their account of what went on in Colombia, no countervailing criticism of those who had killed thousands and forced millions off the land and out of their homes. No highlighting of the kidnappings, the intimidation, the extortion and the protection rackets which, as in Northern Ireland, the terrorists tried to hide behind a veneer of political acceptability.

We developed a plan to help Mauricio in the House of Commons and the House of Lords, and to get him over to Northern Ireland to meet all sides, including former members of the IRA and the UDA. Over the next four years, Henry and I provided briefing notes, drafted articles and gave background analysis as the negotiations progressed on what we believed to be the cleverest ways of influencing public opinion and isolating support for the FARC. We fed everything through Mauricio, who spoke to the president weekly if not nightly, and could decide what to pass on and what to discard.

Juan Manuel invited me to Bogotá for a week, where I met his chief negotiator, Sergio Jaramillo. Sergio who had gained firsts both at Oxford and Cambridge – he was extraordinarily clever but also flexible, shrewd and creative.

At an earlier meeting with Jaramillo at the Mansion House in London in 2012 – when Juan Manuel was on an official visit to the UK and was giving a speech to the City of London in the presence of the Lord Mayor – Henry told him that Colombia had two choices. It could take the route the Sri Lankans had chosen with the Tamils – drive them all into the sea and wait for them to return on some future tide – or do what we had done in Northern Ireland and take the long road to peace.

The negotiations spanned years, during which time there were atrocities that so horrified the public, it was almost impossible to see a way ahead. Such outrages lead to a feeling of repugnance that creates despair, that makes society feel soiled and dirty. It is abhorrent that humans can do such things to one another, to women and children. Such acts lead to revenge, hopelessness, inadequacy, a feeling of an overwhelming need to get away. How – sitting opposite the monsters involved in these crimes – can talks be kept going?

We encouraged the president to press on. *La paz* was inevitable. Its time had come. The FARC wanted to come in from the cold. We had been through it all before in Belfast, and throughout every town and hamlet in

Northern Ireland. The world was willing Santos on.

James O'Keefe, a left-wing lobbyist, together with Baroness Brenda Dean, got Mauricio in front of some of the major Colombian doubters in Parliament and the trade union movement. Mauricio was so clearly an honest, decent and passionate advocate for peace that those he didn't win over he managed to neuter. In a poll in 2013 on the most respected ambassador in London, Mauricio came top.

In February 2014, Mauricio was recalled and replaced by Néstor Osorio, the silver-haired, worldly wise, handsome, multi-lingual perfect diplomat, married to Paola, a beautiful Italian. He carried on where Mauricio had left off.

Five months later, I was contacted by the head of the South America desk at the Foreign Office, Dr Simon Harkin. 'We've been searching for a minister to attend the inauguration of President Santos on August 7,' he began, 'but unfortunately they are all unavailable, most of them on the beach with buckets and spades. Hugo Swire, the foreign office minister in charge of South America, wonders if you would be prepared to represent the Queen. As the visit will be longer than forty-eight hours, we will be able to arrange a business class fare rather than super economy.' I was delighted.

It turned out that I couldn't stay at the British Residence as the ambassador, Lindsay Croisdale-Appleby, wouldn't be in the country. That seemed odd to me – but it turned out that he was being recalled. During the presidential campaign, his Venezuelan-born wife was a vigorous supporter of the opposition candidate. As a result, I would be looked after by Tony Regan, the chargé d'affaires, who had been seconded from the Home Office and would stay at the Hilton.

I phoned up Henry, only to discover that he had already been invited directly by the president and would be on the same flight. For two days we experienced the magnificent and the miserable.

The magnificent included the inauguration ceremony on the Patio de Rafael Nuñez in front of the Casa de Nariño. Together they make Horse Guards Parade and Buckingham Palace look like a dressage arena flanked by well-appointed stables. All the leaders of Latin America were there. King Juan Carlos represented the former colonial power. Sixty-foot-high Colombian flags draped the frontage. Thousands filled the square, sheltering under white umbrellas emblazoned with the dove of Peace. The presidential guard, in full dress uniform and wearing First World

War German Pickelhauben helmets, surrounded the stage on which all the presidents gathered. The speeches boomed and echoed round the buildings reminding me in style, if definitely not substance, of the great political rallies of the last century.

The following morning – after a dreary dinner given by the EU ambassador for EU ambassadors, at which she told us how important she was and how irrelevant the rest of us were when it came to wielding influence in Colombia – we set off on a three-mile journey to one of Bogota's poorest districts.

The trip was to enable us to understand better the work of the YMCA with victims of the armed conflict. Children of poor, displaced families are statistically most likely to join the armed groups, such as the FARC. Some well-intentioned previous mayor had decided to herd all the city's prostitutes into one area. Around three-thousand women and their families were living in tenements. The YMCA was attempting to organise structured activities for the children, with elements of training, learning and sport. They were all football crazy and dying for information on their Premier League idols. The girls were into music, singing and dance but many of them were already drifting into their mothers' profession.

Later we drove to a narrow street of two-storey run-down flats. We were introduced to a mother and her six children, who were aged between three and sixteen. Her brother was in the army and once the FARC had discovered this, a man on a motorbike appeared at her little farm one day and told her she had forty-eight hours to get out or she would be shot. Her husband was already dead. The flat was cold, although it was August – Bogotá is 8,500 feet above sea level – and there was no heating. There were four rooms packed full of hundreds of blue plastic broom heads. The children were attaching the sticks to the heads. It was Dickensian, Theory X, piecework. Repetitive, boring, child labour. At night the mother would squeeze oranges and sell the juice the next morning to commuters in traffic jams heading to the city centre. She used the proceeds to get her children breakfast. *La paz* could not come quickly enough for her and millions like her.

Many of the wives at the British Embassy had joined the YMCA and had become involved with the dispossessed and the abandoned in Bogotá. I was proud of them.

Henry and I flew back the next day. It had never been as bad as that in Belfast.

I have had two good friends who have won the Nobel Prize for peace: Juan Manuel Santos (in 2016) and John Hume (in 1998). The trait that they had in common is that they never gave up. They stuck it out, year after year, disappointment after disappointment, setback after setback. They never lost their sense of humour and in the end they triumphed. Unfortunately so many of those that came after them have been pygmies by comparison.

I had asked Juan Manuel back in 2010 what personal wish he would most like Britain to grant him during his presidency. He said that he had always dreamt of a state visit. My heart sank – these are not easy to come by. There have been two a year in the recent past as the Queen and the Duke of Edinburgh have got older. There is a state-visit-vetting committee that evaluates countries and their leaders' potential political and economic importance to the national interest. I spoke to one of the members of the committee, Sir David Wright, who seemed to think there was a reasonable chance of it coming off.

In November 2016 the call came. The first-ever state visit by a Colombian president. One of Juan Manuel's requests was that his visit should include Belfast as part of the itinerary. This had never happened before. I was asked, along with Jonathan Powell, to travel with the president to Northern Ireland. The night before, at a state banquet at Buckingham Palace, there was a mix-up in the reception line. Sissy and I travelled to the Palace with Tristan Garel-Jones and his wife, Catali. I had the invitations in the car, and when we got there somehow my invitation ended up with Tristan. I was announced as Lord Garel-Jones. Tristan barged past me and bowed. The Queen looked at us and said, 'Make up your minds who you are!' We sat very close to the top table, and my abiding memory is of the Queen and the Duke of Edinburgh chatting away, as if they had not seen one another for a month.

The next morning, I had to enter a side door at the palace to meet up with the president's party to go to Stansted airport. In the lobby there were some extremely attractive, young female officers of the president's entourage and some extremely handsome, hungover Guards officers. 'What time did you get to bed?' I asked.

'3 o'clock,' came the reply.

'Was it a good party?'

'Wonderful! When President Xi came on a state visit we were all in bed by ten.'

In Belfast we visited an equivalent to the YMCA facility in Bogotá. It was built on the so-called peace line, which is in fact a barrier that fences off the Protestant and Catholic communities from each other. It had two entrances on opposite sides of the building, one for Protestants and one for Catholics. It appears that we find it easier to help the Colombians with their difficulties than to sort out our own. Back in London, before the presidential jet took off, we handed him a portrait of himself by the famous painter Jonathan Yeo. It now hangs above his desk.

Two years later and several months after Santos had left office in November 2018, Néstor Osorio rang me. One of Juan Manuel's last executive actions was to appoint me to the Order of San Carlos – Grand Cross. This is a state order that honours both Colombian and foreign citizens who have made an outstanding contribution to the nation of Colombia, especially in the field of international relations. Nestor and his wife held an investiture – followed by a dinner party at which Paola, his wife, did the cooking – for my immediate family and friends at the Colombian embassy. I invited Tristan and Catali Garel-Jones, Chris and Lavender Patten, and Keith and Maria Morris. At the end of the meal Nestor arranged for Juan Manuel to speak to me from New York. I thanked him for the great honour he had bestowed on me.

EPILOGUE

Has Theory Y Worked?

A T THE START of my political and business career, in the treatise I wrote for James Douglas at the Conservative Research Department, I set out my vision of Douglas McGregor's great Theory X and Theory Y idea. I began my thesis with two quotes that I have carried with me throughout my life. From Disraeli:

> My conception of a great statesman is one who represents a great idea – an idea which may lead him to power – an idea which he may develop – an idea which he may and can impress on the mind and conscience of a nation.

And a sentence from John Maynard Keynes's 'Economic Possibilities for Our Grandchildren':

> I see us free, therefore, to return to some of the most sure and certain principles of religion and traditional virtue – that avarice is a vice, that the execution of usury is a misdemeanour and the love of money is detestable.

Fifty years later I have not become a great statesman and the love of money is certainly not yet detestable! I have, however, tried to follow Theory Y throughout my career. At Site Signs, my first business, I proved that employee participation, involvement, transparency and rewarding people for what they had done rather than trying to bribe them worked with young men who had had a minimum of education and motivation when I took them on.

Later when I had responsibility for transforming the towns and cities of

Northern Ireland, I involved local communities at every level. The 1991 Belfast Tall Ships Festival brought unionists and nationalists onto the streets, celebrating a common attachment to their city and its history. The action teams I put together in Northern Ireland were young high-flying civil servants given budgets to support the most deprived and poorest areas. The aim was to empower these distressed communities to gain control over their own lives and to give them power to decide for themselves about the services they relied on for a decent life.

How much has the world moved on since I wrote that treatise? Is Theory Y accepted as the basis on which organisations large and small, public and private conduct their human relations? When it comes to the UK as a whole, the answer is complicated. The collapse of trade union negotiating power has resulted in lower wage rises for many but, paradoxically, has led to lower unemployment as self-employment numbers have exploded. Part-time working, together with zero-hours contracts, has led to a greater flexibility in the workforce but because this way of working offers little certainty or long-term security there is a dearth of training and innovation. No one is responsible for training and motivating part-time workers. As a consequence, productivity has stagnated.

In most larger organisations, ubiquitous HR departments are there to introduce and monitor statutory employment legislation. They help in recruitment and changes to organisational structures, but few HR directors sit on main boards and fewer still influence the levels of top pay, which are determined by remuneration committees of men and women who largely scratch each others' backs.

In some sectors, such as financial services, Theory X still reigns supreme. Bankers maintain that they have to be 'incentivised' and pay themselves eye-watering sums, too often at the expense of their shareholders. In other sectors, such as professional services that require a much greater degree of employee involvement – lawyers, architects, accountants and management consultants, for example – Theory Y management is more embedded but still patchy. Recently the chairman of KPMG, a blunt Australian on £1.7 million a year, had to stand down after telling his hard-pressed staff to stop moaning and dismissing unconscious bias as complete crap! Fifty years ago Theory Y and its associated disciplines were a mainstream course at Harvard and other business schools; now they are part of the leadership programmes.

Does this matter? Of course it does. If we are to be saved at some time in the future from Chinese state capitalism or Trumpist populism, business has to be seen to be fair and the rewards evenly distributed between all those involved. That can only happen in an economy and society where Theory Y is embedded in corporate and management practices. But all is not lost! In some areas of the private sector, Theory Y does seem to be gaining traction, particularly around flexible working practices, sharing information, regular career appraisals and an acceptance that people are the most important resource. There is a growing sector promoting employees' wellbeing and satisfaction. The technology for supporting HR initiatives is one of the most heavily supported areas by investment over the last few years.

The public sector is a much more mixed picture. Trade unions too often foster an atmosphere of distrust in order to hold on to their members. The fire service and the railways are examples of institutionalised, Theory X confrontation. However, few would suggest that policemen, nurses, the clergy, the armed services or even MPs should be incentivised by results! Introducing bonuses in the Civil Service has made little noticeable difference to output and productivity. Following Brexit and the Covid epidemic we are facing a future more uncertain and more challenging than anything we have confronted since the rise of Hitler.

If we are to avoid becoming to the twenty-first century what Spain became to the Europe of the seventeenth century, we have only the skills of our people to fall back on. Never have we needed a society rooted in trust more than now. Trust, which is the foundation of liberal democracy, is too often being shredded by populism, racial intolerance, religious bigotry and increasing wealth disparities. Social media channels have increased division and insecurity for unhappy people in their blinkered bunkers of prejudice and intolerance. But we will find a way though. We always have. Australia and Canada are role models as well as friends. There are others.

Looking at my family, my life and my own career, I am both fearful and excited. I never went to university but all my children did. England has had seventy-five years of relative peace. I've never had to fight in any sort of war as my parents did. My children and grandchildren have travelled the world and gained work experience across continents. They are successful without being arrogant, sensitive without being soft, sharp witted without being spiteful and they are incredibly kind to others.

The most important event in my life was to persuade Sissy to marry me at the absurd age of twenty-two. For almost fifty-six years she has kept the car out of the ditch. I have laughed and cried my way through a life remarkably free of illness and tragedy, and have gone some way to rebuilding the family fortunes. I never reached the summit of my ambitions but I had a good look and got down safely.

I have spent my time in the two separate worlds of business and politics. They are complimentary but they require different skills. I never fully managed to acquire either set but the common thread was the importance of trusting, involving and befriending those I worked with.

It matters not how strait the gate,
   how charged with punishments the scroll,
I am the master of my fate,
   I am the captain of my soul.

William Ernest Henley, 'Invictus'

Bibliography

Benedict, Ruth – *The Patterns of Culture* (1934)

Brown, Professor J.A.C. – *The Social Psychology of Industry; Human Relations in the Factory* (1954)

Burke, Edmund – *Reflections on the Revolution in France* (1790)

Coogan, Tim Pat – *The Troubles: Ireland's Ordeal and the Search for Peace* (2002)

Djilas, Milovan – *The New Class: An Analysis of the Communist System* (1957)

Dobbs, Michael – *House of Cards* (1989)

Fanning, Ronan – *Éamon de Valera: A Will to Power* (2015)

Hobbes, Thomas – *Leviathan* (1651)

Keefe, Patrick Radden – *Say Nothing* (2019)

Kipling, Rudyard – *The Jungle Book* (1894), *Kim* (1901), *Just So Stories* (1902)

Maslow, Abraham – *The Theory of Human Motivation* (1943)

Mayo, Elton – *The Social Problems of an Industrial Civilization* (1949)

McGregor, Douglas – *The Human Side of Enterprise* (1960)

Monsarrat, Nicholas – *The Cruel Sea* (1951)

O'Malley, Padraig – *The Uncivil Wars: Ireland Today* (1983)

Paine, Thomas – *The Rights of Man* (1791)

Pope-Hennessy, James – *The Quest for Queen Mary,* edited by Hugo Vickers (2019)

Popper, Karl – *The Open Society and its Enemies* (1945)

Ramsay, David – *'Blinker' Hall Spymaster* (2009)

Routledge, Norman – *The Strange Life and Death of Dr Turing* (documentary) (1992)

Russell, Bertrand – *The Problems of Philosophy* (1912)

Taylor, Frederick Winslow – *The Principles of Scientific Management* (1911)

Index of People